THE MESOPOTAMIAN SCHOOL & THEODORE OF MOPSUESTIA

by Fr. Andrew Younan

THE MESOPOTAMIAN SCHOOL & THEODORE OF MOPSUESTIA

by Fr. Andrew Younan

Originally a thesis presented to the faculty of the Dominican School of Philosophy and Theology in partial fulfillment of the requirements for the degrees of Master of Philosophy and Master of Theology; Berkeley, California; March, 2004.

ISBN 978-0-578-00615-4
First edition.

Book Description

Two theses are presented in this book. First, that there is an overarching "School of Thought" in Mesopotamia, consistent in its basic tenets, from ancient times to the late middle ages, and that this "Mesopotamian School" is fundamentally realistic as opposed to idealistic. Second, that the Christology of Theodore of Mopsuestia, as read as an expression of this School, is orthodox by the Chalcedonian standard. Included in the Appendices are complete translations of Mar Narsai's 16th and 35th Metrical Sermons, on human nature and the Trinity, respectively, as well as of his "Dialogue Between the Watcher & Mary."

Available at:
http://www.lulu.com/content/5537694

Cover design by Rita Rabban.

He who is estranged seeks pretexts
to break out against all sound judgment.

- Proverbs 18:1

The sleek Brazilian jaguar
Does not in its arboreal gloom
Distill so rank a feline smell
As Grishkin in a drawing-room.

And even the Abstract Entities
Circumambulate her charm;
But our lot crawls between dry ribs
To keep our metaphysics warm.

- T. S. Eliot, *Whispers of Immortality*

Now that you've been broken down,
Got your head out of the clouds,
You're back down on the ground,
And you don't talk so loud,
And you don't walk so proud anymore – and what for?

- W. Axl Rose, *Estranged*

To Mar Sarhad Yawsip Jammo, mentor and friend, without whose insight and inspiration this work could never have been written.

CONTENTS

INTRODUCTION
"What has Athens to do with Jerusalem?"

When Tertullian asked this question eighteen centuries ago, he made an implication that has rarely been examined. That is: do "Athens" and "Jerusalem," as physical places, merely stand as circumstantial symbols for particular types of thought – here "philosophy" and "Judeo-Christianity" respectively – or is there a real connection between a city and a type of thought? A great deal has been written on the "Alexandrian" and "Antiochene" schools of exegesis, as another example, but tracing these "schools" of thought before Philo and Diodore, or following them after Cyril and Theodoret, is a task that has never been attempted. That is one of the tasks of this book, except the city at hand was built before Athens or Jerusalem, and the region is farther east than Alexandria or Antioch. The city at hand is Babylon, and the region Mesopotamia, the Land of the Rivers.

It is, therefore, the first thesis of this book that the thinkers of Mesopotamia, from the earliest pagans to the Christians of the Middle Ages to today, though original in their individual contributions, work along a definite line of thought which can bear the name "The Mesopotamian School."[1] In order to show this, I will divide Mesopotamian intellectual history into segments, beginning with the literary masterpieces of Mesopotamia's ancient paganism, moving through the Babylonian Talmud to the early Church in Persia, and describe each segment in general terms and chronologically, in order to give this "line of thought" the definition adequate to discuss the second thesis of this paper.

---

[1] I have settled upon this term only after a great deal of deliberation. Though its Greek root is certainly alien to the region itself, the word "Mesopotamia" is the only word in English by which we understand trans-historically the region that was called, at various times, Babylonia, Assyria, Persia, Chaldea and (to some extent) Arabia, and which is today called Iraq. In any case, the near-universal reverence given Babylon in the ancient world, and the fame of "Babylonia" even till today, may justify also the term "Babylonian School," but I have used "Mesopotamian School," again, in order to avoid the historical limitations of the former term.

1

The second purpose of this paper is to show that the Christology of Theodore of Mopsuestia, as read as an expression of this School, is orthodox by the Chalcedonian standard. After discussing Theodore, his exegetical method and his Christology in detail, I will turn to the theme of Mesopotamian thought after Theodore, and discuss how the Mesopotamians developed what they inherited from the Syrian-Greek writer.

One important initial note must be made about the first purpose of this thesis. It is assumed in this paper from the beginning that *what constitutes a "School" of thought is* **not** *a set of particular teachings, but rather* **an overall attitude of the mind in its approach to the world** *that may result in varying but existentially similar doctrines in any given generation of thinkers.* Origen, for example, may have taught (apparently) drastically different things from Philo, but it is generally recognized that they were both part of a single overarching "school of thought," and the parallels in their respective *approaches* to, for example, Sacred Scripture, are by far more similar than disparate – especially when both Alexandrians together are contrasted with a Mesopotamian or an Antiochene. Thus my purpose in examining the anthropological assumptions of, for example, the *Epic of Gilgamesh* is not to show that they are exactly the same as those of Mar Narsai of Persia – clearly, the latter taught widely different things about human nature than the former (for example regarding the immortality of the soul) – but rather that they both exhibit similar attitudes toward the human being in the world, enough to justify grouping them together as examples of a single "Mesopotamian School." The meaning of terms like "attitude of mind" and "approach to the world" will, hopefully, become clear as the paper progresses.

CHAPTER 1
THE BEGINNING OF CIVILIZATION AND
THE BEGINNING OF THE MESOPOTAMIAN SCHOOL

Because of the dark and fragmentary nature of the earliest written documents of humanity (the broken tablets written in languages dead now for thousands of years), and the vast, almost infinite socio-historical distance between the modern American student and the ancient Sumerian sage, any attempt to define the beginnings of Mesopotamian thought must be rather realistic and thoroughly self-conscious: we know comparatively little of how the ancient Mesopotamian lived or how he thought, and can therefore hardly expect to interpret what he wrote with strict precision.[2] Even if and when the tens of thousands of tablets from, for example, the library of Assurbanipal, are finally translated,[3] there will always be gaps in our knowledge of Sumerian and Akkadian because of the simple fact that we have absolutely no direct contact with either of the socio-linguistic atmospheres wherein these languages were spoken:

> Ancient Mesopotamia is lost in the faraway past, immense and rough, badly explored, and difficult to explore, and large areas of it remain submerged in the mists of prehistory, while the part of it that emerges still remains, in places, imprecise and indiscernible to us, at such a distance. How can we pretend to draw the portrait of a civilization, attested by half a million intelligible documents at a low estimate, and often by many cultural vestiges that are so rich, so dense, so

---

[2] Admittedly despite the immense progress of cuneiform interpretation in the last two centuries: "Today the Akkadian language may be said to be well – but my no means completely – understood." John Huehnergard, *Harvard Semitic Studies* 45: *A Grammar of Akkadian* (Winona Lake, Indiana: Eisenbrauns, 2000), xxii.

[3] See A. Leo Oppenheim, *Ancient Mesopotamia: Portrait of a Dead Civilization* (Chicago: University of Chicago Press, 1964), 244: "No systematic study has yet been undertaken to establish the contents of the library of Assurbanipal or the provenience of tablets and text groups."

complex, so original, that their enormous vitality has kept them alive for at least three millennia, but from which we are separated by two thousand years of total oblivion?[4]

Indeed, if there are still lacunae in our knowledge of the Old Testament, how many more must there be in our knowledge of the civilization that was already thousands of years old when the Pentateuch was still being formed? Bottero, the scholar quoted just above, describes his book therefore as a "discrete silhouette"[5] rather than any kind of "synthesis" of Mesopotamian thought. If his work is a silhouette, then, an outline of the shadow of the carcass of a dead civilization, let this work be a map and a timeline – however fragmented – showing that this civilization still lives in some sense, or at least that it lived on far longer than previously thought.

In any case, this is all by way of warning: this first chapter must by necessity be as fragmentary as the documents it seeks to interpret.[6] I hope to show, however, that despite every obstacle – even those of historical and cultural distance – the modern scholar can still find and understand real currents of thought which, rising in Eden, are the first currents of genius that initiate the mighty rivers of the Mesopotamian School.

Scholars of ancient Mesopotamian literature and religion, who are, generally speaking, a breed of scholars with particular devotion, are fond of describing the Mesopotamian intellectual personality. Thorkild Jacobsen, for example, in discussing what makes Mesopotamian religion particular – what makes it *Mesopotamian*

---

[4] Jean Bottero, *Mesopotamia: Writing, Reasoning, and the Gods*, tr. Zainab Bahrani and Marc Van De Mieroop (Chicago: University of Chicago Press, 1992), 2. See also Thorkild Jacobsen, *The Treasures of Darkness: A History of Mesopotamian Religion* (New Haven: Yale University Press, 1976), 17-18: "Considering first the absolute distance in time from the end of ancient Mesopotamian civilization shortly before the beginning of our era to the present, it may be noted that it is not only a distance but a clean break. No living cultural tradition connects us with our subject, spans the gap between the ancients and us."

[5] Ibid.

[6] See Oppenheim, 16: "When Assyriologists will be able to follow the fate of individual text groups through the history of their tradition, they will obtain more insight into the workings of this stream and, conceivably, light will be shed some day on ideological preferences and other attitudes that neither the content nor the wording of these texts is likely to reflect directly."

– describes "a tendency to experience the Numinous as immanent in some specific feature of the [religious] confrontation, rather than as all transcendent. The ancient Mesopotamian, it would seem, saw numinous power as a revelation of indwelling spirit, as a power at the center of something that caused it to be and thrive and flourish."[7] Another scholar, Oppenheim, says that "On the metaphysical level, the deity in Mesopotamia is experienced as an awesome and fear-inspiring phenomenon endowed with a unique, unearthly, and terrifying luminosity."[8] A third, already quoted scholar, Jean Bottero, describes the Mesopotamian religious sentiment thus:

> All of [the gods] are considered to be sublime beings, above all dominant and imposing. Before them one bows down, one trembles. Yes, they are merciful, and that is why they are flattered and implored, because it is known that they can do everything. They are especially perceived as being lords and masters: one submits to them. But one is not attracted to them, one does not love them. Religion in Mesopotamia never has anything that is attractive, that one wants to approach, that one has to assimilate to as much as possible.[9]

These are three strong statements given by three major scholars, and each of them says something different.

In order, therefore, to avoid the vague and generic descriptions found in historical surveys, and because the ability to make such descriptions requires a lifetime of study and a broad knowledge and expertise on the matter, both of which I am lacking, my method will be to examine the work of the scholars *on a particular aspect of Mesopotamian thought*, to take a specific piece of Mesopotamian literature on that particular theme, and interpret that one work as representative or at least reflective of the Mesopotamian mind.[10]

---

[7] Jacobsen, 5-6.

[8] Oppenheim, 176.

[9] Bottero, 210.

[10] This is and must be the ordinary course of any study of the "Classics:" to assume that, for lack of anything better, the texts we have in our possession are representative of the culture we wish to study. Jacobsen justifies this method further (3-4): "In the metaphors, therefore, all that is shared by the worshipers of an individual culture or cultural period in their common response to the Numinous

Because "mind" is potentially such a nebulous concept, it will be difficult to be quite clear in what I am discussing unless I focus on *concrete expressions* of the mind which reflect the nature of the School I wish to describe. In order to do this I have decided to concentrate on four specific areas of thought. The four sections of this first chapter, and of most of those following, will therefore be on the topics of: (1) man, or, Mesopotamian Anthropology; (2) the world, or, Mesopotamian Cosmology; (3) the written and spoken word, or, Mesopotamian Dialectics, and (4) the gods, or, Mesopotamian Piety.

Mesopotamian Anthropology – the Epic of Gilgamesh

The human being is at once the most confusing and the most self-reflective creature in the world, and it would be difficult to find a philosopher or thinker who has not made an attempt to understand human nature in one way or another. Nor is this a Modern or even a Classical phenomenon: even among the earliest writings of humanity, there is an attempt to understand, or at least to describe in part, the human lot and our reaction to it, and the earliest writings of humanity were situated at the Cradle of Civilization, between the Tigris and Euphrates Rivers.

The *Epic of Gilgamesh* had, in various versions, been circulating widely throughout Mesopotamia during the second millennium, B.C., but what is known as the "Standard Version" of the Epic was probably authored around 1600 B.C. There are older versions in Old Babylonian and Sumerian, but the Standard work is written in Akkadian, and contains the fullest account of the Epic, though it is itself fragmentary.[11] It is from this first extant Epic of human history

---

is summed and crystallized, and in the summation what is specific and characteristic in the response will stand out. For in its choice of central metaphor a culture or cultural period necessarily reveals more clearly than anywhere else what it considers essential in the numinous experience and wants to recapture and transmit, the primary meaning on which it builds, which underlies and determines the total character of its response, the total character of its religion." I will apply this principle of religious literature additionally to the other themes of anthropology, cosmology and dialectics.

[11] See Jacobsen, 195: "We possess a number of short epical compositions in Sumerian, the originals of which must date to [the third century], but the Gilgamesh Epic proper, with which we are here concerned dates from around 1600 B.C., at the end of the Old Babylonian period, and was composed in Akkadian...This version, made probably toward the end of the second millennium

Mesopotamian, then, *maturity means accepting human limitation and living a good, happy life despite it,*[27] and *immaturity means desiring to change nature and become a god.* This message is what might be called the earliest Mesopotamian "Ethical Theory" or even "Metaphysics of Man."

Mesopotamian Cosmology – Enuma Elish

The precise nature of the Babylonian "Epic of Creation" is not, strictly speaking, that of a book of cosmology. It is more accurately described as a story about Marduk and his ascent to the head of the Babylonian pantheon, wherein the creation of the wo[rld] is described as a sub-story.[28] Still, the creation story within the [*Enuma*] *elish* is "the principal source of our knowledge of Mes[opotamian] cosmology."[29] Nor are we in any sense "forced" to rel[y] merely because there has been little else discov[ered] "creation stories" in Mesopotamia – though [it] makes up only a small portion of the *Enum[a elish]* to Jacobsen, "a very remarkable attempt [at] understanding, and at accepting the u[...]

---

27 Bottero, discussing a[...] commonly called the *Monologue of* [...] "...our author stays in a tr[...] Mesopotamia (present, in m[...] stresses the difference in [...] stresses continuously the h[...] our condition, even of our [...] never have the last word, inclu[...] of our activities, and of our existen[ce...] suffice to keep us tranquil." (267).

28 See Alexander Heidel, *The B[abylonian...]* 1951), 10-11: "*Enuma elish* is not primarily [...] together all the lines which treat of creation[...] granting that most of the missing portion of Tab[let...] they would cover not even two of the seven tablets but only ab[out...] as is devoted to Marduk's fifty names in Tablets VI and VII....E[numa elish is first] and foremost a literary monument in honor of Marduk as the cham[pion of the] gods and the creator of heaven and earth...the story of the creation [of the] universe, was added not so much for the sake of giving and account of h[ow...] things came into being, but chiefly because it further served to enhance the glo[ry of] Marduk and helped to justify his claim to sovereignty over all things visible a[nd] invisible."

29 Ibid., 10.
30 Jacobsen, 167. See also N. K. Sandars, *Poems of Heaven and Hell from Ancient Mesopotamia* (New York: Penguin Books, 1971), 11: "[*Enuma elish*] is about

11

---

that I wish to extract the earliest Mesopotamian "discussion" on human nature. The two particular theses that I will concentrate on, and that I think the Epic author himself chooses to concentrate on, are that human beings are by nature social, and that they are by nature limited.

Before his great journeys began, Gilgamesh, the King of Uruk and hero of our Epic, was wrathful and full of lust, a man who "hoards the wives of other men / for his own purpose."[12] The people of Uruk cry out to the gods, and Anu, the sky god, hears them. He requests, on their behalf, that Aruru, goddess of creation, create Gilgamesh's equal. Aruru grants Anu's request, and fashions Enkidu, the wild-man:

> This Enkidu had neither clan nor race. He went
> clothed as one who shepherds well, eating the food
> of grass, drinking from the watery holes of herds
> and racing swift as wind on silent water.[13]

Enkidu immediately begins terrorizing men hunting outside of Uruk, who in turn go into Uruk to seek the counsel of Gilgamesh. The great king tells them to bring back with them a woman, a temple priestess, named Shamhat:

> who might let him see what charm and force a woman has.
> Then as Enkidu comes again to the watery hole,
> let her strip in nearby isolation to show him all her grace.
> If he is drawn toward her, and leaves the herd to mate,
> his beasts on high will leave him then behind.[14]

The plan works perfectly: Enkidu sleeps with Shamhat, and the wild beasts leave his "new self"[15] behind. When he tries to pursue them, he finds himself weak for the first time. He returns to his lover, still enjoying "the memory that no virgin has,"[16] and she tells him that

Sin-liqi-unninni, is preserved for the most part in copies from around 600 [...] Ashurbanipal in Nineveh." [...] (Wauconda, Illinois:

---

far: the gods smite Enkidu with an illness, and he dies shortly thereafter.[20]

Gilgamesh is distraught at his friend's death, and thoughts of his own mortality make him flee the city in search for immortality. He journeys great distances, meeting such characters as the Scorpion-man and [Sid]uri the wise barmaid, and eventually meets Utinapishtim and hi[s] wife, the only human beings who survived the legendary flood[,] the only humans who are immortal. Gilgamesh asks his [...] the secret to immortality, and Utinapishtim replies with a[...] [initi]al challenge: stay awake for six days and six nights, and be[...] with immortality. The challenge (which Gilgamesh fail[s...] [immediat]ely) is of course a hoax meant to teach a lesson: you cann[ot...] [...]l Sleep! How much less can you avoid Death! Gilgam[esh...] [gr]ave, dejected, and Utinapishtim's wife feels sorry for[...] [...]husband tell Gilgamesh of his last chance at imm[ortality...] [...] eternal life that lives under the sea. G[ilgamesh...] [ti]es weights to himself and dives down in sea[rch...] [...] under the cold water, he takes it (despite[...] [...] it under having touched it) and returns to the surface[...] "life worth having"[21] at hand, G[ilgamesh...] [...] his plans to return to Uruk and s[...] [...] Gilgamesh sets up camp befor[e...] [...] nearby pool. While he is in the[...] [st]eals the plant from him, eats[...] [Gilg]amesh begins to weep, [...] [...]mortality. Urshana[bi...] [...] and Gilgamesh show[...] [...]ment of Gilgamesh[...] [...]ing: the death of h[...] [...]ing: the death of[...] [...]e earth to avo[id...] [...]e seen either[...]

they will go into Uruk, where he will meet and confront Gilgamesh. Enkidu is overjoyed, because now, in his new state, "for the first time he wished for just one friend."[17] He journeys to Uruk with Shamhat and confronts Gilgamesh in a physical battle. The two realize they are equals, and decide to forge a friendship. Almost immediately, Gilgamesh decides to journey to the Cedar Forest and win fame by killing the monster Humbaba.

Several notes may be made here regarding human nature ? society. There is a parallel "education" given to Enkidu Gilgamesh: Enkidu goes from "Wildman" to "civilized"[18] Gilgamesh from "tyrant" to "honor-seeker." Both conversion because of a newfound relationship: Enkidu's relations Shamhat "awakens" him to human consciousness, and G relationship with Enkidu gives him the drive to go beyon current life and seek higher things. In the former case, *be a human being is to be with other humans.* Even on his after lamenting his ever leaving the wilderness, Enki the enormous good he gained in entering the humanity.[19] In the latter case, that of Gilgamesh Enkidu, *developing as a human being is impossible w* to the next point.

Enkidu and Gilgamesh successfully Humbaba and return home to Uruk victorious, in fact, that Gilgamesh att goddess Ishtar, who proposes marria refuses her proposal, citing a list of unfortunate ends. She leaves insul father Anu to send the Bull of Hea He does, and the pair of friends k rips out the bull's thigh and thr

[17] Ibid., I.iv.197.
[18] Jacobsen comments has made his choice, from the fear him and cannot silently Enkidu comprehends som understanding broadened"

Positively, negatively, h maturity: "Gi maturity; he is re plant stands thus fo being a child. It brings and accepting reality." Gilgamesh? What does it n conversation Gilgamesh has refresh the soul," is perhaps the good interpretation to read Sidu very thesis of the whole work.[25]

Remember always, mighty king, that gods decreed the fates of all many years ago. They alone are let to be eternal, while we frail humans die as you yourself must someday do. What is best for us to do Is now to sing and dance. Relish warm food and cool drinks. Cherish children to whom your love gives life. Bathe easily in sweet refreshing waters. Play joyfully with your chosen wife. It is the will of the gods for you to smile on simple pleasure in the leisure time of your short days.

This is the wisdom offered by the *Epic of Gilgamesh*: that mank mortal, is limited – that, in fact, *what it means to be a human being* limited, and that any fleeing or avoidance, much less contra this most bare, basic reality, is the essence of imma

further in depth if one analyzes it not only positively as a flight, an avoidance." (218).
[24] Jacobsen, 219.
[25] It is even the hypothesis of ending itself of the Epic in an earlier contain the Utnapishtim episode Gilgamesh's wanderings…" Epic of Gilgamesh: An 121.4 (2001): 615, fo
[26] Gil

has a first beginning nor…will at a later time suffer destruction.[39]

To see the physical world as eternal is to see it with drastically different eyes from those of any modern American trained and taught by popular science to think of the "beginning" of the world as the Big Bang. Indeed, this fundamental difference in cosmological doctrine seems to reflect a – or even *the* – fundamental difference in philosophical perspective in one's approach to the world.[40]

There also seems to be a connection between anthropology and cosmology in the Epic. The creation of human beings occurs in much the same way as that of the rest of the cosmos; out of a particular need of the gods, Marduk uses parts from a deceased god to create. In the case of the cosmos, the gods wanted a place to live, and so Marduk used Tiamat's body as material for the world. In the case of human beings, the gods wanted servants to work for them and allow them to live a life of leisure, and Marduk uses the blood of Kingu, the head of Tiamat's army of gods, to create humanity:

'Let me put blood together, and make bones too.
Let me set up primeval man: Man shall be his name.

[39] Sandars, 28. She goes further on 61: "In the Babylonian poem there is, strictly speaking, no creation at all. Matter is eternal, Tiamat and Apsu provide, from within themselves, the material of the whole universe."

[40] Sandars concludes her introduction (70): "We can choose today between Continuous Creation and the Big Bang, and the ancient world had the same choice. Creation of the universe *ex nihilo* by Yahweh was a cataclysmic physical event as much as any Big Bang, or series of bangs which may still be whispering round the universe; while the cyclical turnings of time, and the eternal uncreated matter of the Babylonian cosmography, perpetually evolving into greater complexity yet liable to regress into a simpler state, has its counterpart in Continuous Creation. Whatever the nature of the difference, whether theological of physical, it surely represents at bottom a difference of psychological, or mental, tone. We do not know the reason but it is very probably that the antinomy was there from the first beginning of man's thoughts about beginnings." I would like to return to this theme periodically throughout this thesis: that what I call the Mesopotamian School represents or even is merely a representation one of the two primordial and fundamental approaches to the world by the human mind. This will become most evident in the later discussion on Alexandria as the cultural center which later embodies the *other* primordial approach. It will be useful then to describe the two in parallel in order especially to give our School more precise definition by contrast, but for the sake of space the Egyptians must be constricted to one section only.

Let me create primeval man.
The work of the gods shall be imposed on him,
And so they shall be at leisure."[41]

The refinement of the anthropology of the Epic is impressive: though human beings are made from the blood of a god, they are mere servants; though they are mere servants, the work they do is the very work of the gods. The case is the same, though slightly more complex, in the *Ahra-hasis* epic, where Enlil and Mami make humanity, for the same purpose as that described in *Enuma elish*, out of a mixture of a dead god's blood, clay and divine spittle.[42] We will find this motif, that human beings are *by nature* a mixture of greatness with lowliness, throughout Mesopotamian thought, finding its highest expression in Narsai. But the insight here is this: that there seems to be a connection, even a causality, between a basic, heartfelt acceptance of the precariousness of the human condition and an attitude of wonder and gratefulness toward the word. Realism and humility, in other words, lead to wonderment and joy in everyday life.[43]

Not only is the physical universe gazed upon with wonder as made from the body of the oldest goddess, it is also the abode of many of the gods themselves:

Then Marduk the king divided the gods,
The Anunnaki, all of them, above and below.
He assigned his decrees to Anu to guard,
Established three hundred as a guard in the sky;
Did the same again when he designed the conventions of earth,

---

[41] Dalley, 260-261.

[42] W. G. Lambert, "Myth and Ritual as Conceived by the Babylonians," *Journal of Semitic Studies* 13:1 (1968): 104.

[43] The sentiment is expressed beautifully by Chesterton: "The whole point depends upon [man's] being at once humble enough to wonder and haughty enough to defy...We must have in us enough reverence for all things outside us to make us tread fearfully on the grass. We must also have enough disdain for all things outside us, to make us, on due occasion, spit at the stars...Man must have just enough faith in himself to have adventures, and just enough doubt of himself to enjoy them." *Orthodoxy* (San Francisco: Ignatius Press, 1986), 318.

And made the six hundred dwell in both heaven and
earth.[44]

Many of the gods, three hundred to be exact, live on earth. Even
"heaven" here may – and most probably does – refer to the physical
sky rather than a spiritual abode. For the Mesopotamian, there is no
separation, or even distinction, then, between the world of the gods
and our physical world here on earth. Babylon itself was built,
according to our Epic, to be an abode for the gods. Jacobsen
summarizes: "Marduk's first demand upon the gods was that they
build him a city and a house to serve as a permanent royal
administrative center and a place for them to stay when they gathered
for an assembly: a signpost to permanence. Its name was to be
Babylon…They suggested that they themselves move to Babylon."[45]
Marduk grants the request of the Anunnaki, the builders of Babylon:
"'Indeed, Bab-ili[46] is your home too! / Sing for joy there, dwell in
happiness!' / The great gods sat down there, / and set out the beer
mugs; they attended the banquet."[47]

This basic identity between the world of the gods and the
world of human beings has given scholars certain insight into the
practical use for the Epic of Creation in liturgical service as well as a
possible theory as to the inspiration of the creation story itself. As for
the first, Sandars describes the liturgy in which the Epic was read as
not only a re-creation but even a repetition of the legendary events
narrated thereby: "Continual mental and ritual activity were needed
simply to hold the world in equilibrium. Marduk's battle must be
fought year after year. Tiamat is never entirely conquered…" She
continues: "Earth mirrors heaven, and the earthly liturgy echoes the
heavenly. *Ubshukinna*, the Chamber of Destiny, timeless, divine, is
also a room of Marduk's brick palace beside the Euphrates; a mound
of earth in which you can dirty your shoes today. The great *ziggurat* of
Babylon was called the *Etemenanki*, the 'House of the Foundation of
Heaven and Earth,' the common term for the whole universe, which
indeed it was…"[48] Concurrently, Jacobsen describes the physical

---

[44] Dalley, 262.
[45] Jacobsen, 180.
[46] "Bab" is Akkadian for "gate and "ili" the genitive of "ilu," "gods," and
therefore "Bab-ili" means "gate of the gods."
[47] Dalley, 263.
[48] Sandars, 38-39.

phenomenon which may have inspired our author's explanation of the creation of the world:

> The speculations by which the ancient Mesopotamian sought to penetrate the mystery of origins were based, apparently, on observations of how new land came into being. Mesopotamia is alluvial, formed by silt brought down by the rivers. It is the situation at the mouth of the rivers where the sweet waters, Apsu, flow into the salt waters of the sea, Tiamat, and deposit their load of silt, Lahmu and Lahamu, to form new land that has been projected backward into the beginnings.[49]

If this theory is true, it gives us another insight into the Mesopotamian psyche: the physical world and its observable activities today are important enough to tell us even about the creation of the world by the activities of the gods ages ago. Indeed, there is nothing in the documents we have today to suggest that the question "where were the gods when they created the world?" was ever even asked. This should suffice to show that there was, for the Mesopotamian mind, only one world, a physical one, in which both the gods and human beings dwelt.

Our third question was *how was the world as we now know it actually brought into being, and what does this tell us about how we humans should approach it?* We have discussed already how the physical world was brought into being from the body of Tiamat and through the agency of Marduk. Scholars interpret this tension between the old gods and the young, the sleeping and the rowdy, as a personification of the universal principles of Rest and Activity. Heidel summarizes the conflict in the Epic:

> The younger gods, being full of life and vitality, naturally enjoyed noisy, hilarious gatherings. These, however, caused serious distress to their old, inactive, and rest-loving parents and grandparents, Apsu and Tiamat. Peaceful means were tried to diminish the disturbing clamor, but without success.[50]

---

[49] Jacobsen, 169.
[50] Heidel, 4.

Upon this first and most fundamental conflict in the Epic, Jacobsen builds an impressive theory regarding the Mesopotamian's perception of reality. The older powers, Apsu and Tiamat, as we said before, stand for "inertia and rest," while Marduk and his generation stand for "energy and movement."[51] Jacobsen's entire interpretation, involving the historical-political atmosphere of Babylon around the time of the Epic's composition, need not concern us here, except to say that the meaning of the universe for the Mesopotamian, according to Jacobsen, is found in seeing *in the physical world itself* a distinction between inertia and activity.[52]

This distinguishing facility of the Mesopotamian mind works elsewhere, according to Jacobsen, and is of its very essence:

> The characteristic Mesopotamian boundness to the externals of situations in which the Numinous was encountered not only tended to circumscribe it and give it intransitive character, it also led to differentiation. The Numinous was the indwelling spirit and power of many phenomena and situations and it differed with each of them. Thus ancient Mesopotamian religion was conditioned to a pluralistic view, to polytheism, and to the multitude of gods and divine aspects that it recognized. Plurality of numinous power requires the ability to distinguish, evaluate, and choose; and here also the ancient Mesopotamian leaned heavily on external situation.[53]

---

[51] Jacobsen, 183.

[52] Ibid., 191: "As a view of world order this is in many ways impressive. It sees the universe as grounded in divine power and divine will: even those wills traditionally felt as older, more authoritative, or hostile, are unified under the leadership of a single ruler who governs through consultation, persuasion, and conviction. It is religiously of great profundity, leading in its picture of Marduk toward the aspects of awe and majesty. Moreover, it is intellectually admirable in providing a unifying concept of existence: political order pervades both nature and society. Finally, it is humanly satisfying: ultimate power is not estranged from mankind, but resides in gods in human form who act understandably. The universe is now moral and meaningful and expression of a creative intelligence with valid purpose: order and peace and prosperity."

[53] Ibid., 11-12. This phenomenon will be of great importance in Chapter 3, in the discussion on the Medieval Mesopotamian preference for the works of Aristotle over those of the Platonists.

This ability to see and differentiate *in the external situation itself* a real power and meaning allowed the Mesopotamian the intellectual freedom to speculate profoundly about the world around him, while still keeping his speculations in check by constantly grounding them to the physical situation before him.

Before concluding this section, it is worthwhile to examine in this context the phenomenon of *divination*, the belief that an observation of physical substances and events can lead to a real knowledge of the future. It is easy to see why, in the context of such a world vision as that presented by the *Enuma elish*, the Mesopotamian sage would pay close attention to physical events or oddities: if the government of the world is accomplished by the gods themselves, and if the gods have meaning, then the events brought about by their government must have meaning, even if it is not immediately comprehensible to us. The way to *make* seemingly trivial events comprehensible was, for the Mesopotamian, closer observation. Bottero states: "It seems that from very early there was a desire to go further by looking beyond the appearances for an internal connection between the two events which formed an oracle."[54] He comments later:

> In our eyes such "connections" do not exist. They are pure coincidences without importance. We have to believe (and we know it from other sources as well) that such was not the case with the ancient Mesopotamians, especially with their well-known doctrine of the world's government by the gods, and hence the preliminary fixing of the destinies, that is, the names, of all things by these gods.[55]

While we will discuss Bottero's identification between "name" and "destiny" in the next section, we may say here that there is *always*, for the Mesopotamian, a real reason for every event that occurs, whether this reason is known to human beings or not. Or, better, whether it is known to them *yet*. Oppenheim commenting on the practice of divination says, "Because of the belief that whatever happens within perception occurs not only due to specific if unknown causes, but also for the benefit of the observer to whom a supernatural agency is

---

[54] Bottero, 132.
[55] Ibid., 133.

thereby revealing its intentions, the Akkadians of the Old Babylonian period began rather early to record such happenings."[56] In another work, Oppenheim translates what he calls a "Babylonian Diviner's Manual," which is just such a list of recordings of odd events ranging from "If bundles of reeds walk about in the countryside," to "If a wildcat opens its mouth and talks like a man."[57] A telling verse in this work is: "A sign that portends evil in the sky is (also) evil on earth; one that portends evil on earth is evil in the sky."[58]

We may conclude this section, then, by noting that this attitude toward the world requires a tremendous and profound *sensitivity* to surroundings. With this in place, and also with the *humility* of the human subject discussed above, the world becomes a wondrous and exciting place. To the sensitive Mesopotamian mind, then, *the physical world itself has real, true meaning*, and there is no need to posit another world, for example, the Platonic world of ideas, which gives meaning to this one. Moreover, the *wonder* or *curiosity* with which the Mesopotamian viewed the world expressed itself in a real, though realistic, desire to know as much as possible about the universe. This expressed itself, for example, in the long lists of the "divinatory manuals," which show again the paradox of the greatness and the lowliness of the human race: though we wish to know everything, we can *only* know through a painstaking process of memory and sensory perception. Bottero concludes a section of his book: "[Divination] is a new characteristic that places next to the simple passive and detached knowledge of pure observation the desire to know *everything*: not only the observed reality but the possible; in other words the universal. This is a new characteristic that forces us to put forward the term Science."[59]

---

[56] Oppenheim, 210.

[57] A. Leo Oppenheim, "A Babylonian Diviner's Manual," in *Journal of Near Eastern Studies* 33.2 (1974): 203.

[58] Ibid., 204.

[59] Bottero, 36.

Mesopotamian Dialectics[60]

It is an amusing but obvious fact that our knowledge of the beginnings of writing in human civilization is darkened by a lack of texts. We have drawings or pictures of objects on clay, and we then have symbols of *sounds*, writing in the strict sense. The nature of the transition from one to the other is and can only be the object of speculation, though informed and educated speculation ideally. Moreover, what we possess today is only what was able to survive almost five millennia – clay tablets. It is possible that some more perishable medium was used at an earlier date, but we have no way of knowing one way or the other. This being the case, and using all the evidence we have, we guess that the invention of writing occurred in Iraq at the close of the fourth millennium B.C.[61] The writing system is called today "Cuneiform," or "wedge-shaped," because of the shape of the basic elements of the symbols, which were made by impressing a reed stylus onto a piece of clay. It began earlier, as we said, as a pictographical system, where signs were mere drawings of the things they represented, but by the third millennium became a full-fledged syllabic system, retaining elements of the initial pictography until its extinction as a writing system just after the beginning of the Christian era. The fact that pictography, or, more precisely, logograms or symbols representing words rather than sounds, always remained an essential part of the writing system is significant, and it is this significance that allows us entry into the Mesopotamian's attitude about the written and spoken word, or his "dialectic."

Any given cuneiform sign can indicate several different things: an Akkadian or a Sumerian syllable, or both, or several

---

[60] For my use of the term "dialectics" in this context I am indebted to Jean Bottero, who develops the concept brilliantly in his works, and uses the same term: "It is the astonishing and powerful impact of this [cuneiform] script, *precisely in its so-called native shape*, on the point of view, the mentality, and what one may call the "logic" or the "dialectic" and the rules that command the progress of knowledge among the inhabitants of Ancient Mesopotamia. It is as if their spirit had been profoundly marked by the discovery itself." (87). I will be borrowing heavily from the same chapter in this section.

[61] Ibid., 67: "[Cuneiform] is probably the first writing system known, and it is not impossible that it influenced, from afar, the other archaic writing systems: in the west (Egypt, shortly after 3000) and in the east (India, around 2500, and China, around 2000/1500)."

Akkadian syllables or several Sumerian syllables, or both, in addition to an Akkadian or Sumerian *word*, or several, or any combination of any of the above. Thus, for example, the following signs:

"an"   "di"

- The first sign, then, represents: the Akkadian syllable "an." It also represents the Sumerian syllable AN, which means "name," and therefore the symbol also represents the Akkadian word for name "Shamu." The same sign also represents the Sumerian word for god DINGIR, and therefore can also represent the Akkadian word for god "ilum." Finally, it can be placed before any name to indicate that the following word is the name of a divine persona.
- The second sign represents the Akkadian syllable "di," and also the Sumerian syllable DI, which means "judgment." This being the case, the same symbol also represents the Akkadian word for judgment, "dinum." [62]

Thus, the two signs "an-di," can mean a great variety of things, from a mere name to "God the judge." Bottero comments on the dialectic of the name "Asari," given to Marduk in the list of names glorifying him at the end of the *Enuma elish*:

A copyist spelling this name phonetically to write it would never have divided it otherwise than a + sa + ri. But a scholar, who had to analyze it on an entirely different level, not that of script, but that, as he thought, of reality (because he thought that the name was *identical* with the thing), was not bound by the rules of orthography. What counted in his mind was the actual or potential phonetic contents of the name *of which each syllabic element represented a Sumerian word —*

---

[62] See sign list in Huhnegard, 563 and 571.

like all the syllabic values of the characters of the script — *and beyond that word, a reality.*[63]

The seemingly odd claim that Bottero makes that, for the Mesopotamian, the name of the thing was *identical* with the thing itself, that *the name is the thing,* requires explanation. Bottero continues later,

> We have known for a long time that the *name* in ancient Mesopotamia was not, as in our own view, an epiphenomenon, a pure accident extrinsic to the object, a *flatus vocis,* a simple, arbitrary conjunction of a relationship of signification with a group of phonemes. On the contrary, the ancient people were convinced that the name has its source, not in the person who names, but in the object that is named; that it is an inseparable emanation from the object, like a projected shadow, a copy, or a translation of its nature. They believed this to such an extent that in their eyes "to receive a name" and to exist (evidently according to the qualities and the representations put forward in the name) was one and the same. The first couplet of the *Poem of Creation* (I:1f) states:
> When, on high, the heaven had not (yet) been named (and), below, the earth had not been called by a name to indicate the nonbeing, the nonexistence of Heaven and Earth; of Above and Below.[64]

To return to Bottero's illustration using "Asari" as a name glorifying Marduk, he explains how, through a type of linguistic analysis summarized above but the details of which need not be related here, the name Asari "contains" the entire verse of praise to Marduk which follows it: giver of agriculture, founder of the grid of fields, creator of

---

[63] Bottero, 94.

[64] Ibid., 97. He is insistent on this point of identity between things and words: "One did not write first of all the word, then pronounced the name of the thing, but the thing itself, furnished with a name. The name was inseparable from the thing, confused with it, as I have just restated." (99).

cereals and flax, producer of all greenery.[65] Thus, "this entire phraseology, can be *drawn out* of the three syllables of *Asari*."[66]

In this context, the pungent and powerful meaning *of the words* in a text is rather striking as is the closeness of concentration with which author and reader gave every detail of this most physical aspect of their language, impressed painstakingly on clay bricks and then sun-dried to give them greater permanence than human life itself. This especially striking in a world where "breezing through the newspaper" and "sound bites" are the most common forms of transmitting information. We will see later how this aspect of the Mesopotamian personality, this approach to a physical text, becomes the most consistent of all the traits of the Mesopotamian School throughout its phases through the centuries – finding even greater expression, in fact, when there is a *sacred* text at hand. This will of course be developed more fully in the following chapters on the Babylonian Talmud and the Mesopotamian Christian interpreters of the Bible, as well as the so-called "Antiochene School" of Biblical interpretation.

Two more comments should be made regarding the Mesopotamian attitude toward the spoken and written word. First, scribes in ancient Iraq were trained in rather refined schools with severe regimens, without which even *reading* the difficult cuneiform writing (which even Bottero calls a "hellish script"[67]) would be impossible. It is for this reason that the scribes were considered high-level members of the social schema. This strictness in training led the scribes to treat the text which they were copying with great reverence, a fact for which Dalley gives evidence in her introduction: "Because of the looting and copying, tablets found in the cities of Assyria and of Babylonia contain more or less identical versions of myths, and this has led some scholars to deduce widespread conservatism of scribal practice in which texts were faithfully transmitted and

---

[65] See ibid., 95: "Thus all the 'full words,' all these notions included in the gloss in two verses on *Asari*, were found *in* the name in the form of Sumerian words evoked by the phonetic breakdown: *to give* (ru for ri); *agriculture* (sar); *to found* (ra for ri); *tracing/grid* (hydrography of the agricultural fields) (a); *creation* (ra in its reading du); *cereals* (sar); *flax* (sar); *production* (sar, in its value ma) and *greenery* (sar). These notions composed the name; they were an integral part of it: it is thus not surprising that one could extract from the name *Asari* the details of the prerogatives that it accorded to *Marduk*."

[66] Ibid., 88.

[67] Ibid., 93.

variation is all accidental and unintentional."[68] There was a similar reverence for the writing system itself, which by its nature is immensely more difficult to learn and use than the alphabetic systems. Only this textual reverence can possibly explain how long cuneiform lasted in the face of the alphabetic systems surrounding it. Oppenheim explains:

> The alphabetic systems did succeed, from the last third of the second millennium B.C. onward, in crowding out the cuneiform system, restricting it more and more to its home territory, and they eventually invaded the latter. In Babylonia proper, it was the replacement of the Akkadian language by the Aramaic, not the competition with the more efficient and easier system of alphabetic writing, that reduced the use of the cuneiform system to an ever-dwindling number of text categories.[69]

The second note is simply to point out that words for the Mesopotamian were not only meaningful but *powerful*. This is expressed in the famous "Babylonian Magic" which lasted for thousands of years in incantations and spells. W. G. Lambert explains briefly the power of words as used in magic: "To recite an incantation was to bring magic into play. On the magic level, then, a myth within an incantation was part of the means of achieving the end in view, toward which ritual acts were also performed."[70] If the words of human beings contained power, the words of the gods contained infinitely more. Thus, in the Creation Epic, the gods say to Marduk:

> 'May your spoken word destroy the constellation,
> then speak again and may it be intact.'
> He spoke, and at his word
>   the constellation was destroyed.
> He spoke again,
>   and the constellation was (re) constructed.
> The gods, his fathers,
>   seeing (the power of) his word,

---

[68] Dalley, xviii. She limits this observation to Mesopotamia, however.
[69] Oppenheim, 236.
[70] Lambert, 108.

rejoiced, paid homage: "Marduk is king."[71]

It is at this point that we turn to discuss the gods themselves in Mesopotamia.

Mesopotamian Piety

That "Marduk is king" is a sentiment that may summarize, if not the whole, then at least the apex of the Mesopotamian religious tone. It was precisely in those times in history that the political order became more solidly established that the religion in the region underwent major solidifications: when city-states began, the local god of that city-state was the ruler of the rest of the gods; when Hammurabi turned Babylonia into a unified country, Marduk, the local god of Babylon, became king of all the gods of Mesopotamia; when the Assyrians became rulers between the rivers, their god Assur took Marduk's place at the head of the pantheon.[72] There seems to be almost a syllogism at the basis for the theological insight whereby the gods are seen as kings and rulers of heaven and earth: If the shaky, precarious political order we are experiencing now requires a political ruler, by whose agency it is held together; how much *more* must the solid, consistent order we experience in nature require much more solid, consistent rulers![73]

Because of this, it seems that the Mesopotamian religion or religions were always inextricably linked to the polis: religion was *always* official and communitarian, though this did not prevent it from at the same time being personal and intimate, the disjunction between the two is likely a modern, even post-Reformation contrivance. Oppenheim remarks that, "prayers in Mesopotamian religious practice are always linked to concomitant rituals."[74] Again this does

---

[71] Jacobsen, 176.

[72] Bottero, 214.

[73] See ibid., 215: "The Sumerians seem to have tied the supernatural personalities to the functioning of nature and of culture: as if each of the phenomena of both areas presented a problem, in its origin as well as in its functioning, and could be explained only by a supernatural cause that enclosed it and concealed it like a "motor" (in the etymological sense of the word), a "director." Behind heaven there was the god of Heaven: An/Anu; behind the space between heaven and earth, Enlil…"

[74] Oppenheim, 175.

not, for most scholars,[75] prevent them from being intense and personal, even to the non-priestly classes:

> One could think (and many have done so) that these [cuneiform] documents put down in writing and legible only by the literate, reproduce their own religious conceptions and habits but not those of the rest of the population, whether of higher or of lower class, because they were all illiterate. Such a hypothesis, presented in this way, is absurd. It presupposes that the keepers of writing were sequestered in their own circles and were entirely isolated from the rest of their contemporaries. We also have evidence that contradicts this hypothesis. The sanctuaries, for example, were public, even if it was mostly "clergy" who visited them for professional reasons; the common religious spirit is explicitly transparent in the documents that show the life of everyone, not only of the scribes and copyists, as do the letters and many of the administrative "papers." Also, in the sources, the personal names, which in Mesopotamia usually consisted of types of exclamations or theocentric affirmations, confirm for us that the religious sentiments, the ideology, and the behavior did not change substantially from the *majores* to the *minores*.[76]

---

[75] Oppenheim generally has a rather negative attitude toward religion in Mesopotamia: "One obtains the impression – confirmed by other indications – that the influence of religion on the individual, as well as on the community as a whole, was unimportant in Mesopotamia…[the individual] lived in a quite tepid religious climate within a framework of socio-economic rather than cultic co-ordinates." (176), in a chapter called "Why a 'Mesopotamian Religion' should not be Written." This view seems to have been rejected by the academia of Assyriology in general, as expressed in Bottero: "The fad introduced by L. Oppenheim…did not last long, fortunately. The specific arguments of his feigned agnosticism, which could moreover be logically applied to all other cultural aspects of that country and many others, were too clearly contradicted by his book itself, and by the other works of that learned author." (201). It is also obviously contradicted by Jacobsen, whose very book is entitled *A History of Mesopotamian Religion*.

[76] Bottero, 208.

29

What, then, were these religious sentiments or, as I have called it, what was the nature of "Mesopotamian Piety?"

The difficulty in this section of this chapter, more than in other sections, is that a great deal of what can be said is common to all or many types of religions. In discussing what makes Mesopotamian religion unique, then, we will do well to notice what was *predominant* in their prayers and in their attitude toward their gods and to show how these predominant elements related to one another.

At the very beginning of this chapter I quoted Jacobsen saying that a specific feature of Mesopotamian religion was: "a tendency to experience the Numinous as immanent in some specific feature of the confrontation, rather than as all transcendent. The ancient Mesopotamian, it would seem, saw numinous power as a revelation of indwelling spirit, as a power at the center of something that caused it to be and thrive and flourish."[77] This is one of the elements which is noteworthy about Mesopotamian piety: the god or gods were *close by* the worshipper. This feeling expressed itself, for example, in the belief that many of the gods lived in Babylon itself, or, that the statue of the god in the temple in any given city was seen as somehow *actually being* the god or at least that the god *dwelt physically* within the statue. In this atmosphere, then, the gods were trustworthy and merciful rulers who could be supplicated and appeased with sacrifices and prayers, and who were always nearby the believer:

> When one searches through the prayers to establish the topical range of the entreaties addressed to the deity, one discovers a substantial set of requests, each alluding to a specific and very personal experience. This experience is characterized by a feeling of strength and security that is taken to result from the immediate presence of a supernatural power. The experience is consistently described in terms of a pious and god-fearing individual surrounded and protected by one or more supernatural beings charged with that specific function.[78]

The god in question was "charged" with everything from bodily protection to emotional comfort, as shown in this prayer to Ishtar:

---

[77] Jacobsen, 5-6.
[78] Oppenheim, 199.

I have cried to thee,
I thy suffering, wearied, distressed servant.
See me, O my lady, accept my prayers!
Faithfully look upon me and hear my supplication!
Say "A pity!" about me, and let thy mood be eased.
"A pity!" about my wretched body that is full of
disorders and troubles,
"A pity!" about my sore heart that is full of tears and
sobbings…[79]

Here the goddess is asked to take care both of the body and spirit of
the one making the prayer. This trust and closeness is the first
element of Mesopotamian piety that I will discuss.

The second element of religious sentiment in Mesopotamia I
will mention to contrast with the first is that of *fear and awe*. This is
perhaps more consistent with the predominant "ruler" image
discussed above: if the marching soldiers of the king instill fear in his
subjects, *how much more* does the ocean, the thunder and lightning and
terror of nature instill fear in the human being, the servant of the
gods who control them? This fear places the god totally *above and
beyond* anything that the human being can reach or comprehend.
Jacobsen supplies a translation to a hymn to Enlil as the ordering
principle of the universe and the provider of all:

Enlil, by your skillful planning in intricate designs –
their inner workings a blur of threads not to be
unraveled,
thread entwined in thread, not to be traced by the eye
– you excel in your task of divine providence.
You are your own counselor, adviser, and manager,
who else could comprehend what you do?
Your tasks are tasks that are not apparent,
your guise that of a god, invisible to the eye.[80]

This corresponds to the quote from Oppenheim at the beginning of
this chapter: "On the metaphysical level, the deity in Mesopotamia is

---

[79] Jacobsen, 148.
[80] Jacobsen, 151.

experienced as an awesome and fear-inspiring phenomenon endowed with a unique, unearthly, and terrifying luminosity."[81]

Though there are admittedly many ways to understand the psychological and existential relationship between these two semi-opposing sentiments,[82] I would offer a rather simple one: though the gods can be supplicated and appeased, and are merciful and tender and close to the believer, they can never be understood. Though they can aid us, they are utterly beyond us – and that is precisely why they can aid us in the first place. This is the definition of Mesopotamian Piety – to know one's place as a servant of the god, though admittedly a beloved servant. This is beautifully expressed in a prayer to Marduk, god of Babylon, by Nebuchadnezzar II, king of Babylon:

> Without Thee, Lord, what hath existence?
> For the king Thou lovest, whose name
> Thou didst call,
> who pleaseth Thee, Thou advancest his fame,
> Thou assignest him a straightforward path.
> I am a prince Thou favorest, creature of thine hands,
> Thou madest me, entrusted to me the kingship
> over all the people.
> Of Thy grace, O Lord, who providest for all of them,
> cause me to love Thy exalted rule,
> let fear of Thy godhead be in my heart,
> Grant me what seemeth good to Thee;
> Thou wilt do, verily, what profiteth me.[83]

---

[81] Oppenheim, 176.

[82] Jacobsen himself gives two: that the latter is a development and improvement of the former, and that the two come together in the concept of *the god as a parent*. See Jacobsen 158ff.

[83] Jacobsen, 238.

Conclusion

Man is mortal; the world is wonderful; the word is pregnant with meaning and power; the gods are unfathomable. These are the most basic tenets, the first, most primordial streams from which flows the Mesopotamian School. The human being is both great and destined for death, as we learned from the *Epic of Gilgamesh*. Once he maturely accepts his limitations, however, man's perception of the world is made all the more powerful – once humbled and made small, man can look at the world with wonder; and the world is indeed wonderful. This we learned from *Enuma elish*. In his reading, he realizes that everything – even the very sounds by which he forms words – is given a meaning and a destiny by the gods who order the universe. Thus his writing and reading are done with a sense of reverence and honor. Finally, these gods who order the world are not unapproachable, but quite close – but even in being close, they are completely incomprehensible. If one were forced to describe the Mesopotamian School in all its aspects with a single word, that word, however superficial in its modern use, should be *realistic*. It is precisely *realism* that forces a human being to accept that he is not perfect, and never will be despite all his best efforts. It is *realism* that sees the world as, to be redundant, *real* – and not a shadow of something else. It is *realism* – beyond anything today passing for that word – that looks at words as *so* meaningful as to contain worlds of meaning and power within themselves. It is *realism* to know with a dreadful certainty that the gods can never be understood by a mere servant. That is what it means to think like a Mesopotamian.

The Mesopotamian School did not end with the destruction of Babylon. The fall of the Chaldeans to Cyrus the Persian was only a political fall – their culture remained, and though it mixed with outside and alien elements from both East and West, that which made it unique remained and, as I hope to show, became even more defined. The influence of the earliest Mesopotamian thinkers can therefore be seen in much that the Land Between the Rivers produced in the two and a half millennia after the end of its last self-rule until the modern age. The next chapter will be, therefore, a description of the next "phase" of this School, the Jewish phase – that which produced the Babylonian Talmud – which overlaps chronologically both this one and the Christian phase after it.

33

CHAPTER 2
THE BABYLONIAN TALMUD
AND THE JEWS OF MESOPOTAMIA

The fact that the Jews believed that the Father of their forefathers came from Mesopotamia[84] can mean many things, but the least it can mean is that they perceived their cultural heritage as physically originating between the rivers, and that they were inheritors of something that began there. It is not surprising, then, that, centuries later, when they were exiled to Babylonia, and after a few generations freed by Cyrus the Persian, a rather large number of them remained in Babylon – even until the middle of the 20th Century![85]

It is in this cultural center that the Jews produced what would become the greatest masterpiece of Jewish literature: the Talmud of Babylon, or the "Bavli."[86] The Talmud of Babylon, or simply the Talmud, is the compilation of the writings of the rabbis of the Jewish community in Babylon (and also those of Jerusalem) from the years 200 to 600 A.D.[87] It is in its substance a commentary on the Mishnah, a document that began to put the "Oral Torah" into written form, which the rabbis produced and compiled up until its canonization by rabbi Judah around 220 A.D.[88] The Mishnah, most likely a product of Palestine (though the famous Hillel, one of its first

---

[84] Genesis 11:31: "Terah took Abram his son and Lot the son of Haran, his grandson, and Sarai his daughter-in-law, his son Abram's wife, and they went forth together from Ur of the Chaldeans to go into the land of Canaan."

[85] See Geoffrey Khan, "The Verbal System of the Jewish Neo-Aramaic Dialect of Arbel," *Journal of the American Oriental Society* 120:3 (2000), 321-332.

[86] Easily the greatest Jewish scholar of modern times, Jacob Neusner, gives the Talmud this designation: "Few documents in the entire history of the West – the Bible created by Christianity is one, the writings of Aristotle another – have so informed and shaped society in the way in which, within the community of Israel, the Jewish people, the Bavli did." *Talmudic Thinking: Language, Logic, Law* (Columbia, South Carolina: University of South Carolina Press, 1992), 8.

[87] Jacob Neusner, *The Talmud: A Close Encounter* (Minneapolis: Fortress Press, 1991), ix.

[88] Boaz Cohen, *Everyman's Talmud* (New York: E.P. Dutton, 1949), iii.

contributors, was a Babylonian by birth),[89] is a compilation of Jewish law in six sections on six different areas of life:

1. ZERAIM – agriculture.
2. MOED – festivals.
3. NASHIM – women and marriage laws.
4. NEZIKIN – civil and criminal law.
5. KODASHIM – sacrifices and priestly duties.
6. TOHAROTH – ritual cleanliness and purifications.[90]

The purpose of the Mishnah was to make clear the expected lifestyle of the Jew, in order to solidify the Jewish religious identity without the aid of the Temple or of living in Jerusalem.[91] Upon the canonization of the Mishnah, the rabbis in the two major centers of Judaism, Palestine and Babylon, began to comment upon it with great brilliance and enthusiasm. Hence were produced the two Talmuds: the Talmud of the Land of Israel, and the Talmud of Babylon. It is the latter, also called the Bavli, that is unquestionably the more important in Jewish history and almost universally accepted as the superior of the two works, which fact is explained by Cohen:

> The Jewish community [in Babylon] was more numerous and better circumstanced than their co-religionists in Palestine, and they produced or attracted men of superior intellectual powers. At any rate, the teaching in its Schools was deeper and more thorough, and this distinction is clearly evident in the compilation of the Gemara which was made there.[92]

---

[89] See ibid., xxii: "A pioneer who left a profound influence on [the rabbis'] work was Hillel. He was a Babylonian by birth and, so tradition related, a descendent of David through his mother. He migrated to Judea and for about forty years was one of the acknowledged guides of his community." Also, Leo Auerbach, *The Babylonian Talmud in Selection* (New York: Philosophical Library, 1944), 15: "Hillel the Prince, together with some of the Sages, was also a Babylonian."

[90] Ibid., 14.

[91] See Cohen, xv: "Recognizing that the distinctiveness of the Israelite people had always rested on its religion, which had centered around the Temple, they were forced to ask themselves by what means that distinctiveness could be maintained now that the Sanctuary had fallen and the people, resident in a foreign land, were exposed to powerful alien influences."

[92] Ibid., xxxii.

The different approaches of the two Talmuds is a difference of sophistication: "the Palestinians were inferior to the Babylonians in scholastic profundity and ingenuity, and but few of them distinguished themselves therein."[93]

The question I propose to discuss in this chapter, then, in the light of the preceding chapter, is *what is Babylonian about the Babylonian Talmud?* The assumption here is that the Jews in Babylon were in some way influenced by the culture that surrounded them and from which – in one sense or another – they saw themselves as proceeding. (It should be noted also that, though Babylon was at the time of the composition of the Talmud a part of the Persian empire, it remained culturally Babylonian – that is, Semitic[94]). This is not to say, however, that the rabbis read the works discussed in Chapter 1 and utilized them for their own purposes – the influence of Mesopotamian texts on the composition of the Old Testament, for example, is a topic far too broad to even be touched in this short thesis – but rather that we can recognize *in their approach to their subject matter* that they are part of the same culture as the author of, for example, *Enuma elish*. Though this may seem a meager claim (Cohen makes the simple statement: "of course…the rabbis did not live in an intellectual ghetto"[95]), its relevance will, if I am successful, become manifest as this thesis continues.

---

[93] Michael L. Rodkinson, *The History of the Talmud* (New York: New Talmud Publishing, 1903), 18. See also Robert Goldenberg, "Chapter Two: Talmud," *Back to the Sources: Reading the Classic Jewish Texts*, ed. Barry W. Holtz (New York: Touchstone, 1984), 136: "The Jerusalem Talmud is barely half the size of the Babylonian. Dating from a century or two later, the Babylonian Talmud shows the result of more leisurely and more skillful preparation. The arguments in the legal sections are far more elegantly presented, with points made more trenchantly and with the help of a much larger arsenal of standard technical terms and rhetorical devices. The narratives in the Babylonian Talmud also tend to be smoother and more elaborate. In general, studying the Babylonian Talmud tends to be more challenging, but also more gratifying. It is frequently difficult, but the Jerusalem Talmud is often just obscure."

[94] See Jacob Neusner, "How Much Iranian in Jewish Babylonia?" *Journal of the American Oriental Society* 95 (1975): 184: "In Babylonia were various sorts of Semites, Tai Arabs, Mandeans, Syrians, Babylonians, speaking different dialects of Aramaic," and 185: "[The Persians] do not seem to have favored Iranian-speaking people; they moved Romans, Armenians – Jews and Christians – to Iran Proper, so I do not conceive they made a concerted effort to Iranize the lands we now know as Iraq."

[95] Cohen, v.

As in Chapter 1, my method here will be to discuss, through the examination of our primary text, the Babylonian Talmud, its teaching on the four areas of anthropology, cosmology, dialectics, and piety.

Talmudic Anthropology

Upon opening the Talmud for the first time and reading a random page, a reader is struck first by the fact that there are no external structures of organization; the page itself is divided, certainly, into Mishnah and commentary, but aside from that the flow of thought seems almost Joycean: one question left unanswered or given several answers leads to another which does the same. At times the Talmud seems more like an argument between rabbis than a book of instruction – and yet it is both. The argument itself – sometimes producing clear answers, sometimes not – reveals a deeper message within the open-ended structure of the Bavli: that no human being can know all the answers; that there is always another question to be asked. This primordial humility which is expressed in skepticism is at the core of Talmudic thinking:

> What is Talmudic, too, is perpetual skepticism, expressed in response to every declarative sentence or affirmative statement. Once one states that matters are so, it is inevitable that he will find as a response: Why do you think so? Perhaps things are the opposite of what you say? How can you say so when a contrary principle may be adduced? ... Since the harvest of learning is humility, however, the more one seeks to find out, the greater will be one's virtue. And the way to deeper perception lies in skepticism about shallow assertion. One must place as small a stake as possible in the acceptance of specific allegations. The fewer vested convictions, the greater the chances for wide-ranging inquiry. But while modern skepticism may yield – at least in the eye of its critics – corrosive and negative results, Talmudic skepticism produces measured, restrained, and limited insight.[96]

---

[96] Jacob Neusner, "In Praise of the Talmud," *Tradition: A Journal of Orthodox Jewish Thought* 13.3 (1973): 21-22.

Not only is the insight meant for the human being always open to question, it is precisely limited in scope. This is the clear teaching both of the Mishnah and the Talmud. In the following quote (following the practice of the translation of Neusner), the text in bold is from the Mishnah, and the ordinary text is the commentary of the Talmud.

> **C. Whoever reflects upon four things – it would have been a mercy had he not been born:**
> **D. what is above, what is below, what is before, and what is beyond.**
> **E. And whoever has no concern for the glory of his Maker – it would have been a mercy for him had he not been born.**

After the Mishnah text to be discussed is stated, the immediate response is to place it under close questioning:

> I. Might one suppose one may raise questions about what is above and what is below, what is before and what is after?

The authority of the Mishnah is then supported by the authority of the Torah:

> J. Scripture states, "And from one end of heaven to the other" (Dt. 4:32) – thus: "And from one end of heaven to the other" you may raise questions, but you may not raise questions about what is above and what is below, what is before and what is after.
> K. [12A] *Now that that fact is derives from the language*, "And from one end of heaven to the other" (Dt. 4:32), *then what need do I have for the language*, "Since the day that God created man upon the earth" (Dt. 4:32)?

Another rabbi is then appealed to as further support:

> L. *It is in accord with what R. Eleazar said, for* said Eleazar, "The first Adam was from earth to the firmament: 'Since the day that God created man upon

the earth' (Dt. 4:32). But when he went sour, the Holy One, blessed be he, put his hand on him and cut him down to size: 'you have fashioned me after and before and laid your hand upon me' (Ps. 89:5."[97]

The relationship between the respective texts of the Torah, Mishnah and Talmud will be discussed later, in the section on Dialectics. The point to be made here is that the Talmud teaches – in accord with the Hebrew Bible and the Mishnah – a strict limitation to speculation that is based on the created order established by God and manifest in revelation. In a phrase, one may say that it is prudence, or the Practical Intellect, that guides the Speculative Intellect. The mind first reflects on itself and its limited nature before beginning a reflection on anything else. This point is repeated a bit later in the same section of the Talmud:

> 23. A. Of matters up to this point you have every right to speak, concerning matters from this point onward, you have not got the right to speak, for so it is written in the book of Ben Sira: "Don't seek things that are too hard for you, and don't search out things that are hidden from you; the things that have been permitted to you are what you should think about, and you have no business with things that are secret" (Ben Sira 3:21-22).[98]

Thus the exact sign of a mature mind – of a true rabbi – is this realism regarding the mind and its limitations, but, as stated earlier, the fruit of this realism is a mature, piercing insight into the true though limited range of human thought. Neusner continues in his discussion: "Articulation, forthrightness, subtle reasoning but lucid expression, dialectic and skepticism – these are the traits of intellectuals, not of untrained and undeveloped minds, nor of neat scholars, capable only to serve as curators of the past, but as critics of the present."[99] Finally, this is not a singular circumstance in the

---

[97] Genesis Rabbah, "Babylonian Talmud, tractate. Hagigah, Ch. Two, Folio 11B-20B," from Jacob Neusner, *The Talmud of Babylonia: An Academic Commentary* (Atlanta: Scholars Press, 1994), 44-45.

[98] Ibid., 51.

[99] Neusner, "In Praise," 21.

Talmud, but rather the overarching attitude of the entire work, as Cohen states, referring to the same passage quoted above: "That is typical of the Rabbinic attitude."[100] Humble and realistic acceptance of limitation, again, then, is the core attitude toward the human situation in Mesopotamia – and, just as their Pagan predecessors in that Land, the Jews of Babylon expressed this attitude with acute insight. Not, however, that this is an *exclusively* Mesopotamian trait – certainly many thinkers from varied places shared this attitude. Nevertheless, not all thinkers did, and the point here is that, when the question of whether the human mind is to soar to the heights of divinity by its own nature, or be sober and humbly accept its limitations, Mesopotamia chose the latter decisively and consistently.

Talmudic Cosmology

The six divisions of the Mishnah referred to above which supply the core of the discussion of the entire Talmud, which are, to repeat:
1. ZERAIM – agriculture.
2. MOED – festivals.
3. NASHIM – women and marriage laws.
4. NEZIKIN – civil and criminal law.
5. KODASHIM – sacrifices and priestly duties.
6. TOHAROTH – ritual cleanliness and purifications,
show, by means of their specificity, a universal assumption of the inherently social nature of the human being. Laws about agriculture, social festivals, marriage and so on, making up such a large part of the Mishnah and therefore the Talmud, betray a real concern for the social life of the Jew. As Neusner states in an article entitled "The Talmud as Anthropology,"

> One route to the interpretation of a system is to specify the sorts of issues it chooses to regard as problems, the matters it chooses for its close and continuing exegesis. When we know the things about which people worry, we have some insight into the way in which they see the world.[101]

---

[100] Cohen, 27.
[101] Jacob Neusner, "The Talmud as Anthropology," *Religious Traditions* 3.2 (1980): 28.

This being the case, and assuming that "the purpose of Talmudic literature, as Talmudists have always known, is to lay out paradigms of holiness,"[102] we must ask *why it is that such a precise ordering of social and physical actions is so important to Talmudic thinking?* That is, what is it about ordering physical life that is holy?

The answer to this anthropological question is cosmological. To begin with the text of the Talmud itself, there is a notable passage which discusses the nature of angels from Genesis Rabah which we should quote in full:

> 18. A. One verse of Scripture states, "Each one had six wings" (Is. 6:2), and another, "Each one had four wings" (Ez. 1:6)!
> B. *No problem*, the one [Is. 6:2] speaks of the time that the house of the sanctuary was standing, the other, the time that the house of the sanctuary was not standing. It is as though the wings of the living creatures were diminished on account of its destruction.[103]

What is remarkable here is that the earthly sanctuary affects the creatures of heaven. This same idea is repeated a little later:

> 19. A. One verse of Scripture states, "Thousand thousands ministered to him, and ten thousand times ten thousand stood before him" (Dan. 7:10), and another, "Is there nay number of his armies" (Job 25:3).
> B. *No problem*, the one speaks of the time that the house of the sanctuary was standing, the other, the time that the house of the sanctuary was not standing. It is as though the heavenly family were diminished on account of its destruction.[104]

There is, for the Talmud, no separation between earth and heaven; the one affects the other, all parts of creation are tied together in the one glorious ordering of the Creator. Cohen remarks on this point:

---

[102] Ibid., 14.
[103] Genesis Rabbah, 54.
[104] Ibid., 55.

"On this point there was unanimity, viz. that the world being the production of God Who is perfect must itself be perfect in every respect."[105] Cohen supports himself by quoting a different passage from Genesis Rabbah:

> 'Even such things as you deem superfluous in the world, e.g. flies, fleas, and gnats, are necessary parts of the cosmic order and were created by the Holy One, blessed be He, for His purpose – yea, even serpents and frogs.'[106]

This is the first step toward answering our question: for the Jews of Babylon, just as for their Pagan predecessors, it is the order of creation that is remarkable and worthy of wonder.

It is not only, however, worthy of wonder. Its perfection, which comes from the perfection of God, is also worthy of *emulation*. That is, because the human being is, biblically speaking, the image of God, he should imitate God; and if God's activity is perfect in every detail, so therefore should be the activity of every human being. Neusner makes this clear:

> If the rabbis of the Talmud studied and realized the Divine teaching of Moses, whom they called "our rabbi," it was because the order they would impose upon earthly affairs would replicate on earth the order they perceived from heaven...and what they saw projected from heaven to earth was, as I have said, the order and rational construction of reality.[107]

An important note to make, however, is that this situation is not merely natural – that is, even if the "rational construction" of the world is overwhelming, that we should imitate it in our activity *because we are God's image* is not itself self-evident. This insight is one that is revealed only by a direct communication of God to Moses.[108]

---

[105] Cohen, 38.

[106] Cohen, 39.

[107] Neusner, "In Praise," 19.

[108] See ibid., 18: "The discipline does not derive from the perception of unifying order in the natural world. It comes, rather, from the lessons imparted by the supernatural, in the Torah."

Moreover, it is rather interesting to note the longstanding rabbinic belief that God consulted the Torah when creating the universe![109] Though this seems to say more about the importance of the Torah for the rabbis than their conception of the manner of the world's creation, the fact still seems to be that there is no dichotomy between the created world and the revelation of God to Moses. It may be even more to the point to say that the creation of the world was concurrent to the composition of the Talmud. For example, when the Talmudic authors discuss why the Torah begins with the letter "Beth," the second letter of the alphabet, and not the first, teach this is so,

> Because *beth* is the initial of *berachah* (blessing) and *aleph* is the initial of *arirah* (curse). The Holy One, blessed be He, said, I will only create My Universe with *beth*, that they who come into the world shall not say, "How can the world endure since it was created with a letter of ill omen?" Behold, I will create it with a letter of good omen, peradventure it will endure.[110]

The point here is that, though it is conceptually difficult for us today to grasp, *the world itself and not only the Torah begins with the letter "Beth."* This will be discussed in greater detail in the next section.

This is then the answer to our question: *the reason that physical ritual and close control of every physical action is so important is because by ordering our actions we imitate God and thereby make our actions holy*:

> So even the placing of a napkin at a meal is turned into a discipline for living, a discipline which requires that logic and order everywhere prevail, and demands that concerns for a vast world of unseen, principled relationships come to bear. Humble and thoughtless action is elevated and made worthy of thought, shown to bear heavy consequences.[111]

---

[109] See Cohen, 29, who quotes again Genesis Rabbah: "So did the Holy One, blessed be He, look into the Torah and created the universe accordingly."

[110] Ibid., 39.

[111] Neusner, "In Praise," 16. Interestingly, the physical act seems to have been even more important than the intention behind the act for the pious Jew: "The very indecisiveness of the Talmudic discussions does permit one firm

Cosmologically speaking, therefore, the physical world is filled with meaning – just as our actions should be. Herman Mueller brings all these ideas together:

> For a Jew, all things sensible are meaningful and all creation is a discourse with a vocabulary everyone can understand. That is the reason he likes parables so much. Man does not have to flee the sensible in order to reach the intelligible; the meaning is contained in the concrete reality.[112]

G. Sarfatti, in an article entitled "Talmudic Cosmography," discusses the various cosmological expressions in the ancient world – the Greek, the Egyptian, etc. His conclusion is this: "The cosmographical information revealed in Talmudic and Midrashic sources is based on the Babylonian system, which reached the Rabbis by direct and indirect (= the Bible) contact."[113] If this is the case, one wonders whether the Talmud contains anything of the astrological or even magical practices that were prevalent in Mesopotamia for so long. The simple answer is that it does, despite a mixed attitude toward magic, astrology, and divinatory techniques in general. This is, to a great extent, merely a cultural necessity: "Magic, astrology, and other occult sciences…were as attractive to Jews as they were to pagans and Christians; these were regarded as advanced sciences, and, to reject them, the Jews and their leaders would have to ignore the most sophisticated technological attainments of contemporary civilization."[114] The struggle *against* such practices in Judaism, however, goes back much further than the reign of the rabbis:

> Even though astrological beliefs can be traced back to at least 1000 B.C. (*Enuma Anu Enlil*), the OT documents were not influenced by them but rather

---

conclusion: for the people who produced these discussions, the act took precedence over the thought." Robert Goldenberg, "Command and Consciousness in Talmudic Thought," *Harvard Theological Review* 68:3 (1975): 270.

[112] Herman Mueller, "The Ideal Man as Portrayed by the Talmud and St. Paul," *The Catholic Biblical Quarterly* 28 (1966): 281.

[113] G. Sarfatti, "Talmudic Cosmography," *Tarbiz* 35 (1965): 137-148.

[114] Neusner, "How Much Iranian in Jewish Babylonia?" 189.

contain disputations against astrology (e.g., cf. Isa 47:13-14). But, as we shall soon see, by the time of the Babylonian Talmud in the sixth century A.D. – prior to the full-blown astrological teachings by the eighth-century Jewish Messahala and the ninth-century Christian Ibn Hibinta – astrological images and beliefs were assimilated into some segments of Jewish culture.[115]

Though the attitude towards such practices today among Jews (and Christians) is entirely negative, it is easy to see how they can, properly interpreted, fit in perfectly with what we have already said about the implicit cosmology of the Talmud. If God so orders the world as to make it nearly burst with meaning, why *shouldn't* there be some way to find a deeper meaning in events like the movement of the stars? In fact, the type of meaning given to the physical universe takes its most powerful form, as we shall see, in the Talmudic attitude towards words.

Talmudic Dialectics

Because much of what needs to be said about the Talmudic approach to a written text has been said in the previous two sections, I will restrict this section to two specific issues.

In order to discover how the Babylonian Jewish intellectual approached a written text, the first question to ask ourselves is: what text was he looking at? The answer to this is clear: the text which the Talmud examines is the Mishnah. Neusner states: "The Mishnah presented itself to [the authors of the Bavli] as constitutive, the text of ultimate concern."[116] We will discover how the Talmud regards the written word, then, by examining how it deals with the text of the Mishnah. In the same work, Neusner continues, stating the thesis of his book:

The principal and paramount proposition the framers of the Bavli set forth in infinite detail is that the

---

[115] James H. Charlesworth, "Jewish Astrology in the Talmud, Pseudepigrapha, the Dead Sea Scrolls, and Early Palestinian Synagogues," *Harvard Theological Review* 70 (1977): 185.

[116] Neusner, *Talmudic Thinking*, 131.

Mishnah is a perfect piece of writing, exhibiting no flaws such as mar the writings of ordinary men. That proposition yielded two corollaries. First came the blatant and unsurprising principle that the Mishnah's construction of reality accurately portrayed how things really were, that is, the hierarchical classification of all being. What the Mishnah said in general, not only in detail here and there, was so. Second emerged the more subtle, because merely implicit, proposition. It was that the masters whose opinions are represented in the Mishnah – and, therefore, their disciples even down to the very present – were entirely consistent in what they said, so that the deepest premises of their rulings cohered in a unitary composition (not a composite), governing all things.[117]

Thus the single thesis of the entire Talmud, though it expresses itself in many ways, is that the Mishnah is a perfect text. How does the Talmud set out to prove this? First, by taking each statement of the Mishnah and grounding it firmly on Sacred Scripture: "In demonstrating the perfection of the Mishnah, our sages first of all exposed the scriptural sources or foundations for the rules of the Mishnah."[118] But showing that it is founded upon Scripture is not enough to prove it a perfect text. The Mishnah must also be free of all internal inconsistencies.[119] What this produces is a severely acute reading of the text of both the Mishnah and the Bible. We have seen this in the quotation above from Genesis Rabbah that begins "Whoever reflects upon four things..."

That the rabbis had a real consideration of the power of the written word is reflected in this example, the message of which we have already discussed:

To the question, Why does the story of Creation begin with the letter *beth*? the answer is given: 'In the same manner that the letter *beth* is closed on all sides

---

[117] Ibid., 133.

[118] Ibid., 134.

[119] See ibid., 164: "The document is perfect in that it rests upon Scripture and exhibits no flaws of inconsistency."

and only open in front, similarly you are not permitted to inquire into what is before or what was behind, but only from the actual time of Creation' (p. Chag. 77c).[120]

This is easily illustrated: this is what the Hebrew letter "B" looks like:

The simple message of this section is that the *beth* is closed on three sides and open on only one. Because Hebrew writing is from right to left, the book of Genesis would have begun with the top, bottom, and "back" of the first letter closed off, indicating, to the rabbis of the Talmud, "you begin here and nowhere else." Though precisely this type of "letter-splitting" is not extremely common in the Talmud, the attitude of close reading is the very essence of Talmudic exegesis.

Talmudic Piety

During the time when theologians of all sorts – from Christians to Pagans to Alexandrian Jews – were making great strides in their descriptions of God, the rabbis of the Babylonian Talmud remembered their own rule: "ask not what is above." Because of this, commentators today are able to remark that, "all things considered, the Talmud for a 'religious' text pays remarkably little attention to God."[121] This is again an example of the sort of Mesopotamian realism that expressed itself throughout the early paganism of that land, as well as in the overall attitude of the Talmud itself.

Nevertheless, there is still a deep and insightful theology within the pages of the Talmud. Though their main purpose was not to break into the Mystery of God's Essence, their discussions did lead them there on occasion. In discussing what I have called "Talmudic Piety," then, I will concentrate on the specific question of God's transcendence and immanence, and how the rabbis deal with that problem.

---

[120] Cohen, 27.
[121] *Back to the Sources*, 171.

God's transcendence is attested in a rather long, almost tiresome passage from the Genesis Rabbah. Its very length, in fact, seems to exist for the sake of stressing God's utter transcendence over the created world:

24. A. *It has been taught on Tannaite authority:*
B. Said Rabban Yohanan ben Zakkai, "What answer did the echo give that wicked man when he said, "I will ascend above the heights of the clouds, I will be like the Most High' (Is. 14:14)?
C. "The echo came forth and said, 'Wicked man, son of a wicked man, grandson of Nimrod the evil, who through his dominion brought about a rebellion by the entire world against me! How long does a man live? Seventy years: 'The days of our years are three score years and ten, or even by reason of strength fourscore years' (Ps. 90:10). But isn't it a journey from heaven to the firmament of five hundred years? And the thickness of the firmament is a journey of five hundred years. And so too, between each firmament and the one above it. And now, above them are the holy living creatures, and the feet of the living creatures are equal to all of them together, the ankles of the living creatures are equal to all of them together, the legs of the living creatures are equal to all of them together, the knees of the living creatures are equal to all of them together, the thighs of the living creatures are equal to all of them together, the bodies of the living creatures are equal to all of them together, the necks of the living creatures are equal to all of them together, the heads of the living creatures are equal to all of them together, the horns of the living creatures are equal to all of them together. Now above them is the throne of glory. The feet of the throne of glory are equal to all of them together, and the throne of glory is equal to all of them. Above them dwells the King, the living and eternal God, high and exalted. And yet you say, "I will ascend above the heights of the clouds, I will be like the Most High" (Is. 14:14)? No, "you shall be brought

down to the nether world, to the deepest parts of the pit."[122]

The simple point that the rabbis make is "God is above the universe," but the manner in which they make this point is severe: they wish there to be absolutely no question about the approachability of God.

On the other hand, God's immanence and nearness to creation is brought out in Cohen:

> Much more prominent, however, in the Talmudic literature is the conception of God's immanence in the world and His nearness to man. It follows as a corollary from the doctrine of His omnipresence. How happily the Rabbis synthesized the two aspects of Deity is illustrated by this extract: 'An idol appears to be near at hand but is in realty afar off. Why? "It is borne upon the shoulder, it is carried and set in its place; but though one cry to it, it cannot answer, nor save him out of his trouble" (Is. xlvi. 7). The end of the matter is, he has his god with him in his house, but he may cry unto it until he dies without its hearing or rescuing him from his plight. On the other hand, the Holy One, blessed be He, appears to be afar off, but in reality there is nothing closer than He.' There follows a reference to the immeasurable distance of His dwelling-place from the earth, as cited above, and then the moral is drawn: 'However high He be above His world, let a man but enter a Synagogue, stand behind a pillar, and pray in a whisper, and the Holy One, blessed be He, hearkens to his prayer. Can there be a God nearer than this, Who is close to His creatures as the mouth is to the ear?'[123]

The conclusion here is remarkably similar to the one reached upon examining the Pagan Mesopotamian, except here containing a moral precept: God is afar off to those *who desire to comprehend him or reach him*

---

[122] *Genesis Rabah*, 51.
[123] Cohen, 41.

with their own efforts, but is close to those *who approach him with humility and supplication.*

Conclusion

Though the Talmud of Babylon is an enormous and complex document, we may, through the help of the scholars, discover in it a real continuation of the type of thought – the attitude toward the world and God – that we found in Mesopotamia only a few centuries earlier. *Realism*, here in the Talmud expressed as a guiding of the Speculative Intellect by the Practical Intellect – though not in those terms – is the central principle yet again. The children of Abraham never forgot their roots.

In turning to Christianity, however, the situation becomes much more difficult to analyze. As large as the Talmud is, it is still one document, representative of the thinkers, named or not, which worked on its composition. The Christian Church in Mesopotamia, on the other hand, supplies us with a much greater variety of documentation. The method of our analysis must therefore be altered accordingly.

CHAPTER 3

THE FIRST CENTURIES

OF THE CHURCH OF THE EAST

Samuel Hugh Moffett begins his large first volume on the *History of Christianity in Asia* thus:

> The following survey of early Asian Christianity is undertaken with the hope that it may serve as a reminder that the church began in Asia. Its earliest history, its first centers were Asian. Asia produced the first known church building, the first New Testament translation, perhaps the first Christian king, the first Christian poets, and even arguably the first Christian state. Asian Christians endured the greatest persecutions. They mounted global ventures in missionary expansion the West could not match until after the thirteenth century.[124]

What he means, of course, by "Asian Christianity" is Christianity east of the Euphrates River, the most consistent border between the Roman and Persian Empires, and therefore between Western and Eastern Christianity.[125]

My purpose in this chapter is to examine the first five centuries of the Church in Persia, which called herself the "Church of the East," and trace the continuation – ideological if not chronological[126] – of what I am calling the "Mesopotamian School."

---

[124] Samuel Hugh Moffett, *A History of Christianity in Asia* (New York: Orbis Books, 1998), xiii.

[125] The ordinary conception of "East" and "West" regarding the Christian Church is that the "Eastern Church" centered around the "New Rome" of Constantinople, while the "Western Church" centered around Rome itself. This schema leaves out entirely the Church which had neither Constantinople nor Rome for her center, but rather Selucia-Ctesiphon and later Baghdad, and which indeed considered the Greek Church to be "The Western Church."

[126] That is, although most of the documents to be examined in this chapter are concurrent with or even prior to the composition of the Babylonian

In other words: **what is Mesopotamian about the Church in Mesopotamia?**

In beginning this chapter, I should explain why I must avoid the question of *intellectual influence*: the question "if it is the case that Christians and Jews and Pagans (and, later, even Moslems) in Mesopotamia exhibit similar modes of thought and intellectual attitudes towards the world and towards their respective faiths, does this mean that they read one another's works and were consciously affected by them?" While it seems rather likely that, for example, Aphrahat had some interaction with the Rabbis who composed the Talmud, the question itself is far too broad, and the documentation far too sparse, to come anywhere near a real answer. Whether, for example, any fourth-century Rabbi was familiar with the *Epic of Gilgamesh*, or any ninth-century Moslem was familiar with the homilies of Narsai, is simply too difficult a historical question to examine in this paper. Moreover, it is outside its scope: the purpose of this thesis is to expose the evidence that there is an overarching mode of thought and intellectual attitude that is pervasive in Mesopotamian culture through several millennia. It does not seek to answer the much more difficult question of *why* this is the case. Be it the overall culture, or the Semitic language, or even the land itself, the question of the *reason for* or the *method of transmission of* the Mesopotamian School must be left to another time.

While the ancient Pagan literature of Mesopotamia is rather sparse and information about the social and cultural interactions within it and across its borders is almost nonexistent, and while the Jewish community in Babylon lived in relative comfort and semi-isolation, the cultural situation surrounding the Christian community in Mesopotamia is extremely complex. While the documents from this time-period are not abundant, they are ideologically rather variant, ranging from the Gnosticism of the "Thomasine Literature" of the Gospel and Acts of Thomas to the Dualism of the Manicheans to the orthodox practicality of the Synods of the Church of the East. The Christians of Mesopotamia in these first centuries lived and interacted with many different ideas and cultures, and sifting out

---

Talmud (though it is difficult to tell precisely), I will treat them as in some sense coming "after," as Christianity comes "after" Judaism not only chronologically but ideologically.

what is authentically Mesopotamian in this clash of cultures is a difficult task.

My method, therefore, will be as follows: I will give a short description of some of the major ideological or religious movements or documents that either began or had some significant influence upon Persian intellectual life in the first five Christian centuries. Because dating such documents is shaky at best, the ordering of these sections must be approximate: I will begin with the official religion of the Persian Empire, Zoroastrianism; there will then be a discussion on Manichaeism. After these religious movements, I will discuss pieces of literature produced by smaller religious communities: the works called "Thomasine Literature," the *Doctrina Addai*. I will then move to individual writers: Tatian, Bardaisan, Aphrahat, and Ephrem. Finally, I will make a few comments on the earliest Syriac translations of Aristotle. Once there is an appreciation of the complexity of the historical and cultural situation in which the Church of the East first found herself, I will turn to the Church's own self-expression as a representation of authentic Mesopotamian Christianity, for, as I hope to show, every other movement that was alien to the Church of the East was alien to Mesopotamia itself, and *in every case*, from the *Acts of Thomas* to Zoroastrianism, *ceased to have any intellectual or religious significance* except for exceptional and tiny minorities. The documents which I will examine as representative of the Church of the East and therefore of authentic Mesopotamian thought are: the Liturgy, especially the Eucharistic Prayer of Addai and Mari, and the Canons of the Synods of the Church of the East.

Zoroastrianism

The official Roman paganism that persecuted the Christian Church in the West was paralleled in the East, that is, in Persia, by Zoroastrianism, the official religion of the Persian Empire. The Zoroastrian religion at the time when the Church of the East began to exist was, in fact, a *revival* of a religion that had fallen into relative disuse before the rule of the Sassanians:

> How far the Zoroastrianism of the Sassanians resembled the ancient faith they thought they were reviving no one knows. Little can be said about the origins of that ancient religion with any certainty

55

except that Zoroaster has always been revered as the
Iranian prophet of Persia's heroic age.[127]

The date of Zoroaster's life is generally placed between 700 and 1000
B.C., and it was not until well after a millennium that his teaching, or
what was thought to be his teaching, which had been handed down
until then only orally, was put into written form in the Avesta.[128] At
that time, the revival of a "truly Persian" religion was at the forefront
of the Shahs' minds,[129] and the identification of being a "real" Persian
citizen with being a Zoroastrian slowly began to take shape. It is no
wonder, then, that when Rome, the old enemy of Persia, became
Christian with the conversion of Constantine, Persia reacted against
the Christians in her own territory with great violence; the Christians
in Persia were, as far as the Empire was concerned, Roman spies.
Hence began, in 340, what is called by historians the "Great
Persecution:"

> Persia's priests and rulers cemented their alliance of
> state and religion in a series of periods of terror that
> have been called the most massive persecution of
> Christians in history, 'unequalled for its duration, its
> ferocity and the number of martyrs.' The description
> is probably true, though the traditional accounts may
> exaggerate the numbers and usually fail to mention
> that the persecution was not concentrated in one long
> forty-year outburst of hate but occurred in at least
> two shorter but no less tragic periods of madness
> separated by an interval of comparative peace.[130]

---

[127] Moffett, 106.

[128] Ibid., 106-107.

[129] See ibid., 107-108: "The first shah, Ardashir, passed on to his son,
Shapur I, his ideal of an empire stabilized and united by a truly Persian religion. His
dying charge may not be genuine, but it became a governing tenet of imperial
Sassanian policy for the next four hundred years: 'Never forget that as a king you
are at once the protector of religion and of your country. Consider the altar and the
throne as inseparable; they must always sustain each other. A sovereign without a
religion is a tyrant; and a people who have none may be deemed the most
monstrous of all societies.'"

[130] Ibid., 138-139.

Indeed, prior to the Christianization of the Roman empire, the Christians in Persia lived in relative tolerance, depending on the period.

Our concern here, however, is not so much with the physical influence of the persecution by the Persian government, but with the intellectual influence by the Persian culture that predominated in every official forum in the first centuries of Christianity. In other words: how much did Persian culture, expressed in its religious form by Zoroastrianism, influence the native population of Mesopotamia over which it was ruling as an alien force? As I said earlier, my method in this chapter in discussing the survival of the Mesopotamian School despite the permanent end of Mesopotamian self-rule in 587 B.C., will be to examine what *lasted* in Mesopotamian thought and culture over the centuries, and despite the physical force of what was, in essence, alien to it.

What was, then, the Zoroastrian religion, at least in its final form? Again, it is difficult to reconstruct the actual teaching of Zoroaster, and so we must examine the religion as it is confronted: as a mixture and a dilution, even after the "reform:" "Noble as much of this [reform] truly was, nevertheless the teachings of Zoroaster had been diluted, and not a little was gross paganism."[131] Moffett describes the religion itself in these terms:

> However much of the *Avesta* is later addition to Zoroaster's lyric search for truth, there was a religious power in its mystic, cosmological dualism of two warring gods in eternal conflict and in its high ethical demand that the good people of the realm must follow the good god, Ahura-Mazda (or Ormuzd), and worship him in fire. Their reward is eternal life; but the evil ones, possessed by Ahriman, the god of darkness, will be punished in "the house of lies."[132]

As I hope to show in the next section, on Manichaeism, this basic dualism of Zoroastrianism, or what I will call the "Persian element," was decisively rejected by the inhabitants of Mesopotamia, the authentic adherents to the Mesopotamian School. Suffice it to say

---

[131] A. T. Olmstead, *History of the Persian Empire* (Chicago: University of Chicago Press, 1948), 475.
[132] Moffett, 107.

here that, for various reasons, both Zoroastrianism and Manichaeism had an extraordinarily short life-span in Mesopotamia when they were not enforced by civil authority. Jacob Neusner posits a reason for this:

> [The Persians] do not seem to have favored Iranian-speaking people; they moved Romans, Armenians – Jews and Christians – to Iran Proper, so I do not conceive they made a concerted effort to Iranize the lands we now know as Iraq.[133]

This is, of course, only to say that the Persians were more concerned with military control than with cultural predominance. Moffett, on the other hand, is pithy on this point: "Both [Zoroastrianism and Manichaeism] claimed Persia and both eventually lost Persia, but the first losers were the Manicheans."[134]

Manichaeism

While the Persian Empire eventually used the excuse of nationalism and national religion to persecute Christians, the Manicheans were the first to feel the brunt of Persia's force:

> Mani himself, at first in favour at the Persian court, developing a type of thought which to some extent resembled Gnosticism, but introducing as a prominent factor the Persian theory of dualism – of two rival deities, the good and the bad – was crucified about the year 275.[135]

It is precisely this mixture of anti-material Gnosticism and Persian dualism that sets Manichaeism apart as a religion. Elements of Buddhism, Christianity, and even Pagan folklore also add bits and pieces to its complex cosmogony.[136]

---

[133] Jacob Neusner, "How Much Iranian in Jewish Babylonia?" 185.

[134] Moffett, 110.

[135] De Lacy O'Leary, *The Syriac Church and Fathers* (Piscataway, New Jersey: Gorgias Press, 2002 [reprint of the 1909 edition]), 73.

[136] See "Manichaeism," *Catholic Encyclopedia* (www.newadvent.org/cathen/0959a.htm): "[Manichaeism] purported to be the true synthesis of all the religious systems then known, and actually consisted of Zoroastrian Dualism,

Though the life of its founder Mani, whether legendary or historical, is fascinating, it is not our concern here, except to say that he was the son of a famous Mandaean reformer, Mandaeans being a small but severe sect of followers of John the Baptist living south of Babylon.[137] It was here that he apparently learned his disdain for the body, an element of spirituality that was to become one of the basic tenets of his mature teaching. When he grew to adulthood, he traveled through India propagating his teaching and founding communities, and finally returned to Persia to meet with short-lived success and finally crucifixion. Mani's teaching is summarized thus by Moffett:

> The basic motif was a Zoroastrian dualism: Light against Darkness. In the world of matter Darkness holds prisoner particles of the Light. The Power of Light has always yearned to redeem the elements of Light held in the demon grip of the human body and from time to time has sent prophets of truth to proclaim the way of liberation: Adam, Noah, Abraham, Zoroaster, Buddha, and Jesus. The last and greatest of all was Mani. Mani taught that the way of salvation is the way of the ascetic. The body must be broken and subdued, for only so can the particles of Light break free to return to the home of Light.[138]

This summary is only a basic outline of the extremely complex cosmogony of Mani. Indeed, it seems that much of the attraction of Manichaeism was in the very complexity and thoroughness of its description of the universe:

> It had an answer for everything and despised Christianity, which was full of mysteries. It was utterly unconscious that its every answer was a mystification or a whimsical invention; in fact, it gained mastery

---

Babylonian folklore, Buddhist ethics, and some small and superficial additions of Christian elements."

[137] Ibid.

[138] Moffett, 110.

over men's minds by the astonishing ⟨...⟩
minuteness, and consistency of its asserti⟨...⟩

It was within the completeness of this system ⟨...⟩ soteriology found a place: the soul is trapped ⟨...⟩ can only be freed if it masters the body by a ⟨...⟩ meat, alcohol, sex or physical labor.[140]

Having said already that Manicha⟨eism⟩ unsuccessful in Mesopotamia where it was fo⟨...⟩ fact, much more successful both East an⟨d...⟩ homeland[141] – it is worthwhile to ask *why*. Beca⟨use⟩ Manichaean documentation – and of document⟨...⟩ in general – the following can only be regarded ⟨...⟩

Let us contrast the basic discipline ⟨of⟩ Mesopotamian thought both before and after – quoting first from Siduri's speech in the *Epic of Gilgamesh* and second from the Canons of the Synod of Isaac in 410, the first successful attempt of the Mesopotamian Church at self-organization.

To begin, we look at Mani's view on marriage:

> [The Manicheans] regarded [marriage] as an evil in itself because the propagation of the human race meant the continual imprisonment of the light-substance in matter and a retarding of the blissful consummation of all things; maternity was a calamity and a sin and Manichaeans delighted to tell of the seduction of Adam by Eve and her final punishment in eternal damnation.[142]

To this we may add Mani's description of Adam's first self-awareness: "Adam looked around and wept. He mightily lifted up his

---

[139] *Catholic Encyclopedia*, ibid.

[140] See ibid.: "They were forbidden to have property, to eat meat or drink wine, to gratify any sexual desire, to engage in any servile occupation, commerce or trade, to possess house or home, to practice magic, or to practice any other religion."

[141] See ibid.: "Its greatest success was achieved in countries to the east of Persia…in Persia and Babylonia proper, Manichaeism seems never to have been the predominant religion." Also, "In no country did Manichaeism enter more insidiously into the Christian life than in Egypt."

[142] Ibid.

voice as a roaring lion. He tore his hair and struck his breast and said, "Cursed be the creator of my body and he who bound my soul and they who have made me their slave.'"[143] Clearly, then, the body is an evil for Mani, created by an evil god for malicious purposes.

In strong contrast to this is Siduri's advice to Gilgamesh:

> What is best for us to do
> Is now to sing and dance.
> Relish warm food and cool drinks.
> Cherish children to whom your love gives life.
> Bathe easily in sweet refreshing waters.
> Play joyfully with your chosen wife.
> It is the will of the gods for you to smile
> on simple pleasure in the leisure time of your short days.[144]

A greater difference in attitude can hardly be imagined: in Mani's view, the body is to be scorned and marriage avoided. For Siduri, the simple pleasures of leisure and family life are the very essence of happiness – they are the *best* thing!

The very thesis of this paper is, of course, that the basic tenets of the Mesopotamian School, including the attitude toward physical life, continued in authentic Mesopotamian thought well after the end of the Neo-Babylonian period. I will here cite a single example of this from the Synod of Isaac, and give a fuller treatment of the theme in the section devoted to the Synods themselves. The ordering of the Canons of the Synod of Isaac, like those of any Synod, must be assumed indicative of importance. This being the case, it is notable that the Second Canon concerns a very severe condemnation of eunuchs: "any man who willfully makes himself a eunuch and damages his fruitful nature, the same shall not be received into the church."[145] Here a deliberate damaging of one's "fruitful nature" is thought of as such an evil as to *prevent entry into the church itself.* Where the body is condemning for Mani, *hurting* the body is condemning for the Church of the East.

It is a little wonder, then, that Manichaeism was not nearly as successful as Christianity in Mesopotamia, despite the fact that both

---

[143] Ibid.

[144] *Gilgamesh* X.iii.87-99.

[145] *Synodicon Orientale ou recueil des synodes nestoriens*, ed. J. B. Chabot (Paris, 1902), translation by Mar Bawai Soro, unpublished. Hereafter *Synodicon.*

were persecuted, and both very severely. It appears that the "mystification and whimsical invention" of Mani was too much to swallow for the cultural inheritors of the *Epic of Gilgamesh*.

Thomasine Literature

The term "Thomasine Literature" refers to the apocryphal works attributed to or about the Apostle Thomas, which were influential to both Manichaeism and the Monasticism that took root, with varying degrees of success, in northern Mesopotamia.[146] The three main works that fall under the name "Thomasine" are the *Gospel of Thomas*, the *Book of Thomas*, and the *Acts of Thomas*. Because of its greater antiquity and the fact that it has been given greater attention by modern scholarship, I will concentrate most on the *Acts of Thomas*, though the philosophical attitude therein is representative of all three: "All three works are unified by their focus upon the search for oneself together with an ascetic approach to the world."[147]

There is a great deal of debate over the dates of composition of the three works in question. Barnard posits the composition of the *Gospel of Thomas* as early as 140 in Edessa,[148] and Moffett claims 200 as the year when the *Acts* was written, calling it "the oldest narrative account of a church in Asia beyond the borders of the Roman Empire."[149] The precise date of composition concerns us rather little here, suffice it to say that these works were written in Mesopotamia during that dark and often tumultuous time before the Christian Church east of the Euphrates was able to "breathe," so to speak – that is, before the time of Church organization and relative freedom which began during the reign of Yazdegerd I, who allowed the Church to call its first ever successful council in 410.[150] The reason that the date of composition need be no more precise is that, as I

---

[146] *Catholic Encyclopedia*, ibid.

[147] Patrick J. Hartin, "The search for the true self in the Gospel of Thomas, the Book of Thomas and the Hymn of the Pearl," *Hervormde Teologiese Studies* 55.4 (1999): 1008.

[148] L.W. Barnard, "The Origins and Emergence of the Church in Edessa During the First Two Centuries A.D." *Vigiliae Christianae* 22 (1968): 165.

[149] Moffett, 25.

[150] Ibid., 152: "The first Persian church council after the persecutions was the Synod of Isaac, which met in 410, the that Alaric the Goth burned Rome. It was a year of stunning grief in the Christian West, but of celebration for Christians in the East. How often joy in one empire was mirrored by agony in the other."

hope to show, the oddities of the teachings of Thomasine literature, especially those regarding marriage and the goodness of the created world, were rejected with great force as soon as the Church gained the freedom of self-expression.

The clear Gnostic tendencies of the *Acts of Thomas* are shown in the summary of Thomas' teaching in the story given by Thomas Anikuzhikattil:

> Jesus, the exalted Voice that arose from the perfect mercy, savior of all, and liberator and administrator of the world, and strengthener of the dead, is the Right Hand of the Father, who has hurled down the evil one to the lowest limit, and collected his possessions into one blessed place of meeting. If He offers Himself to humankind, it is in order to provide an exit out of the carnal world, out of the world of appearances.[151]

The *Gospel of Thomas* gives a similar soteriology of escape from the physical world, whereby salvation comes from a severe separation from all bodily things. Even more Gnostic in its teaching, the *Gospel of Thomas* places the agency of salvation in *knowledge*:

> Knowledge of oneself brings with it the understanding that one must take seriously the duality between the material and spiritual worlds. Salvation consists for the human in escaping from the material, from the body and from the world. If one is too closely connected to the body and to the world, one will continue to be associated with them at death.[152]

The disassociation from the body which is demanded by this knowledge of the duality between body and soul takes the form of, among other things, absolute abstinence from all sexual activity, which is seen as bestial and sinful of its very essence. The *Gospel of Thomas* itself places these words in the Apostle's mouth: "Does the body not derive from intercourse like the body of the beasts? If it too

---

[151] Thomas Anikuzhikattil, "Syriac Soteriology in the *Acts of Judas Thomas*," *Ephrem's Theological Journal* 6 (March 2002): 34.
[152] Hartin, 1011.

derives from intercourse, how will the body beget anything different from the beasts?"[153]

This introduces two points that will help guide us through the currents of this tumultuous time when the rivers of the Mesopotamian School are difficult to see, being surrounded on all sides by marshes and swamps. The first guiding post is this: that **the teaching on marriage in a given text or writer betrays most clearly whether it is what I have called "authentically Mesopotamian."** Thus if a text is positive toward marriage, reflecting the teaching in the Talmud or in *Gilgamesh*, then it is an expression of the Mesopotamian School. If it condemns marriage in any way, as the Thomasine Literature we are examining, then it must be seen as an alien teaching, produced by something quite external to the Mesopotamian School. The case with Thomasine Literature is quite clear: even if (what is quite unlikely) the books were composed by the Apostle Thomas himself, or came from a tradition that traces back to him, Thomas was not a Mesopotamian, and need not necessarily reflect the culture to which he preached. This latter fact is affirmed quite strongly when we consider how seldom Thomas' name is mentioned in the Breviary of the Church of the East, and how late an addition to the calendar is his feast day. It is odd, to say the least, for the supposed founder of an entire Church to be thus avoided – unless there was some reason to do so. And we find this reason in the fact that the Literature associated with Thomas influenced a very specific group of people in northern Mesopotamia: the monks, and that these monks were forbidden from preaching by the official Church for their overly ascetic and, later, Monophycite tendencies.[154]

The second principle this research suggests is regarding the very special place of the city of Edessa in the schema of the Mesopotamian School, in which city were probably composed most of the Literature connected with Thomas, as well as the Diatesseron of Tatian (which we will examine later) and other very important early Syriac literary works. Edessa was on the very edge of Mesopotamia – it was, in fact, the border city between the Persian and Roman Empires for many years. Being thus so metropolitan, it was a city where every culture, philosophy and religion was allowed

---

[153] Quoted in ibid.

[154] This will be treated in detail in the section on the Synods at the end of this chapter.

for at least some time to flourish and take root, from Judaism to Manichaeism.[155] That being the case, **we must be very careful not to attribute every production of the blessed city of Edessa to the Mesopotamian School.**

With these two principles in mind, then, we move on to another work produced in Edessa, though at a much later date: the *Doctrina Addai*.

The Doctrina Addai

Moffett dates the composition of the *Doctrina Addai* between 390 and 430,[156] although he makes passing reference to an "earlier version that may have been the source of Eusebius' abbreviated account of the story" of the visit of Jude Thaddeus to King Abgar the Black of Edessa. Drijvers also claims an earlier source: "It is most likely that our version of the *Doctrina Addai*, the text of Eusebius, and the Greek papyri all go back to that Syriac original, which must date back to the second half of the third century."[157] Moffett summarizes the story in its pages aptly:

> *The Doctrine of Addai*, written between 390 and 430, tells how Addai came to Edessa and in the apostolic missionary manner first sought out the Jewish community, lodging with "Tobias the son of Tobias." The king heard of his arrival, sent for him, and was miraculously healed. The next day he ordered all his people to assemble to hear Addai explain the source of his great powers and tell "the history of the coming of Christ," and "all the city rejoiced in his doctrine."[158]

---

[155] See Moffett, 46-47.

[156] Moffett, 48.

[157] Han J. W. Drijvers, "Facts and Problems in Early Syriac-Speaking Christianity," *The Second Century: A Journal of Early Christian Studies* 2 (Spring, 1982): 160. Drijvers shifts his dating slightly a few years later in "Jews and Christians in Edessa," *Journal of Jewish Studies* 36.1 (1985): 91: "[The *Doctrina Addai*] dates back to the end of the third century."

[158] Moffett, 48-49.

The doctrine of the book, according to the old Catholic Encyclopedia, is "not unorthodox,"[159] and contains nothing of the condemnation of the physical world or of marriage whereby we dismissed Thomasine Literature as being un-Mesopotamian. Rather, the *Doctrina Addai* presents a practical, peaceful Christianity where faith in the crucified Messiah and gathering into community for worship are central themes. This message comes through, however, in the midst of attacks against the other faiths in Edessa, and the fact is that, as a whole, the work is explicitly polemical.[160]

In fact, the *Doctrina Addai* can be read as nothing but a work of polemics against both the Jews and the Manicheans of Edessa, and mainly the latter. In the already-quoted "Facts and Problems in Early Syriac-Speaking Christianity," Drijvers makes the claim that the character of Addai is portrayed precisely as an "Anti-Mani," that is, as the true Apostle of the Truth of whom Mani is the corruption. Since the details of his argument need not concern us here, his summary should suffice:

> The whole structure and various motifs of the *Doctrina Addai* should be explained against the background of a historical situation in Edessa in which the Manichaean version and interpretation of Christian belief was the most powerful rival of a nascent "orthodox" version of the same tradition.[161]

If this interpretation of the document is valid, then we have in the *Doctrina Addai* an explicit and early Christian Mesopotamian rejection of Manichaeism, which is, for everything we know of it, the embodiment of everything opposite the teaching of the Mesopotamian School.

---

[159] *Catholic Encyclopedia*, "Doctrine of Addai."

[160] See Drijvers, "Jews," 94-95, who quotes one of the sermons from the *Doctrina Addai*: "Beware, therefore, of the crucifiers and do not be friends with them, lest you be responsible with those whose hands are full of the blood of the Messiah. Know and bear witness that everything which we say and teach in regard to the Messiah is written in the books of the Prophets and is laid up with them...They do not know that when they rise up against us, they rise up against the words of the Prophets."

[161] Drijvers, "Facts," 166. The same essay proposes that several of the *Odes of Solomon* were written as explicit polemical works against Mani and his followers.

Incidentally, the problems we cited above regarding the apostle Thomas and his lack of a feast day and direct reference in the Liturgy of the Church of the East for so many years, do not apply to the apostle Addai – in fact, the earliest Eucharistic Prayer of the Church of the East (and, in fact, the oldest still used by any Church in Christianity), is attributed to him and his disciple Mari. This Anaphora will be examined in some detail at the end of this chapter. For now, we will shift from looking at documents to looking at individuals, and the first of these is Tatian the Assyrian.

Tatian

The most interesting figure in Christianity east of the Euphrates (though he did not remain there) in the second century is Tatian (ca. 110-180). Moffett describes him thus:

> This remarkable biblical scholar, linguist, and ascetic was born of pagan parents in the ancient Assyrian territory of northern Mesopotamia (modern Iraq). About 150, having come to Rome for study, he became a pupil of that firm defender of orthodoxy Justin Martyr.[162]

Not only did Tatian travel from Iraq to Rome (and, later, back to Iraq), in the second century, but it is possible that, after the martyrdom of Justin, Tatian opened his own theological school there.[163] Around 172, however, Tatian abandoned Rome and returned to his homeland, where he founded a Christian community and, in Moffett's terms, "brought the Bible, not philosophy, to the Church of the East."[164] Tatian's only work that survives in its full form is his *Address to the Greeks*, a polemic against Hellenic culture which betrays at least one reason why he returned to Assyria from Rome: he simply believed that the East was better than the West:

> Where did the Greeks learn their astronomy? He asks. From Babylon. Their alphabet? From the Phoenicians. Their poetry and music? From Phrygia.

---

[162] Moffett, 72.
[163] Ibid.
[164] Ibid.

Their postal system? From Persia. "In every way the East excels," said Tatian, "and most of all in its religion, the Christian religion, which also comes from Asia and which is far older and truer than all the philosophies and crude religious myths of the Greeks."[165]

This pungent style of writing is typical of Tatian, whom one author describes as "violently hostile, harshly dogmatic."[166]

The form in which Tatian introduced the Gospels to the Church in what was then called Persia was his Syriac harmonization of the Gospels called the *Diatesseron*:

> There is some dispute as to which is the oldest translation of the Gospels from the original Greek. Some say the Old Syriac separate Gospels. Some say the Old Latin. But an emerging conclusion by many scholars is that the earliest of all was Tatian's *Diatesseron*, about A.D. 170.[167]

The *Diatesseron* is a meticulous harmonization of the four Gospels in Syriac, of which we have only fragments of the original, and the complete work in Arabic translation, as well as a Commentary by St. Ephrem. The work was immensely popular in the Syriac-speaking world, even more so than the Gospels themselves for over two centuries.[168] Tatian's influence upon the Church in Mesopotamia, therefore, came mainly through his composition of this Gospel harmony.

---

[165] Ibid.

[166] Gerald F. Hawthorne, "Tatian and His Discourse to the Greeks," *The Harvard Theological Review* 57 (1964): 162. The entire quote: "The tone of the Discourse is violently hostile, harshly dogmatic. On the surface, at least, Tatian condemns all of the ancient civilization: philosophy is folly, secular morality is immorality, pagan literature is frivolity, etc. Tatian here wears the garbs of sophist and cynic: of a sophist in that he exhibits a frenetic desire to be original at any price; of a cynic in that he is harsh and vehement. So thinks Puech, who says: 'Tatian does not reason...he uses invective; he does not defend himself, he heartily takes the offensive; he does not bother to examine doctrines, he attacks persons.'"

[167] Moffett, 72.

[168] See Barnard, 169: "Tatian's *Diatesseron* for nearly two and a half centuries was the *only* version of the Gospels which was used in Syriac-speaking Christianity."

We have in Tatian a case of a Mesopotamian moving to Rome for some twenty years and returning to teach his countrymen what he learned abroad. Indeed, one author even considers Tatian a Westerner: "during this period the Church in Mesopotamia was greatly influenced by people from the West, like Marcion and Tatian."[169] Still, if we follow our method closely, we may distinguish between the authentically Mesopotamian and the alien elements in Tatian's thought.

For one thing, the eminent practicality of the *Diatesseron* seems to be in perfect conjunction with the School of thought which found expression in the Babylonian Talmud. Four Gospels, with some (perhaps) minor or seeming contradictions, are not exactly ideal for teaching the simple people in the villages of northern Mesopotamia.[170] Much more significant, however, is Tatian's belief, expressed in the very act of composing the *Diatesseron*, that the Scriptures, especially the Gospels, are the very core of the Christian Faith. Though this is certainly not a new idea today, it is remarkable during a time when the Canon of Scripture was yet unsettled. We will later see that the absolute primacy of Scripture in teaching and understanding the Christian Faith – even over the apparent teaching of the Councils and certainly over the novelties of philosophy – is perhaps *the* trademark of the mode of thought of the Church of the East.

What seems quite alien to Mesopotamian thought as we have described, however, is Tatian's teaching against marriage (among other things), which has been given the name "Encratism." Though the documentary evidence is scant, and the accusations against Tatian, especially those of Jerome,[171] seem exaggerated, most authors seem to agree that there is some basis for believing that Tatian

---

[169] Anikuzhikattil, 33.

[170] See Hawthorne, 164: "It seems to me that Tatian's real motive for producing his Harmony was his belief that disagreement between two accounts of the same historical incident renders it impossible for one to believe in the truth of those accounts."

[171] See Moffett, 75, where he quotes Jerome: "Tatian…the very violent heresiarch of the Encratites, employs an argument of this sort: 'If anyone sows to the flesh, of the flesh shall he reap corruption'; but he sows to the flesh who is joined to a woman; therefore he who takes a wife and sows in the flesh, of the flesh shall he reap corruption."

regarded marriage as at least comparable to fornication.[172] It is this only this fact, in my opinion, that can explain why the Church of the East never considered Tatian a saint, despite the fact that she used his *Diatesseron* for two hundred and fifty years as her main Gospel book.[173]

Bardaisan

"No two people could be more unlike each other than Tatian of Assyria and Bardaisan of Edessa, Asia's first theologians." [174] Thus does Moffett describe Bardaisan, the son of wealthy pagan parents who was born in about 154 in Edessa. He was educated with a young man named Bar-Manu, who later became Abgar, the first Christian king of the city.[175] His friendship with the king was lifelong, and allowed Bardaisan, after his conversion to Christianity, to have significant influence upon Church events in his city.

Moffett does not exaggerate in describing Bardaisan's personality as totally unlike that of Tatian: where Tatian was the severest of ascetics, Bardaisan "was clearly no ascetic, but dressed in Oriental finery 'with berylls and caftan,' according to St. Ephrem."[176] Clearly, then, his attitude toward the material world was quite positive, and even the oddities of his cosmology which, later, earned him condemnation as a Gnostic from some, never suggested that matter was evil:

> The description of Bardaisan as a Gnostic is due to Greek writers who may have derived their information from his followers, or from works now lost, or may have misunderstood his references to

---

[172] See Hartin, 1018: "[Tatian's] ascetical practices led him to reject marriage which he denounced as fornication." Also, see Peter M. Head, "Tatian's Christology and its Influence on the Composition of the Diatesseron," *Tyndale Bulletin* 43 (1992): 121: "It was [Tatian's] stance against marriage which caused him to be regarded as a heretic by many Western Church Fathers."

[173] Indeed, Tatian's name seems all but forgotten for the Church of the East: "the remarkable thing is that the Syriac-speaking Church preserved no tradition about Tatian, except to identify the author of their Diatesseron with the Tatianus mentioned by Eusebius." Hawthorne, 165.

[174] Moffett, 72.

[175] O'Leary, 37.

[176] *The Catholic Encyclopedia*, "Bardesanes and Bardesanites."

angels, etc., and to the planets, and so confused his teaching with the Gnostic theory of aeons.[177]

Nor was his teaching on marriage anything like that of Tatian: he was married himself, and had three children even after his ordination to the deaconate or priesthood.[178] So positive, in fact, was his view toward marriage that he believed the sexual act to be "purifying"[179] – a stark contrast with the apparent teaching of Tatian. Moffett summarizes Bardaisan's teaching: "Unlike the Gnostics and even most Syrian Christian writers of the early centuries, Bardaisan's theology was a theology of freedom and not of ascetic restraint."[180]

Aside from his *Book of the Laws of Countries*, a defense of free will against the teaching of astrologers that the planets determine every act on earth, we have only a few fragments of Bardaisan's work, mostly in the form of defenses of the Faith against the Marcionites and hymns which were so popular in Edessa as to be replaced two hundred years later only by those of Ephrem himself.[181] Bardaisan is described even by Ephrem, who spent so much of his life attacking the doctrines of his followers, as "seemingly orthodox" on the surface: "There is such a reasonable sound to the man's writings that common people do not see the 'madness' beneath."[182]

This "madness" came in the form of an odd cosmology, gleaned, apparently, from Bardaisan's early studies with Babylonian astrologers and Indian mystics, into which he attempted to fit the Christian faith, in an attempt to make it intelligible to his contemporaries in Persia. For the Church, and especially for later Church writers, it was a failed attempt.[183] Moffett summarizes Bardaisan's "worldview:"

---

177 O'Leary, 40.

178 *The Catholic Encyclopedia*, ibid.

179 Quoted in Moffett, 67.

180 Ibid.

181 See *The Catholic Encyclopedia*, ibid.: "[Bardaisan's hymns] became famous in the history of Edessa: their words and melodies lived for generations on the lips of the people. Only, when St. Ephrem composed hymns in the same pentasyllabic metre and had them sung to the same tunes as the psalms of Bardesanes, these latter gradually lost favour."

182 Moffett, ibid.

183 See ibid., 69: "[Bardaisan] may have thought he was using secular and pagan learning only to make the gospel intelligible to an unbelieving world, but the Greek and Persian lions did not lie down as peaceably with the Christian lamb as he

Above is God and below is darkness. In between are the four pure elements, white light, red fire, blue wind, and green water. When chance disturbed the primeval harmony of these pure elements, darkness entered the mixture and evil came into the world. Only the coming of Christ, "the First Thought" (the Logos), was able to restore order in the resulting chaos.[184]

As odd as it seems to us today, for a Persian in the second century attempting to make sense of the Christian Faith, this is a rather sober cosmology – a glance at the cosmology of Iamblichus, a Pagan of Syria living less than a century later, or that of any of the Neo-Platonists in the first centuries of Christianity, proves this sufficiently.

Still, Bardaisan was rejected by the official Church, and, like Tatian before him, was forgotten and unnamed, except as the supposed founder of a sect of heretics against which Ephrem and others debated for centuries. Where did this seemingly orthodox man – respected in some way even by his adversaries – go wrong in the eyes of the Mesopotamian Church? Again, having an odd cosmology and the belief in some form of astrology seemed to have been part and parcel with being a thinker in the ancient world – even Aristotle believed that the planets effected life on earth in some way.

It is my view, supported by Moffett, that Bardaisan was wrong precisely where Tatian was right: Scripture. Where Tatian saw the importance of Scripture clearly enough to work so meticulously as to produce the *Diatesseron*, Bardaisan draws rather little from Holy Writ, and instead introduces ideas and modes of thought exterior to Scripture:

> His root error, as seen from an orthodox position, would seem to be not so much any particular doctrine but rather the whole philosophical and cosmological foundation of his worldview, a view he had derived from outside Scripture and into which he tried to fit his new Christian worldview.[185]

seemed to expect, and the ill-matched combination brought on him the condemnation of the church."

[184] Ibid., 68.

[185] Ibid.

It seems that having a view of harmony between heaven and earth, and believing in the ultimate goodness of matter and of marriage is not enough to be a thinker acceptable to the Mesopotamian Church. One must be grounded firmly not only on earth, but also in the Bible. As I hope to show in the next chapter, the primacy of Scripture which was ignored by Bardaisan later becomes, for the Church of the East, the definitive catalyst for her Christological debate with the Church of Alexandria.

Aphrahat

The "Persian Sage" lived first in the region of northern Mesopotamia around Adiabene, before he became bishop of a town called Mar Mattai which is near the Mosul of today. His only surviving works are the *Demonstrations*, which are basically twenty-three homilies on various aspects of Christian life. He was the son of noble Persian parents, and a convert to Christianity.[186] Aphrahat is unique in being the only Christian writer of inner Persia whose works we have today who wrote during the Great Persecution. Though he was a contemporary of Ephrem, Ephrem lived on the border between Persia and Rome, under better circumstances and closer to the influence of the Western Church. It is an accident of history that, once Aphrahat took the name Jacob upon his entry into the Church, his works were for centuries attributed to his friend Jacob, the bishop of Nisibis.[187]

Aphrahat was a practical, well-educated, and, in the words of Jacob Neusner, a man with a "powerful, independent mind."[188] Sebastian Brock makes this remark regarding Aphrahat's influence on the later Church: "It is evident that Aphrahat exerted a continuing influence on Syriac spirituality, especially during the sixth to eighth centuries, for his homilies are tacitly quoted by a number of writers."[189] Modern authors generally affirm his orthodoxy: "[Aphrahat has] from antiquity an unblemished reputation for

---

[186] Ibid., 125.

[187] *The Catholic Encyclopedia*, "Aphraates."

[188] Jacob Neusner, "Aphrahat and Judaism: The Christian-Jewish Argument in Fourth-Century Iran," *Studia Post-Biblica* 19 (1971): xi.

[189] Sebastian Brock, *The Syriac Fathers on Prayer and the Spiritual Life* (Kalamazoo, Michigan: Cistercian Publications, 1987), 3-4.

orthodoxy."[190] And the *Catholic Encyclopedia* remarks on Aphrahat's early affirmation of "the perpetual virginity of the Blessed Virgin and her Divine Maternity, the foundation of the Church on St. Peter...the existence of all the sacraments except Matrimony, which is not mentioned...[and] the Holy Eucharist, which Aphrahat affirms to be the real Body and Blood of Christ."[191]

Because he was writing during the time of the Great Persecution, Aphrahat found himself debating the rabbis of the Jewish communities to which many in his flock, dismayed at their own plight and attracted by the relative freedom of the Jews in Persia at the time, were converting.[192] Though the range of his debates with the Jewish rabbis[193] – whether they physically took place at all or were merely the fruits of his own reflection – goes from the question of "are the Jews alone the people of God" to "are the current persecutions of the Christian Church proof of God's disfavor," I will follow the guideline established earlier, and concentrate on his debate regarding marriage.[194]

In the 18th *Demonstration*, Aphrahat writes about an accusation made by a Jew against one of his parishioners:

> I write you my beloved concerning virginity and
> *kadishuta* [holiness] because I have heard from a
> Jewish man who insulted one of the brothers,
> members of our congregation, by saying to him: You
> are *tame'in* [impure] who do not marry women; but we
> are *kadishin* [holy] and better, who procreate and
> increase progeny in the world.[195]

---

[190] William L. Petersen, "The Christology of Aphrahat, the Persian Sage: An Excursus on the 17th *Demonstration*," *Vigiliae Christianae* 46 (1992): 244.

[191] *The Catholic Encyclopedia*, ibid.

[192] Moffett, 126.

[193] Some authors are convinced that there must have been some sort of give-and-take between Aphrahat and the rabbis. See Naomi Koltun-Fromm, "A Jewish-Christian Conversation in Fourth-Century Persian Mesopotamia," in *Journal of Jewish Studies* 47.1 (1996): 48: "Aphrahat's writings are as much a key to understanding the rabbinic texts as the rabbinic texts are in understanding Aphrahat's *Demonstrations*."

[194] My main sources for this are Moffett and Naomi Koltun-Fromm, "Sexuality and Holiness: Semitic Christian and Jewish Conceptualizations of Sexual Behavior," *Vigiliae Christianae* 54 (2000): 375-395.

[195] Koltun-Fromm, "Sexuality," 373.

It is easy to see how such an accusation would shake the faith of Christian in fourth century Persia. Making reference to God's commandment in Genesis to multiply and subdue the earth, the rabbi accuses Christians – the elite of which were celibates comprising a proto-religious order called "Sons and Daughters of the Covenant"[196] – of disobeying God's command in their acceptance of celibacy. The dichotomy is real and severe: the holiest lifestyle for the Christian is one condemnable for the Jew.

Aphrahat's reply takes the form of a close reading of the Old Testament. Beginning with Moses' example in the tent of meeting in Exodus 33:11. Noticing that, while serving God in the tent, Joshua, and not Moses' wife, served Moses, Aphrahat makes the simple conclusion that Moses was celibate during that time. Going further, Aphrahat notes that:

> Concerning Joshua's marital status, this same verse continues: '[Joshua] never quit the tent.' Aphrahat argues, since women were not allowed into the tent of meeting, how could Joshua have been served by a wife if he never left the tent? Hence, Joshua too was celibate. Furthermore Aphrahat contends, the priests were required to be celibate, i.e., 'remain in their sanctity,' during their days of service.[197]

Citing many other examples of temporary celibacy in the Old Testament, Aphrahat argues that, for Christians who are in the Presence of God perpetually, celibacy is of the highest propriety.

This teaching has prompted some to accuse Aphrahat of condemning marriage, or of requiring celibacy for baptism, but modern scholarship has shown that this is not the case. Koltun-Fromm, for example, repeats several times in her article that "[Aphrahat] never condemns the Jews outright for their sexual practices, nor does he ever denounce Christian marriage," and "Aphrahat is unwilling to condemn marriage completely."[198] Another author, Skiry, also states that "there is general agreement that Aphrahat did not require celibacy for Baptism," quoting Aphrahat

---

[196] For a description of the Sons and Daughters of the Covenant, the "Bnay Qnayma," see Moffett, 97-100.

[197] Koltun-Fromm, "Sexuality," 380.

[198] Ibid., 385.

directly: "Far be it from us, however, to debase marriage, constituted in the world by God himself."[199]

Still, this is a far cry from the usual Mesopotamian view of marriage. The fact that Aphrahat *tolerates* marriage – even begrudgingly – shows the influence of a greater force than the culture around him, and that force is Scripture itself. Though Aphrahat is careful not to cite New Testament sources in his debates with the Jews,[200] it is clear that the Sons and Daughters of the Covenant drew the inspiration for their celibate lifestyle from the life of Christ and the example of St. Paul. We here find, for the first time, a tension between what I have posited as two representative tenets of the teaching of the Mesopotamian School: the goodness of the physical world and especially of marriage, and the authority of Scripture as the source of Christian doctrine. While Scripture certainly never suggests that marriage is a bad thing, it does suggest, both in the Gospels and in Paul's writings, that celibacy is somehow superior.

His attitude toward Scripture becomes definitive for the Church of the East, which always avoided allegory: "[Aphrahat] was concerned to interpret Scripture in an ordinary, plain sense. His biblical interpretation largely follows a historical and typological approach, and refrains from allegorical interpretations."[201] And again in Neusner:

> When [Aphrahat] cites the Hebrew Scriptures, he ordinarily refrains from fanciful or allegoristic reading of them, but, like the rabbis with whom Jerome dealt, stressed that his interpretation rested solely on the plain and obvious, factual meaning at hand.[202]

We will find both in Ephrem and in the Synods of the Church of the East how this tension between the authority of Scripture and the established Mesopotamian view regarding marriage finds a better balance between the two tenets than did Aphrahat.

---

[199] Jaroslav Z. Skira, "Circumcise Thy Heart: Aphrahat's Theology of Baptism," *Diakonia* 31 (1998): 124.

[200] Neusner praises him on this point: "[Aphrahat] rarely cites the New Testament in his demonstrations on Judaism." *Rabbinic Judaism's Generative Logic* (Binghamton, New York: Global Publications, 2002), 22.

[201] Skira, 117.

[202] Neusner, ibid., 22.

Ephrem

"The Harp of the Spirit" was born around 309 in or around Nisibis, a city to whose literary fame Ephrem contributed greatly, and which he himself associated with the ancient (now thought to be lost) city of Akkad.[203] The ancient sources diverge on whether he had pagan or Christian parents, but it is quite clear that he himself grew up in Nisibis a Christian, and spent almost his entire life there – moving to Edessa only in 363, after Nisibis had been taken by the Persian Empire.[204] His time in Nisibis was spent serving the Church faithfully as a writer, the head of a Christian theological school in Nisibis, a defender of the faith, and a counselor to the three successive bishops who were his close friends: Jacob, Babu and Vologeses. It is well known that Ephrem refused to be elevated to any Ecclesiastical office higher than that of deacon, despite pressures from the Church.[205] Though thus affirming his active service to the Church in his day contradicts many of his ancient biographies, which claim he was a hermit unconcerned with outside affairs, there is a great deal in his writings to support his active role in the Church, and little to suggest that he was in fact a hermit.[206]

After having been forced to move to Edessa for the last ten years of his life, Ephrem continued to write, and even more prolifically than before, for it was in Edessa that he encountered all the heresies against which many of his works were targeted: Arianism, Marcionism, Bardaisanism, and especially Manichaeism.[207] Mathews summarizes his literary activity in Edessa thus:

> The majority of [Ephrem's] surviving hymns and commentaries seem to stem from this period. Tradition also maintains that Ephrem set up a school in Edessa after the manner of the one he had directed in Nisibis. His biblical commentaries, probably

---

[203] See his *Commentary on Genesis*, VIII.1. The fact is mentioned in the General Introduction to *St. Ephrem the Syrian: Selected Prose Works*, v. 91 of *The Fathers of the Church*, tr. Edward G. Mathews (Washington, D.C.: The Catholic University, 1994), 26.

[204] Ibid., 35.

[205] Ibid., 29.

[206] The question is thoroughly dealt with in ibid., 12-37.

[207] Ibid., 35.

written during this period, were long used as the
standard commentaries in this school.[208]

Though he was extremely prolific both as a theologian-poet and a
Biblical commentator, I will concentrate on his poetic works as being
most representative of Ephrem's theological teaching and personal
genius.

Sebastian Brock, in a paper on *Ephrem on Christ as Light*,
quotes the Dominican S. Tugwell, who describes Ephrem as "one of
the great religious poets of the world."[209] Ephrem is officially
recognized as a "Doctor" of the Catholic Church, and considered by
most scholars to be the greatest hymnodist in Christian history. So
powerful is his religious poetry that the historian Sozomen and St.
Jerome both remark with surprise how beautiful are Ephrem's
writings even in translation.[210] My method in this section, then, will
be to examine, in summary, Ephrem's religious poetry as an authentic
representation of the thought of the Mesopotamian School. Thus, I
will reinstate three of the four categories which I used in Chapters I
and II: Cosmology, Dialectic and Piety. The first category of
Ephrem's thought, Anthropology, should be made clear in the other
three.

Ephrem on Cosmology: the Wonders of Creation

In the eighteenth of the *Hymns on Faith*, Ephrem uses several
images, drawn both from nature and from Scripture, to describe the
centrality of the Cross of Christ in the Christian faith. The sixth
stanza uses the image of a flying bird:

> If a bird contracts its wings and denies
> the outspread symbol of the Cross, then the air too
> denies it, and does not carry it
> unless its wings proclaim the Cross.[211]

---

[208] Ibid., 36.

[209] Sebastian Brock, "St. Ephrem on Christ as Light in Mary and in the
Jordan: Hymni De Ecclesia 36," *Eastern Churches Review* 7 (1975): 137.

[210] Cited in Mathews, 39.

[211] Tr. Peter Yousif, "St. Ephrem on Symbols in Nature: Faith, the Trinity
and the Cross (Hymns on Faith, No. 18)," *Eastern Churches Review* 10 (1978): 53.

As a poetic image, describing the bird as representing the Christian, and its motion as the necessary embrace of the Cross to which every Christian is called, is attractive and appropriate, and nothing extraordinary by modern standards of religious poetry. What is extraordinary to the modern mind, however, is the metaphysical assumptions that underpin Ephrem's use of the bird image in this way. For Ephrem, it is not merely coincidence that the bird stretches its wings the way Christ stretched his arms out on the Cross – it is the case because of the deliberate desire of the Creator. It is no accidental resemblance, in other words, but a real piece of evidence for the providential guidance of the world by God, who created the bird and its flight patterns in order to reflect the glory of the Cross.

This is the meaning of the word "type" or "symbol" – the Syriac *tupsa*. In the twentieth of the *Hymns on Virginity*, Ephrem tells us that "wherever you look, God's symbol is there; wherever you read, there you will find His types. For by Him all creatures were created, and He stamped all His possessions with His symbols when He created the world."[212] For Ephrem, every detail in the physical cosmos (and, as we will see, in the Scriptures) is a pointer to the God who created it. Nor are creatures empty in themselves, as if their value lay only in God to whom they point: "types and symbols are not simply pointers, for to Ephrem 'the symbol contains within itself the actual presence of that which it symbolizes' – a view by no means confined to Ephrem, but one common to the Fathers, leading to an essentially sacramental view of the world."[213] And these "sacramentals" are innumerable enough to lead Ephrem to exclaim "this Jesus has so multiplied His symbols that I have fallen into their many waves."[214] Kathleen McVey summarizes the point thus:

> No person, thing or event in the world exists without a mysterious relation to the whole...Each moment of life is governed by the Lord of life and is an opportunity to see oneself and the community in relation to that Lord. So not only the events described in scripture but all historical events must have

---

[212] Quoted in Mathews, 49.
[213] Sebastian Brock, "The Poet as Theologian," *Sobornost* 7:4 (1977): 245.
[214] Quoted in Mathews, 53.

profound religious significance...Nature, too, is replete with intimations of the presence of God.[215]

This obviously leads the individual to the same type of wonder at the physical world which we find in the *Enuma Elish* and in the Talmud: "As Ephrem regularly points out, [the] right attitude is essentially one of an awesome wonder that finds expression in thanksgiving and praise."[216] Reflecting once more on the beauty of the physical creation, and of daily life, Ephrem is forced to exclaim:

> Let us see those things that He does for us every day!
> How many tastes for the mouth!
> How many beauties for the eye!
> How many melodies for the ear!
> How many scents for the nostrils!
> Who is sufficient [to explain] the goodness
> of these little things![217]

Not only does Ephrem have seemingly no dialectic against the world and worldly things, he continuously praises – and enjoys – the beauty of creation that reflects and reveals its Creator at every moment.

Ephrem on Dialectic: the Centrality of Scripture

Brock introduces his book on *The Syriac Fathers on Prayer and the Spiritual Life* with a general description of the early Church east of the Greek world: "Early Syriac Christianity can justly be described as the product of a creative and fruitful meditation upon Scripture."[218] Theology is, for the authors at hand, drawn directly and exclusively from the Bible: "time and time again, the starting point for distinctive developments is to be located in the biblical text itself."[219] This is poignantly the case with Ephrem, whose hymns Bock describes as being "soaked in Scripture."[220]

---

[215] Tr. Kathleen McVey, *Ephrem the Syrian: Hymns* (New York: Paulist Press, 1989), 41.

[216] Sebastian Brock, "Humanity and the Natural World in the Syriac Tradition," *Sobornost* 12:2 (1990): 139.

[217] Quoted in Mathews, 47.

[218] Sebastian Brock, *The Syriac Fathers on Prayer and the Spiritual Life*, xxxiii.

[219] Ibid.

[220] ibid., 31.

Scripture is, for Ephrem, the second book written by God in order to reveal himself to creatures. The first, of course, is nature itself:

> In his book Moses described
> The creation of nature,
> So that both the natural world and his book
> Might testify to the Creator,
> The natural world, through humanity's use of it,
> The book, through their reading of it.[221]

Scripture thus testifies to nature, while standing in itself as a special testimony to the God who reveals himself in these manifold ways.

Ephrem's exegetical method may be described as "symbolical" or "typological." That is to say, in reading a passage of Scripture, he is neither allegorical nor literal. Mathews gives us his own description in modern scholarly terms:

> Ephrem's emphasis on the obvious sense of the words of Scripture, and his treatment of the two economies of salvation and the two Adams places him in a position much closer to the Antiochian tradition of scriptural exegesis than to the Alexandrian which preferred the allegorical method.

But Ephrem is no mere literal reader of Scripture:

> Taking for granted the dynamic convergence of the Old and New Testaments, Ephrem shows his true genius by the way he draws out the full significance or the inner sense of the words and sets them in their typological context within the rest of the sacred text. The bond that unites the two Testaments is so intimate that there is virtually no incident or detail in one which does not have its typological parallel in the other.[222]

---

[221] Quoted in Brock, "Humanity," 138.
[222] Mathews, 47.

Thus Ephrem contradicts Marcion, who rejected the Old Testament, and the Arians, who read Scripture in a slavishly literal fashion, without recourse to the fanciful "allegorism of the Alexandrian school."[223] The strict difference between typology and allegory will be treated in detail in the next chapter, suffice it to say here that allegory in the sense that Ephrem rejects it tends to ignore the actual event referred to by the text of Scripture in order to leap immediately to the "spiritual meaning" hidden behind the text, whereas typology looks at the event itself as revealing the spiritual message.

Finally, the point of all types, Scriptural or natural, is Christ himself, "the one who reveals their true meaning, whom Ephrem calls 'the Lord of the Symbols.'"[224] I will conclude this section, therefore, by simply quoting part of the tenth of Ephrem's *Hymns on the Faith* as an illustration both of the intrinsic interrelation between the Old and New Testaments, and of Ephrem's genius in composition and symbolic theology.

> For even if the great John cried out,
> 'I am not worthy, Lord, of the strap of your sandals,'
> then I like the sinner-woman must flee
> to the shade of your garments, to start from there.
>
> And like her who feared yet took heart when she was healed,
> Heal my fear of terror, let me take heart in you;
> Let me pass from your garment to your body,
> That to the best of my power I may speak of it.
>
> Your garment, Lord, is a fountain of healing.
> In your visible dress dwells your hidden power.
> A little spittle from your mouth
> Was a mighty wonder, for light was in the clay it made.
>
> In your Bread is hidden a Spirit not to be eaten,
> In your Wine dwells a Fire not to be drunk.
> Spirit in your Bread, Fire in your Wine,
> A wonder set apart, [yet] received by our lips!
>
> When the Lord came down to earth, to mortals,

---

[223] Ibid., 48.
[224] Ibid., 53.

A new creation he created them, like to the Watchers.
He mingled fire and spirit in them,
To make them fire and spirit within.

The Seraph touched not the coal with his fingers;
Only Isaiah's lips did it touch.
He neither held it nor ate it;
But to us, see! our Lord has granted both.

Bodily food for angels of spirit
Did Abraham bring, and they did eat;
New wonder! Our mighty Lord gives to bodily creatures
Fire and Spirit as food and drink.

Fire came down in anger on sinners and ate them up;
The Fire of Mercy has come down on bread, to stay.
Instead of that fire eating men up,
You have eaten Fire in the Bread and found life.

Fire came down on Elijah's sacrifice and ate it up;
The Fire of Love has become our living sacrifice.
Fire ate up the offering;
In your Offering, Lord, we have eaten Fire.

'Who has ever grasped the wind in his hands?'
Come and see, Solomon, what your father's Lord has done!
Fire and Spirit, against their nature,
He has mingled and poured into his disciples' hands.

'Who has ever,' he asked, 'gathered the waters in a cloth?'
See, a cloth, in the lap of Mary, the Fountain!
Enclosed in a cloth, your handmaids take
From the Cup of Life, a drop of Life![225]

---

[225] From "A Hymn of St. Ephrem to Christ on the Incarnation, the Holy Spirit, and the Sacraments," tr. Robert Murray, S.J., *Eastern Churches Review* 3 (1970-1971): 143-144.

Ephrem on Piety: Loving the Unknowable God

The first stanzas cited in the hymn above reveal the first of Ephrem's two guiding principles in his theology: fear of approaching God too closely: "heal my fear of terror." This principle is expressed throughout Ephrem's theology as a tendency to avoid definition: "Ephrem's method deliberately eschews any definition of the divine nature. Ephrem considers any attempt to define God as a setting of limits on that which is limitless."[226] This places Ephrem outside the category of Systematic Theologian, a categorization which Ephrem would not have minded.[227]

Still, Ephrem's theology is not entirely – or even mainly – negative. Although God's nature is entirely beyond human comprehension, God himself has chosen to reveal it to the human mind, as we said above, through the books of nature and Scripture. These revelations, solidifications or physical manifestations of the Divine Essence, "dim the divine brightness for the sake of humanity," though "God Himself loses absolutely nothing of His nature or His majesty."[228]

Moreover, there is, for Ephrem, a powerful inner drive in human nature which pushes the mind and heart toward God, the natural fear of God notwithstanding. This dynamic tension in Ephrem's thought is beautifully brought forth in his *Hymn on the Church* number 9, titled *Dialogue of Reason and Love*.[229]

In this dialogue, it is Reason which takes up the voice of negative or apophatic theology, since "Reason insists – almost brutally – that the attempt to penetrate the nature of God is both folly and blasphemy."[230] Love, on the other hand, "simply has to praise and respond to the revelation and experience of himself which

---

[226] Mathews, 49.

[227] See Brock, "The Poet as Theologian," 243: "But [Ephrem] is certainly not a systematic theologian, or one who is continually seeking for definitions. Indeed, the search for precise definitions on topics that belong to areas beyond the experience and capacity of the human intellect is, in Ephrem's eyes, something that only prying rationalists (in his case the Arians) indulge in, and their example should not be imitated."

[228] Mathews, 51.

[229] I will be using the translation given by Robert Murray in "St. Ephrem's Dialogue of Reason and Love," *Sobornost* 2:2 (1980): 26-40.

[230] Ibid., 27.

God himself has given."[231] It is Robert Murray's thesis that "Ephrem's way of holding and expressing this tension can truly be said to anticipate what was to become the classic doctrine of 'analogy' in speaking of God."[232]

The dialogue begins recalling the lowliness of human nature:

> Never, when I would draw near [you],
> Can I forget my nature's weakness;
> When I contemplate you in silence
> It would be too much for me if I could understand.[233]

Thus cold, sober reason speaks. Love, however, is not so sober:

> Your teaching is new wine,
> Which ennobles everyone who becomes drunk with it;
> Through it he forgets his weakness
> And fearlessly dares to speak.[234]

Speaking henceforth becomes the mark of Love, while Silence is the mark of Reason. The argument is thus about whether we should dare say anything about God, or only adore him without words in contemplation. Reason continues boldly:

> 'It is enough for you, O Weakling,
> To offer praise in silence.'
> Blessed be He who through insight
> Has made silence mightier than the tongue![235]

Love replies, citing several Scriptural examples of people who won favor with God and true knowledge of him by speaking up and asking for insight, especially John the Beloved Disciple, who "fearlessly...leant on the breast of Power and asked the hidden secret and received the revealed explanation."[236] Reason responds with other Scriptural examples which show human beings harmed by

---

231 Ibid.
232 Ibid.
233 Ibid., 31.
234 Ibid., 32.
235 Ibid.
236 Ibid., 33.

drawing too close to the Mystery, such as Daniel who "lost his wits" when he saw an angel.[237]

The argument, now "saturated with Scripture," begins to refine itself. Reason allows for an understanding of creation, but limits even that, taking the voice of God which spoke to Job:

> 'Interpret [all] creatures for me
> and explain to me all that is visible;
> when this sun sets, how does it come back?
> By what road does it return
> To the place from where it rises?'[238]

But Love answers by recalling how God chooses, in his abundance, to grant great gifts to those whom he loves, enjoining the reader to: Load up with his riches to your capacity and do not presume to restrict his treasure!"[239] The dialogue approaches its conclusion in this stanza, which summarizes the truth of both combatants:

> All things have their measure; Love gave
> The rule for the measure of words,
> As Reason in its turn gave me
> The rule for the measure of silence.
> Like masters they imparted to me
> The pattern for silence and speech,
> That my mind might not drown in silence
> Nor yet in speech make too bold,
> Prying and presuming to explain
> The Sun's nature, seen and unseen,
> Whose visible light we may love
> But whose hidden power we must fear.
> Blessed be he who through two masters
> Made me a discerning learner![240]

This "measure" of both silence and speech, of Love and Reason, each active in its own place, is the essence of true piety for Ephrem.

---

237 Ibid., 34.
238 Ibid., 35.
239 Ibid.
240 Ibid., 37.

It was just in the century after the time of Ephrem that we find the earliest translations of the Aristotelian corpus into Syriac, which were done almost entirely by the Christians of Mesopotamia. When looking at any history of western philosophy, there is usually little or no mention of what happened to Aristotle's works before the advent of Islamic philosophy and Western Scholasticism. Marias, for example, usually fairly detailed in his descriptions, states only that "The great role of the Arabs and Jews was as the transmitters of Aristotelian thought." He continues, in greater detail,

> In the seventh century, during the Abbasid Empire, the Syrians introduce Aristotle's thought to the Arabs in rather indirect fashion. The Aristotelian texts are translated – not always accurately – from Greek to Syriac, from Syriac to Arabic, and sometimes also pass through the Hebrew Language. These extremely indirect Arabic translations are in turn translated into Latin and then come to the attention of the Scholastics.[241]

Though this is an accurate description of the train of languages through which the corpus was translated, Marias is missing any reference – besides the ambiguous word "Syrians" – to *who* actually did the translations, and the fact that these translators were all Christians in Mesopotamia. He does, however, make reference to Syriac, which was the dialect of Aramaic, that was spoken and taught in the theological schools of Nisibis and Edessa.

Another historian of philosophy, Msgr. Glenn, is even more vague:

> From the Byzantines in the early 13th century, the Scholastics of Western Europe received the original and complete works of Aristotle which they had

---

[241] Julian Marias, *History of Philosophy* (New York: Dover Publications, 1967), 153.

known hitherto only in imperfect and interpolated Arabic translations of Syriac versions.[242]

Again, we find much missing in this description, but another interesting point made, which was that, while the East Syrians were the original translators of Aristotle, it was the Byzantines who were the preservers of most of the original Greek texts.

A look at a third and most prestigious history of philosophy should suffice to show the general tendency of western historians of philosophy to pass over the fact of the Christian Mesopotamian translators of Aristotle's works. Frederick Copleston, S.J., in his voluminous work, makes no mention of the translation of Aristotle besides a passing reference to the Arabs, and even goes so far as saying that

> The rediscovery of Aristotle and the translation of the leading Islamic thinkers in the second half of the twelfth century and the first part of the thirteenth brought to the knowledge of the Christian mediaeval thinkers for the first time a developed system which was the work of a pagan philosopher *and which owed nothing to Christianity.*[243]

That the history of Aristotelian philosophy "owed nothing to Christianity" is false, assuming the Christian translators played an important part therein. The question is, of course, whether the Christian translators were simply slavish literal translators simply working for the Arab courts, or were also interpreters, reading Aristotle for their own sake, and therefore commentators as well. Why it was that Christians, mainly Nestorians or "East Syrians" and some Jacobites or "West Syrians," were the first translators of Aristotle's works in the East may be answered in several ways, depending upon the historical point of the particular translation. To put it simply, there were two "phases" of translation. The first began in the fifth century, the second peaking in the eighth and ninth centuries.

---

[242] Paul J. Glenn, *The History of Philosophy* (New York: B. Herder Book Co., 1934), 218.

[243] Frederick Copleston, *A History of Philosophy* (New York: Image Books, 1962), v. 3, 414. Italics mine.

Ironically, while it is difficult to find any reference to the Mesopotamian Christian translators of Aristotle in any western history of philosophy, there is usually an abundance of references thereunto in histories of Arab philosophy. F. E. Peters, in his work *Aristotle and the Arabs*, begins the third chapter, "The Eastern Translation Movement" with a parallel between East and West: in both cases, there was a gradual movement of translation of, specifically, Aristotle's works of logic. These translations in the West, "began about AD. 355 with the Latin translations of the *Categoriae* by Marius Victorinus."[244] Only about a hundred years later, "The Eastern translation of Aristotle began about A.D. 450, not, however, into Arabic, but into Syriac. It was about this time that a certain Probha translated the *De interpretatione* and the *Analytica priora* into Syriac."[245] Being years before the Arab conquest, the reason motivating the early translators was hardly Arab benefaction. In his *A History of Islamic Philosophy*, Majid Fakhry states simply that these early translations of the logical works "were dictated by the need to probe more deeply into the meaning of theological concepts and the dialectical processes involved in the Christological debates of the time." And earlier on the same page, "the study of Greek had been cultivated chiefly as a means of giving the Syriac-speaking scholars of those venerable institutions access to Greek theological texts emanating chiefly from Alexandria." In other words, Nestorians needed the vocabulary and systematic thought of these works in order to debate the Jacobites, and the Jacobites needed them to debate the Nestorians. Fakhry continues,

> It is significant, however, that the translators did not proceed beyond the *Isagoge* of Porphyry, the *Categories*, the *Hermeneutica*, and the *Analytica Priora*. As borne out by a tradition associated with al-Farabi's name in the Arabic sources, logical studies were not pursued beyond the *Analytica Priora* because of the dangers inherent in the study of demonstrative and sophistical arguments.[246]

---

[244] F. E. Peters, *Aristotle and the Arabs* (New York: University Press, 1968), 57.

[245] Ibid.

[246] Majid Fakhry, *A History of Islamic Philosophy* (New York: Columbia University Press, 1970), 13.

There was a limit, therefore, to these early translations in the number of books making up the entire Aristotelian corpus, to basically his *Organon*. But was this movement limited simply to translation? Fakhry notes that, in the early phase of translation, most of the important scholars were members of a particular "monastery of Qinnesrin," naming many Christian translators and listing the works each translated and wrote commentaries on. During the sixth and seventh centuries, several commentaries each on the *Analytica Priora*, the *Hermeneutica*, and the *Categories* were written.[247] Thus even this early on there is a definite connection between Aristotelian thought and the Church of the East.

One objection may be that, at this point, the East was only keeping up with the West. After all, Aristotle's logical works were known in the west during the same time, and were translated just as early on or earlier. Answering this is what I call the "second phase" of translation, which overlapped the first. It is marked by the foundation of the Nestorian school of Jundishapur in 555, near Baghdad. The school at Jundishapur, was originally a school of medicine:

> In Persia, at [Ju]ndishapur, we find an Institution for philosophical and medical studies established by Khosrau Anosharwan (521-579). Its teachers were principally Nestorian Christians; but Khorsau, who had an inclination for secular culture, extended his toleration to Monophysites as well as to Nestorians. At that time, just as was the case later at the court of the Caliphs, Christian Syrians were held in special honour as medical men.[248]

It nevertheless became the largest center for philosophical translation in all of Mesopotamia for the next five centuries. Beginning under Persian rule and before the founding of Baghdad, it would survive Arab conquest and the Abbasid caliphate, and become, after 754, closely united to the academic desires of the caliphate.[249]

---

[247] Ibid., 14.

[248] T.J. DeBoer, *The History of Philosophy in Islam* (New York: Dover Publications, 1967), 14.

[249] Peters, 59.

When consulting, again, the histories of Arab philosophy, there is nearly universal detail given to the names of each of the translators of this school, again all Mesopotamian Christians, and each of the works they translated. Such a list would be inappropriate here, but a short summary may be helpful. Peters organizes the translators of this second phase into "three distinct phases." The first began in the middle of the eighth century, in 765, a date Peters calls "probably the single most important one in the translation movement," due to the caliphate officially hiring one of Jundishapur's physicians as a court medic. This first phase is marked by severely literal translations from Greek to Syriac, and then into Arabic. The second phase began about a hundred years later, and involved a refinement from purely literal translation to a more "polished" work. The third phase, beginning about 900 and extending until 1020, involved final revisions of older translations. Peters states:

> These later versions bear witness not only to the heightened technical mastery of the apparatus of textual criticism, but also to more purely philosophical and pedagogical interest than had their ninth-century predecessors, an interest directly connected with the beginning of more formal philosophical studies in Baghdad.[250]

Hence the translators were also interpreters and therefore, to a certain extent, philosophers. Peters continues, "By the middle of the eleventh century the translation movement was over; during its three-hundred year duration it carried into Arabic every extant Aristotelian treatise except the *Politica*."[251] A particularly notable accomplishment during this period of translation is the commentary of the Christian Ibn-al-Bitriq of the *De Anima*, which, says Fakhry, "played a decisive role in the development of the Arab conception of Aristotle's psychology, and especially his doctrine of the intellect."[252]

Interestingly, the policy of the Mesopotamian translators was to translate the original Greek text first into Syriac, then later into Arabic. This habit probably has several facts as its cause. For one

---

[250] Peters, 61.
[251] Ibid.
[252] Fakhry, 21.

thing, a practical problem was finding translators who had mastered Greek, Syriac, and Arabic. Most of the *Organon* was preserved only in Syriac, and the other works, found in monasteries or bought from Byzantium,[253] were only in Greek. One set of translators, therefore, would work from Greek to Syriac, and another from Syriac to Arabic, with masters checking the accuracy at every step, as well as comparing original manuscripts for authenticity and precision. Another reason the translation was done with a Syriac intermediary between Greek and Arabic was that the more flexible Syriac language lent itself grammatically more to Greek than did the rigid Arabic.[254] A third reason could be that "Arab scholars held Syriac to be the oldest, or the real (natural) language."[255] Hence the caliphs tolerated this inefficiency in their translators out of respect for this ancient language. A fourth possibility is that, just as the Nestorians required the use of the logical and hermeneutical works in order to debate the nature/person Christology problem against the Jacobites, so did the Nestorians and Jacobites require the use of more sophisticated concepts in order to debate the Three Persons/ One God problem against the Moslems. As Jammo put it, Mesopotamian Christians "did not learn Greek so they could translate for the Arabs."[256] They needed it for their own studies, and to some extent, at least for a time, the school at Jundishapur worked independently of any government sponsorship.

It is unfortunate that little or no study has been done to examine the precise effect of the Aristotelian corpus on the theology of the Church of the East. Any student of philosophy, however, should note the strong correspondence between Aristotelian and Mesopotamian Realism (if the reader will excuse such vague phrases), and should not, assuming the validity of anything claimed thus far in this paper, be surprised that the people of Mesopotamia were so interested in Aristotle and his thought.

---

[253] Ibid., 22-24.
[254] Peters, 63.
[255] DeBoer, 17.
[256] Fr. Sarhad Jammo, Ph.D., personal interview on 4/15/01.

Perhaps the most conspicuous aspect of this text of the "Holy Mysteries" of the Church of the East is its sensitivity to Holy Scripture. I thus include this short description of the Eucharistic Liturgy of the Church of the East to show how the official Church reflected her constitution in the Mesopotamian School in her close reading and celebration of the revelation of God given in the New Testament.[257]

The general layout of the Liturgy is based very precisely on Luke 24:13-35, the story of the journey to Emmaus. There are therefore two main sections of the Liturgy, within the bookends of the Lord's Prayer at the very beginning and end (as with all of the rites of the Church of the East): the Instruction and the Anaphora, following the two sections of this passage from Luke: the road to Emmaus and the breaking of the bread.

The Instructional section of the Liturgy, just as the Scriptural pericope, begins with "Moses and the prophets," that is, two Old Testament readings. This is followed by the interpretation of God's word as found in the writings of Paul, and a description of Christ's words actions from the Gospels (Lk 24:27-29). After the homily, the Eucharistic Rite begins.

The Anaphora follows the basic outline of verse 30 of Luke 24: "When he was at table with them, he took the bread and blessed, and broke it, and gave it to them." Thus the four sections of the Eucharistic Rite follow the four verbs in this verse: he *took*, *blessed*, *broke* and *gave*.

The Offertory: Jesus Took

The gifts of bread and wine are prepared before the Liturgy begins, in a short, separate rite. The pre-Mass preparation of the gifts is in accord with the command of Christ in Lk 22:8: "Jesus sent Peter and John, saying, 'Go and prepare the Passover for us, that we may eat it.'" The gifts come either in procession from the Bema, a platform in the middle of the Nave, or from a side table. They are

---

[257] My sources for this section are an article by Sarhad Jammo, ""The Anaphora of the Apostles Addai and Mari: A Study of Structure and Historical Background," in *Orientalia Christiana Periodica* 68 (2002): 5-35, and a private lecture by the same author given in January, 2003.

brought up to the opening of the Sanctuary, the bread on the right (as one faces the Altar) and the cup on the left. The priest takes them from the deacon and turns facing the Cross behind the altar, and crosses his arms, keeping the positioning the same, so that the cup is always underneath the representation of Christ's right side, out of which blood and water spilled. After placing the gifts on the Altar, the priest leaves the Sanctuary and, facing the people, begins the Nicean-Constantinopolitan Creed. This is followed immediately by the Kiss of Peace.

Both the Creed and the Kiss of Peace being done at this point are references to Christ's command in Matthew 5:23-24: "If you are offering your gift at the altar, and there remember that your brother has something against you, leave your gift there before the altar and go; first be reconciled to your brother, and then come and offer your gift." The understanding here is that there are two types of division: that of faith, reconciled by the Creed, and that of love, reconciled by the Kiss of Peace.

The Rite of Consecration: Jesus Blessed

This could perhaps be called the "Anaphora Proper." After the gifts have been placed on the Altar and the reconciliation made among the community in faith and love, the gifts of bread and wine are consecrated. The Anaphora Proper begins with the usual Sanctus-Benedictus, and the priest ceremonially washes his hands in preparation. The basic structure of the Anaphora in Mesopotamian Tradition is as follows: 1) Praise and Glorification of God for the creation of the world; 2) Thanksgiving to God for the redemption through Christ; 3) Remembrance of the graces given to the Church that has gone before us. Recent studies[258] have shown that this structure is borrowed from an ancient Jewish food blessing called the *Birkat Ha-Mazzon*, which has the following structure: 1) Blessing God for the food and for creation; 2) Thanksgiving to God for the land; 3) Supplication for Jerusalem. The early Anaphorists, then, took this basic form and "Christianized" it for their own purposes. The earliest form of the Anaphora of Addai and Mari, according to the most recent scholarship, is therefore as follows:

[258] Ibid.

94

Glory to you, O adorable and glorious Name (of the Father and the Son and the Holy Spirit), who created the world in his grace and its inhabitants in his compassion, who has redeemed mankind in his mercy and has effected great grace toward mortals.

We give thanks to you, O Lord, we your lowly, weak and wretched servants, because you have effected in us a great grace which cannot be repaid, in that you put on our humanity so as to quicken us by your divinity; lifted up our poor estate and righted our fall; raised up our mortality and forgave our debts; justified our sinfulness and enlightened our understanding and, O Lord and God, vanquished our enemies and made triumphant the lowliness of our weak nature through the abounding compassion of your grace.

And for all your help and graces toward us, we lift up glory, honor, thanksgiving and adoration to you, now and forever and ever, amen.

O Lord, through your unutterable mercies, make, in the commemoration of your Christ, a gracious remembrance of all the upright and just fathers who have pleased you, the prophets, apostles, martyrs and confessors, bishops and priests and deacons, and all the children of the holy catholic Church, who have been marked with the sign of holy baptism.

And grant us your tranquility and your peace all the days of the age, that all the inhabitants of the earth may know you, that you alone are the true God and Father, and that you have sent our Lord Jesus Christ, your beloved Son, and that he, our Lord and our God, taught us through his life-giving Gospel all purity and holiness.

And for all your wonderful economy for us, we give you thanks and glorify you unceasingly in your Church, redeemed by the precious blood of your Christ, with open mouths and unveiled faces, as we offer up praise, honor, thanksgiving and adoration to your holy and life-giving Name, now and forever and ever, amen.[259]

The Breaking Rite: Jesus Broke

The Gifts now having been consecrated, the priest needs further purification if he is to handle them; thus the thurible is brought by the deacon, and the priest is incensed to cleanse his heart while repeatedly acknowledging his unworthiness to approach the Saving Mysteries on the Altar in a prayer of gratitude. The Breaking Rite is performed in the following order: 1) the Body of the Lord is broken in half over the Chalice ("In the Name of the Father, the Son and the Holy Spirit), the particles mingling with the Precious Blood; 2) half of the host is laid on the paten, and the other half is dipped into the Chalice in the sign of the Cross ("In the Name…"); 3) the half of the host soaked with the Precious Blood is then used to "sign" the half of the host on the paten in the sign of the Cross ("In the Name…"). This threefold commingling of the Holy Elements is to indicate that the Body and Blood that are on the Altar are not separate, like those of a dead man, but are united in the resurrected, living body of Christ.

The Communion Rite: Jesus Gave

After the Consecration, the Mysteries are again "left on the Altar," for a second reconciliation of faith and love in the form of a prayer, to prepare the people and the priest to receive "the Holy." The community then together prays the Lord's Prayer and receives Holy Communion. There is then a final blessing, and the people are dismissed.

Jesus "took, blessed, broke and gave." These four words constitute the entire anaphora for the Church of Mesopotamia, and such is the sensitivity of the Mesopotamian to the words of Scripture that each word is given an individual rite within the Sacred Liturgy.

---

[259] Ibid., 18-19.

I have mentioned above how the Synod of Isaac, the first official self-expression of the hierarchy of the Church of the East, anathematizes anyone who makes himself a eunuch, on the grounds that he is thereby "damaging his fruitful nature."[260] Indeed, the attitude of the Church of the East regarding marriage is almost infamous among some scholars – notably those who study the history of clerical celibacy[261] – because it was the Synod of Mar Aqaq in 486, which Synod was given support again by the Synod of Mar Babai in 498, that explicitly allowed any cleric, "from him who is patriarch to him who is lowest in standing" to "apply [themselves] to pure marriage."[262]

In this section, however, I will concentrate on one particular Canon of the Synod of Aqaq – the Second Canon, which sets forth the opinion of the official Church as regards the ascetics who lived in the mountains around the dioceses of the respective bishops in attendance. It is the attitude toward these monks set forth in this Canon and implicitly affirmed in later Synods that, in my opinion, best sheds light on official Mesopotamian Christianity's stance on (or against) the teachings of the movements and documents discussed earlier in this chapter.

The title for the Second Canon begins thus: "Concerning the dishonest men about whom we made mention above…"[263] The description of these men is found, then, in the First Canon:

> It was reported to us that there are men who are corrupt of mind in this land…who are clothed in the garb of mourning…who go about in many places, corrupting simple minds and doing harm to the true confession of faith of the catholic and apostolic

---

[260] *Synodicon*, 7.

[261] Among the most famous are: Roman Cholij, *Clerical Celibacy in East and West* (Hereford, England: Gracewing/Fowler Wright Books, 1989); Christian Cochini, *The Apostolic Origins of Priestly Celibacy* tr. Nelly Marans (San Francisco: Ignatius Press, 1990); Stefan Heid, *Celibacy in the Early Church* tr. Michael J. Miller (San Francisco: Ignatius Press, 2000); Alfons Maria Cardinal Stickler, *The Case for Clerical Celibacy: Its Historical Development &Theological Foundations* tr. Brian Ferme (San Francisco: Ignatius Press, 1995).

[262] *Synodicon*, 43.

[263] Ibid., 36.

church. While they are sick with the doctrine of the heretics, and the filth of every heresy inheres in them...they draw upon themselves the name and reputation of those concerning whom the Holy Spirit spoke through the blessed Paul: "In the last times some will depart from the faith...they will forbid marriage and withdraw from foods which God created for the use – with thanksgiving – of those who believe and know the truth."[264]

Not only do these "men who are corrupt of mind" teach against marriage, but they adhere, as is said later in the First Canon, to the heresy of the Monophycites: "But our faith in the dispensation of Christ should...be in a confession of two natures of divinity and humanity, none of us venturing to introduce mixture, commingling, or confusion into the distinctions of those two natures."[265] These are, then, precisely the monks mentioned above, who were so heavily influenced by the *Thomasine Literature* and perhaps even by the Manichaeans, who, at this later time, denied the perfect humanity of Christ.[266]

To return to the Second Canon, then, we have the stern response of the bishops to these men whom they see as misleading their flock. "Concerning the dishonest men," then,

We command thus: if they are truly disciples and children of those blessed men and follow them in dress and manners, let their way of life be, like those (of old), in places suitable to their dress: they are not permitted to enter in order to live in towns or villages which have in them priests, bishops, presbyters and deacons, and become a cause of strife or produce tumult between priests and their flocks or (between) teachers and their disciples. They may not form a congregation in them, offer oblations in them, or give baptism, or corrupt the orders of the church as they have done hitherto. Instead, let them go to

---

[264] Ibid., 35. The Scripture quote is from 1 Tim 4:1-3.
[265] Ibid.
[266] See Moffett, 75-77.

98

monasteries and to places which are far from cultivated land.[267]

Moreover, there are harsh penalties for members of the official Church who help these ascetics or invite them into their town or village:

> Henceforth, any bishop, presbyter, or deacon, or any
> faithful layman who receives them and assists them to
> do any of those things which have been prohibited –
> (whether) in his town, or on his estate, or in his house
> –and to make tumult in the church, shall be bound
> and anathematized.[268]

Thus the official Church dealt with severity against those who taught against marriage and against the real and perfect humanity of Christ, showing themselves to be true Mesopotamians, faithful to the spirit of *Gilgamesh*.

---

[267] *Synodicon*, 36.
[268] Ibid.

Conclusion

We have seen how, in every case, that document or movement which was antithetical to the tenets of what I have described as the Mesopotamian School was rejected outright by the official Christian Church of Mesopotamia, and how those writers, Ephrem mainly but Aphrahat as well, which were respected by the Church were consistent with the Mesopotamian School.

As we move to the next chapter, we will examine a writer who was revered, as an exegete, above all others by the Church of the East: Theodore of Mopsuestia. But before we move west to Antioch and its School (though I hope to show how the "School of Antioch" is but a temporary extension of the Mesopotamian School), it is worthwhile to reexamine the common categorizations of early Christianity which modern scholars have used. One example of this type of categorization are the correlative terms "Hellenistic" and "Semitic" Christianity, or "Greek" and "Syriac" Christianity. If there is indeed such a thing as the Mesopotamian School, these categories might not be as worthwhile as has been thought in the past. Indeed, the Jewish Christians of Palestine are just as Semitic as the pagan converts of Mesopotamia, and the Greek of Philo or Origen is just as Hellenistic as that of Theodore, and in both cases the contrast is at least equal to the comparison. Using such linguistic distinctions to categorize types of Christian thought may therefore be re-thought if the category is to represent the reality.

Even less helpful are the terms "East Syrian" and "West Syrian." As I hope to have shown in this chapter, the Church in Mesopotamia was an authentic expression of the thought *of Mesopotamia*, and not of Syria, east or west, assuming this geographical division ever existed in the first place. In place of these either too-generic or misnamed categories, I would suggest fitting the category to the school of thought, and thus the real categorization would be between "Mesopotamian Christianity" and "Alexandrian Christianity," and those movements and thinkers which they influenced outside their own respective regions. The next chapter will examine the differences between these two Schools in detail.

CHAPTER 4
THEODORE OF MOPSUESTIA
AND THE MESOPOTAMIAN SCHOOL

Life and Works

Theodore of Mopsuestia, called "the Interpreter," was born in Antioch around 350 AD. After his education first as a lawyer under the Sophist rhetorician Libanius, then under the biblical scholar Diodore, he entered religious life, an act owed perhaps in great part to the passionate pleading of his lifelong friend St. John Chrysostom.[269] He was well respected throughout his life as a wise and moderate teacher and exegete, and was raised to the Episcopal See of Mopsuestia in 392. He served in this capacity until his death in 428, the same year Nestorius was raised to the See of Constantinople. Theodore died a well respected bishop in peace and communion with the Church. A. Minanga, in the introduction to his translation of Theodore's *Commentary on the Nicene Creed*, describes the reverence given to Theodore's name even after his death:

> Death did not put a stop to the fame of Theodore. It is recorded in Tillemont that Meletius, Theodore's successor to the see of Mopsuestia, asserted that he would have endangered his own life if he had uttered words detrimental to his predecessor. Even Cyril of

---

[269] See Sozomen's *Ecclesiastical History* VIII.2: "Theodore was well conversant with the sacred books and with the rest of the discipline of rhetoricians and philosophers. After studying the ecclesiastical laws, and frequenting the society of holy men, he was filled with admiration of the ascetic mode of life and condemned city life. He did not persevere in the same purpose, but after changing it, he was drawn to his former course of life; and, to justify his conduct, cited many examples from ancient history, with which he was well acquainted, and went back into the city. On hearing that he was engaged in business and intent on marriage, John composed an epistle, more divine in language and thought than the mind of man could produce, and sent it to him. Upon reading it, he repented and immediately gave up his possessions, renounced his intent of marrying, was saved by the advice of John and returned to the philosophic career." (The text of this work is accessible at www.newadvent.org).

101

Alexandria whose views in the Incarnation were not in harmony with those of Theodore was obliged to avow that in the Churches of the East one often heard the cry: "We believe as Theodore Believed; long live the faith of Theodore!" The same Cyril of Alexandria informs us that when a party of bishops was found ready to condemn him, the answer of the bishops of Syria to them was: "We had rather be burnt than condemn Theodore." Leontius Byzantinus informs us also that Cyril of Alexandria advised against the condemnation of Theodore because all the bishops of the Eastern Church considered him an eminent Doctor, and if he were condemned there would be serious disturbance in that Church.[270]

A certain North African bishop Facundus even recalls that Cyril once referred to Theodore as "the great."[271] There is, indeed, absolutely no historical debate regarding Theodore's death in good reputation and in full communion with the Church. Considering this, one can hardly blame the Church which was alive and well in what was then called Persia, most commonly named the Church of the East, for seeing in Theodore an upright and articulate representative of what was already her own preferred method of exegesis and interpretation of the Holy Scriptures. Thus, very early on, the works of Theodore began to be translated into Syriac.[272] Indeed, due to the posthumous condemnation of Theodore and his writings in 553 and the burning of his works within the Roman Empire after the Council of Ephesus in 431, a great deal of Theodore's extant works are available to us only in Syriac translation – though due to the consistent hardship

---

[270] A. Minanga, "Introduction" to his translation of Theodore's *Commentary on the Nicene Creed*, vol. V of *Woodbrooke Studies* (Cambridge: W. Heffer & Sons, 1932), 3-4.

[271] Quoted in Dimitri Z. Zaharopoulos, *Theodore of Mopsuestia on the Bible* (New York: Paulist Press, 1989), 27: "The great Theodore has written perhaps twenty ample books against the Arian and Eunomian heresies, and besides these he has interpreted the gospel and apostolic writings."

[272] See ibid., 28: "The Christians of eastern Syria made themselves the heirs of Antiochian biblical scholarship, and the writings of the Mephasqana were so much esteemed that after the Council of Ephesus in 431 several of Theodore's compositions were translated into Syriac by the teachers at the school of Edessa, thus becoming the literary heritage of the Nestorian church of Syria and Persia."

faced by the Church of the East, even these have become scarce.[273] At any rate, even a cursory glance at his extant works[274] will show the main point: Theodore was first and foremost a student of the Bible; insofar as he was a theologian, he was one secondarily and even then totally within the context of Scripture.

Whatever the case, despite the universal respect given to Theodore during his life and at his death, and the perpetual honor given him and his writings in the East, he was condemned, in his person and his teaching, along with Nestorius and Theodoret, at the second council of Constantinople in 553, a hundred and twenty-five years after his death. The council calls Theodore "mad," "blasphemous," "impious," and ultimately "heretical."[275] A great deal has been written on the fact that the condemnation of a dead man's person is less than acceptable (Cyril of Alexandria himself objected to the idea)[276] as well as on the blatant political motives behind these condemnations.[277] Suffice it to say here that the Emperor Justinian had a great deal to gain in backing the Egyptians within his Empire

---

[273] See Minanga, 6: "When 'Abdisho' wrote his Catalogue in about A.D. 1298 all the works of Theodore were found in the churches and monasteries of his day, and probably also in his own library at Nisibin. The numerous persecutions inflicted since that date on the eastern Christians by Mongols, Turks and Kurds have, however, resulted in their complete disappearance even in East Syrian lands."

[274] Among them: Commentaries on the Psalms, the Minor Prophets, the Gospel of John, the Epistles of Paul, and fragments of commentaries on the other three Gospels, Genesis, catechetical homilies, etc. His "systematic" works include a commentary on the Nicene Creed, one on the sacraments of Baptism and Eucharist, a polemical work "Against the Macedonians," and several fragments of "On the Incarnation." As will be shown, even the latter "systematic" works are based solidly and almost entirely on the Bible and utilize almost exclusively Biblical terms. Full citations of the publications of these works can be found in the bibliography.

[275] *Anathemas against the "Three Chapters"* Canons 4, 5, 6, 12. *Decrees of the Ecumenical Councils* ed. Norman P. Tanner (Washington D.C.: Sheed and Ward, 1990).

[276] See L. Patterson, *Theodore of Mopsuestia and Modern Thought* (London: Macmillan, 1926), 5: "To do him justice, Cyril was restrained by feelings of Christian charity and human decency from defaming the character of the dead. He urged that it would be sufficient to condemn the opinions of Theodore without anathematizing him, as he had gone to his rest."

[277] See John L. McKenzie, S.J., "Notes on the Commentary of Theodore of Mopsuestia on John 1:46-51," *Theological Studies* 14 (1953): 83: "The political and ecclesiastical *Sitz im Leben* of the Fifth Ecumenical Council emits a bad odor which can still be perceived after fourteen centuries. It will not go away if we pretend it is not there."

and nothing to lose in condemning "the Interpreter" honored mainly by those outside it. At any rate, nearly no one would debate that the condemnation of Theodore's *person* so long after his respectable death is unjust and basically meaningless.[278] The present question, however, is deeper than this. As Francis Sullivan said in defending his book *The Christology of Theodore of Mopsuestia*: "this study is not a judicial process, to decide whether Theodore was guilty of formal heresy. It is rather a theological study, to see whether or not his objective teaching, as it has come down to us, conformed with the essential truths of revelation."[279] In other words, did the second council of Constantinople interpret Theodore fairly and accurately, or was the heresy condemned even at Ephesus that of a straw man? Though this is indeed the question at hand in this chapter, we must be careful lest we place Theodore within a debate which began only after his death. The plain fact is that Theodore never wrote a "Commentary on the Council of Ephesus" or on the Acts of Chalcedon, and for us today to judge his works merely by comparing them with terminology and formulae made explicit well after his death would be the height of anachronism. Nevertheless, with this in mind, it is left to us today to examine with the utmost care the remnant of his work and balance it not against posthumous definition and dogma, but against the true faith of the universal Church, the comprehension of which is ultimately beyond the limitations of human expression.

This all having been said, I would suggest that a fair and accurate appraisal of Theodore's orthodoxy would require, first, an examination of the differences between the two distinct – but ultimately complimentary – exegetical and theological "schools" within Christianity, and the acknowledgement that these two methods originate not in Antioch and Alexandria but within human

---

[278] Rowan A. Greer, in *Theodore of Mopsuestia: Exegete and Theologian* (Westminster: The Faith Press, 1961), 47, quotes Gibbon's *Decline and Fall of the Roman Empire* vol. IV: "If these bishops, whether innocent or guilty, were annihilated in the sleep of death, they would not probably be awakened by the clamour which, after a hundred years, was raised over their grave. If they were already in the fangs of the demon, their torments could neither be aggravated nor assuaged by human industry. If in the company of saints and angels they enjoyed the rewards of piety, they must have smiled at the idle fury of the theological insects who still crawled on the surface of the earth."

[279] Francis A. Sullivan, S.J., "Further Notes on Theodore of Mopsuestia: A Reply to Fr. McKenzie," *Theological Studies* 20 (1959): 274.

nature itself, both finding expression even within the Scriptures; second, the realization that Theodore was first and foremost an interpreter of the Bible, and that his Christological teaching must be read as an application of his Biblical exegesis; third, an explanation of the relevance of the fact that both Theodore's exegetical method and his Christological formulation were expressed in a cultural and philosophical framework that was decisively different from that of the Alexandrians. Finally, I will suggest that the current ecumenical movement between the Catholic Chaldean Church and the Assyrian Church of the East is particularly relevant in that the patrimony of the Church of the East represents the true continuation of all that was positive in the "Antiochene School" of interpretation and theology that was all but lost in the West due to the condemnations of the Councils, and also that the patrimony of the Church of the East, which I have called the "Mesopotamian School," though holding Theodore and other Antiochenes in high honor, never limited itself to their interpretation, but took what it saw as good in them and perfected what was flawed, precisely as the Western Church perfected what was flawed in early Alexandrians such as Origen. Thus the exegetical and theological refinements of the Mesopotamian School may, if studied in this light, add a great deal to contemporary Biblical exegesis and theology.

Two Exegetical Schools

Any reader will be struck with the sharp contrast between the first verses of the three Synoptics on the one hand and those of the Gospel of John on the other. Where Matthew and Luke begin with an explanation of the Lord's earthly birth, and Mark with the preaching of the Baptist, John begins with the Lord's eternal existence: "In the beginning was the Word..." This is certainly not a matter of contradictory doctrines between the Gospels, but rather of a difference in *method*. The *person* whom the four evangelists are describing is the same, and the Holy Spirit who inspired them guarantees that there be no confusion or falsehood in their description. Yet the approaches are varied, and this variation adds a richness to the New Testament that would have been absent had there been only one approach or only one evangelist. Matthew, Mark and Luke *begin* with a description of a man whose words and actions, in the end, could not be explained except by affirming that this man is in fact the Son of God. John, on the other hand, *begins* with the Son of God descending to take flesh – in other words, the logical conclusion of the Synoptics is the first premise of John.

These two schools found within the New Testament find further expression within the history of the Christian Church.[280] Though it is an enormous oversimplification to say simply that "Alexandria represented the Johannine method" and "Antioch represented the Synoptic method,"[281] the fact is that the writers of note of these respective "schools" did indeed use different methods in approaching Scripture, and that there are similarities running throughout their interpretations that do bear some of the weight of this admitted generalization. My method in this section will be first to attempt to describe each of these methods within their historic outline with special attention to their origin; second, to explicate the details of each method by looking at the characters that are generally seen to be their representative examples, Theodore and Origen; third, to examine the further development of the two methods after these writers. It will be seen throughout that what I have called the Synoptic method is best and most consistently represented, both in its historical origin and in its refinement and perfection, not by Antioch but by Mesopotamia. The significance of this claim will be made clear when the question of Theodore's Christology is examined, and the question of which cultural framework he should be read in is asked.

In his chapter on "Theodore's Exegetical Method," Rowan Greer describes the different schools of Jewish Scriptural interpretation in the context of which Christian exegesis was born and flourished. Though many of the details of his analysis need not concern us here, his descriptions of the types of interpretation found among the Jews of Alexandria on the one hand and Babylon on the other are worth noting. Regarding Alexandria, Greer discusses Philo as its representative Jewish thinker: "In Alexandria a quite different method of exegesis had grown up, a method undoubtedly influenced

---

[280] For an account of the varying schools of interpretation in the Jewish tradition, and their respective "seats" in Alexandria and Babylon, see Greer, Chapter 5.

[281] See O'Keefe, "A Letter that Killeth: Toward a Reassessment of Antiochene Exegesis, or Diodore, Theodore and Theodoret on the Psalms," *Journal of Early Christian Studies* 8 (2000): 90: "Cyril of Alexandria and Theodoret of Cyrus used essentially the same methodology in their interpretation of the Minor Prophets."

by Hellenistic allegory. Philo is the best representative of this allegorical school. He attempted to see in the Hebrew Scriptures the Platonic philosophy he held on other grounds."[282] Thus, the interpretation of the Scriptures mainly as *allegory* seems characteristic of the Alexandrian school. Philo read the words of the Hebrew Bible not to draw new wisdom out of them, but rather to justify what he already knew and believed about God and the world. We may draw an analogy here with the Gospel of John: John recalls the words and deeds of Christ within the context of his knowledge of Christ's Divinity. That Jesus is the Son of God is for John an *a priori* in writing; for the Synoptic writers, Christ's Divinity is the *conclusion* the reader must reach when reading about his words and actions.[283] Similarly, Philo reads the words and actions of God in the Old Testament *already knowing*, for example, God's loving providential care for Israel, his omnipotence and his perfection, whereas the redactors themselves of the Jewish Bible seem to set out to *prove* these things to their reader. It is not the historical proof that interests Philo, but the eternal truth to which they point: "Philo really had no interest in the Scriptures as records of Jewish history or experience. He was simply interested in using them as a springboard for the Platonic, moralistic philosophy he believed."[284] This, generally at any rate, is the cultural context which Origen and other Alexandrians inherited.[285]

In contrast to this stands the Babylonian Talmud, which we have discussed already in Chapter II, and which, as we have seen, approaches Scripture in a severely practical and literal manner. Thus there is, very early on, a correspondence between Mesopotamia and what is simply, even vaguely, called "literal interpretation." This style of interpretation will be given a more detailed description later. Whatever be the case, the literary output of the Babylonian Talmud

---

[282] Greer, 89.

[283] See Frederick McLeod, S.J., "Theodore of Mopsuestia Revisited," *Theological Studies* 61 (2000): 461, where he connects Theodore to the "Synoptic method:" "[Theodore's] is the approach we find in the Synoptic Gospels where Jesus is visibly portrayed as acting in divine ways and gradually realized to be divine."

[284] Ibid., 89.

[285] On Ibid., 86, Greer suggests that, while Jewish Alexandrian allegorical method is a source for Christian allegory, a possible source for *Jewish* allegory is classical Greek allegory: "Alexandrian Jews were more directly influenced by such Hellenistic phenomena as Stoic allegorization of Homer."

indicates at least a preference in Scriptural interpretation in the group of Jews that would later become the basis for the first Christian community in Mesopotamia.

The Church of the East that was initially founded on these Jewish communities between the Tigris and Euphrates saw in Theodore a fine example of her own preferred method of Scriptural exegesis: the high honor in which she holds him is proof enough of that. The "enormous influence"[286] of Origen especially on the Alexandrian school, despite any problems in his theology, I think justifies naming him as the reasonable Alexandrian representative. Thus a comparison between the exegetical methods of Theodore and Origen should give us a clear enough idea of what each method entails, and, for this paper's purposes especially, how Theodore's method influenced and even defined his Christology. Thus, if we use the four categories of the first and second chapters of this thesis, this entire chapter would fall under the category "Dialectic," since Christology for the Mesopotamian, and also in Theodore, is an entirely Biblical enterprise.

In order for us to avoid being vague to the point of obscurity in a subject in which it is easy to be so, we propose to describe the two exegetical methods in contrast to each other and, hopefully, without the aid of phrases like "literal" and "historico-grammatical" that serve as mental crutches and which in the end give little insight into the nature of the problem. We begin from Origen's *de Principiis*, Book IV:

> But just as providence is not abolished because of our ignorance, at least not for those who have once rightly believed in it, so neither is the divine character of scripture, which extends through all of it, abolished because our weakness cannot discern in every sentence the hidden splendor of its teachings, concealed under a poor and humble style.[287]

Thus for Origen what is "divine" in the Scriptures is precisely what is "hidden." The "poor and humble" face value of the text itself is merely a hurdle to be overcome on the way to discovering the eternal truth beyond it. The superiority of this "spiritual reading" is made

---

[286] Ibid., 92.
[287] Quoted in Greer, 91.

108

clear by what sort of person appreciates it: "the uneducated should be edified by the letter itself, by what we call the obvious meaning; while he who has ascended a certain way may be edified by the soul. The perfect should be edified by the spiritual law, which has a shadow of good things to come."[288] Thus the "soul" of Scripture, meant for those who have "ascended" above the "uneducated," is the moral sense, and the "spiritual law," meant for the "perfect" is the allegorical sense.

In contrast to Origen,[289] Diodore of Tarsus, who was Theodore's teacher in Scripture and spirituality, shows a different approach:

> We do not forbid the higher interpretation and *theoria*, for the historical narrative does not exclude it, but is on the contrary the basis and substructure of loftier insights... We must, however, be on our guard against letting the *theoria* do away with the historical basis, for the result would then be, not *theoria*, but allegory.[290]

Both Greer and Zaharopoulos[291] interpret *theoria* here to mean what is commonly called "typology." The main difference between typology and allegory as understood in the early Church is that, while allegory ignores or considers irrelevant the historicity of the event described in the text, typology assumes it. That is, allegory abstracts from the words to the "spiritual sense" directly; typology seeks first to understand the event on its own terms, and then build a "spiritual sense" not on the words, but on the event itself and its *resemblance* to a spiritual reality. We have seen this already in the section on Ephrem. Thus, for example, the crossing of the Red Sea in Exodus as an event resembles the sacrament of Baptism, but it is still first and foremost

---

[288] Again from the *de Principiis*, quoted in Zaharapoulos, 109.

[289] Indeed, "in contrast" is here meant to be very literal. In the fourth and fifth centuries of Eastern Christianity, there was hardly a force to contend with as much as Origen. Ibid., 92: "It is against the background of Origen's enormous influence that any discussion of Theodore's method must take place." Though Origen's influence is not, in this case, a positive one; ibid., 110: "Certainly Theodore was in an Antiochene tradition which was largely uninfluenced by Origenism save by way of reaction."

[290] Greer, 93.

[291] Zaharopoulos, 112.

an event. For Origen, "the literal meaning of the text is really beside the point."[292] The crossing of the Red Sea *means* that the soul, after passing through the waters of Baptism symbolized by the Sea, leaves her sins, symbolized by the Egyptian soldiers, destroyed. This, for Origen, is the *primary* meaning of Scripture, while for Theodore and others the event itself is the primary meaning meant by the words of that particular passage, and the similarity to Baptism is a meaning that is secondary and built upon the meaning of the event itself. And though Theodore did not consider this connection between event and spiritual reality to be merely accidental, he was very careful in making it himself. McLeod states:

> [Theodore] recognized that God could foresee and contrive that at times a real relationship exists between two historical persons or events. He insisted, nevertheless, that this relationship had to be confirmed by a New Testament passage. For instance, the First Adam and the Second Adam, Sarah and Hagar, and the Hebrew and the Christian covenants...can be seen as type and archetype. Their relationships are acknowledged as such by Paul. Being approved and inspired, these types and archetypes could be used to illumine the meanings of each other...If, however, neither of these poles were grounded in reality, Theodore considered such an instance to be an allegorical interpretation spun out of one's vivid imagination.[293]

There was thus great reverence given to the words of Scripture as having *in themselves* the saving power of God when rightly understood. Because of this, there is little need to read "beyond" the words to the "spiritual sense," because the "obvious sense" by itself is sufficient; besides, it is very easy to fall into imaginative fabrication when pursuing the allegorical sense beyond any particular passage. Overall, and very generally, the matter may be summed up thus: while Origen sought the meaning of the text in what it did *not* say, Theodore sought the meaning of the text through what it *did* say. This led Theodore to consider the words of the passage very closely, to the

---

[292] Greer, 92.
[293] McLeod, 452.

point of comparing different translations to find the most accurate rendering, to examine the text within the historical framework in which it was written, and to compare the meanings of words in different parts of Scripture – all very modern exegetical techniques.[294]

If the problem with Origen was a fanciful imagination in some of his interpretations, the problem with Theodore is perhaps too rigid a limitation on the use of Biblical texts. The example that O'Keefe gives of this is Theodore's commentary on the Psalms, a work which Theodore himself later admitted was carelessly written.[295] In it, Theodore makes the claim that only four of the Psalms (2, 8, 45 and 110) directly refer to Christ in their meaning, and that the bulk are rather to be read within the context of David's historical rule over Israel.[296] O'Keefe shows convincingly enough how Theodore, in the instance of Psalm 28, failed to render even an acceptable historical interpretation, and blames this fact on the rigidity of Theodore's exegetical method, and his general unwillingness to allow for a "Christ-centered figural reading of the Old Testament."[297] Though this is I think a valid criticism in itself, it does not seem to sustain the sweeping dismissal of "Antiochene" exegesis that concludes O'Keefe's article. At any rate, as we shall see, the negative notes of Theodore's method may and will be put aside by those who hold him in high regard in later generations, while the enormous positive side is retained; those who condemn him outright, on the other hand, lose even what is good in his method, only to return to find value in it hundreds of years later.

In looking at the further development of each of these schools, it will be interesting to note how through time they grew closer to one another, each one taking (or at least admitting in theory) what was positive in the other. The particulars to be compared are Augustine as the thinker who in theory improved what was flawed in Origen, and the Church of the East as the body that perfected what was lacking – or, better, took only what was good – in Theodore and the other Antiochenes.

Augustine represents a more moderate example of allegorical Scriptural interpretation. In writing on the proper ways to interpret Scripture in the third book of his work *de Doctrina Christiana*, he

---

[294] This is summarized well in Zaharopoulos, 111.
[295] Patterson, 7.
[296] O'Keefe, 97-104.
[297] Ibid., 96.

discusses when and how a phrase in the Bible should be taken as figurative:

> But in addition to the foregoing rule, which guards us against taking a metaphorical form of speech as if it were literal, we must also pay heed to that which tells us not to take a literal form of speech as if it were figurative. In the first place, then, we must show the way to find out whether a phrase is literal or figurative. And the way is certainly as follows: Whatever there is in the word of God that cannot, when taken literally, be referred either to purity of life or soundness of doctrine, you may set down as figurative. Purity of life has reference to the love of God and one's neighbor; soundness of doctrine to the knowledge of God and one's neighbor.[298]

For Augustine, then, there are rules of when something in Scripture is to be taken as a figure: one may read a phrase as figurative if it contradicts charity or the truth of the faith. Nor does he leave it at that. The interpreter of Scripture must be careful lest he make himself the rule:

> Now Scripture enjoins nothing except charity, and condemns nothing except lust, and in that way fashions the lives of men. In the same way, if an erroneous opinion has taken possession of the mind, men think that whatever Scripture asserts contrary to this must be figurative.[299]

The ordinary, erroneous opinions of men must not guide Scripture, then, but rather men must be guided and fashioned by Scripture. This is not to say that Origen would have disagreed with this – he certainly would not have. It is not the principle itself but the *attitude* of approaching the words of Scripture that sees them as a guide to which the mind must bend itself (or, rather, straighten itself), as opposed to seeing them as a kind of "raw material" which the minds

---

[298] Augustine, *de Doctrina Christiana*, Book 3, Chapter 10, Section 14. Available at www.newadvent.org.

[299] Ibid., Section 15.

of the "enlightened" must fashion. Not to leave the impression that Augustine leaves allegory behind, I supply also this quote from a chapter of *de Doctrina Christiana* entitled "It is a Wretched Slavery which Takes the Figurative Expressions of Scripture in a Literal Sense:"

> For the saying of the apostle applies in this case too: "The letter killeth, but the spirit giveth life." For when what is said figuratively is taken as if it were said literally, it is understood in a carnal manner. And nothing is more fittingly called the death of the soul than when that in it which raises it above the brutes, the intelligence namely, is put in subjection to the flesh by a blind adherence to the letter. For he who follows the letter takes figurative words as if they were proper, and does not carry out what is indicated by a proper word into its secondary signification; but, if he hears of the Sabbath, for example, thinks of nothing but the one day out of seven which recurs in constant succession; and when he hears of a sacrifice, does not carry his thoughts beyond the customary offerings of victims from the flock, and of the fruits of the earth. Now it is surely a miserable slavery of the soul to take signs for things, and to be unable to lift the eye of the mind above what is corporeal and created, that it may drink in eternal light.[300]

This is sufficient to show in a cursory fashion the way Alexandrian-style exegesis developed in Augustine.

Though the Mesopotamians who saw in Theodore a fine example of their preferred style of exegesis honored him, and honor him still today, they never limited themselves to him – the Church of the East never divinized Theodore.[301] They indeed saw a great good

---

[300] Ibid., Book 3, Chapter 5, Section 9.

[301] Nor was Theodore, during his life, a fan of those whom he saw as "Syrians." He knew little or no Syriac, and considered the Peshitta at times a rather inauthentic translation of the Bible. Zaharopoulos quotes Theodore's commentary on Habakkuk on p. 59: "Some have said that the Syrian version reads "peg"; but it would be nonsense to disregard the voice of the Hebrew – in which the prophets spoke...and pay attention to the Syrian who has altered the voice of the Hebrews into that of the Syrians. Besides he [the Syrian] often wants to raise his own

in him, and one to be retained, but they had no difficulty simply omitting what they saw was flawed. Regarding exegesis, this meant a rejection of Theodore's limitation of the typological sense to that which is specifically referenced in the New Testament. The liturgical life of the Church bears witness to this. Among a thousand examples, a few will suffice to illustrate the point. In the liturgy for Christmas, the appointed Psalm for the vigil Mass is Psalm 87, the center of which, in the Syriac, reads:

> This man was born there, and of Zion it is said: the great man is born in her and he will establish her. The Lord will count the people in the registry: this man was born there.

The liturgical context in which this Psalm is used is clearly a reference to the birth of Christ. Needless to say, Theodore's commentary on the Psalms hardly lends itself to this type of usage. This freedom in using typology to illustrate a theological point in order to enrich the life of the Church does not lessen the importance of the "ordinary sense" of Scripture: this use of typology is based solidly upon the historical reading of the Bible.

The Divine Office of the Church of the East for the feast of Our Lady on the day after Christmas contains a long selection from a hymn about Mary by the thirteenth century writer Mar Warda. Besides being a magnificent Mariological treatise, the work utilizes with the utmost freedom a typology between Mary and several images in the Old Testament. A few verses of the work will manifest the point:

> If I compare her to the Garden with four rivers going out to the four corners [of the Earth], as there is in creation, out of which a spring went forth that did not save man from death, and in which the Tree of Life was set up whose location no one knew: from Mary came the Spring who was preached with four mouths, and from whom the whole Earth drank, and budded forth with praise to his name... She is the Ark of

---

mistakes to a linguistic law, without knowing what he is talking about." Again, in commenting on the book of Jonah (57): "Here again they say that the name Jonah in Syriac means dove; these Syrians are marvelous legend tellers."

flesh, in whom the true Noah rested – he who gave our race freedom from the sentence of the enemy... In her womb she was pregnant, and in her flesh she was the glorious tabernacle; in her soul the Spirit was compassionate, and in her whole being she was heaven. Do not blame me, O reader, for saying she is like heaven – indeed, I am convinced that she is more precious, greater, and more exalted than heaven: our Lord was hidden in heaven for six thousand years, and he did not save the human race until *she* became his dwelling.

Though he is clearly using typology and not allegory (as he begins "comparing" Mary to actual historical things), Warda feels absolutely free to compare Mary to a great number of Old Testament types, a few of which are seen in the above selection. The point is that the type of exegesis preferred by his Church never prevented him, or anyone else, from freely comparing the events and figures of the Old Testament with those of the New, and even to claim that those of the New are greater than and fulfill those of the Old.

A writer of the Church of the East, Isho'dad of Merv, discusses what is for him the difference between the interpretation of his Church and that of Origen, who "tainted all the books of the Bible by an enigmatic interpretation:"

The psalms and the prophets, who speak of the captivity and the return of the people of Israel, he explained as teaching the captivity of the soul... Those insane people have not perceived that the apostles in quoting the sayings of the Old Testament do not quote them in only one way; sometimes they quote them to show their fulfillment, at other times as an example for the exhortation and correction of their readers, or else to confirm the doctrine of the faith, although these sayings were uttered for other purposes according to the historical circumstances.[302]

It is interesting to note the parallel between Augustine and Isho'dad in their concentration not on method *per se*, but on its use for

---

[302] Zaharopoulos, 114-115.

fulfilling the purposes of Scripture: teaching the faith and moral exhortation.

Thus far we have seen (1) what it means to say that there are two methodologies within Scripture itself, (2) how these methodologies revealed themselves in the history of Judeo-Christianity and within the writers Theodore and Origen, and (3) how these schools developed after these two thinkers. With all this in mind, we must return to the original question of Theodore's orthodoxy, and re-examine his Christological thought in the light of his exegetical method, before we turn to examining his eventual Scriptural formulation within his cultural context, and how the Church of the East developed and perfected his Christological thought.

Theology as Exegesis

The two most common mistakes made in attempting to understand Theodore, say, in an introductory Christology class, are, first, asking whether Theodore depicts Christ as "too human," and, second, taking one of Theodore's phrases describing the union of natures in Christ and asking "is this enough to explain the unity of Christ satisfactorily?" Regarding the first approach, one can and must reply that if Christ's humanity is complete in any sense, as it was defined at Chalcedon,[303] then there can be no such thing as describing Christ as "too human." There are several problems with the second approach. First, as we said, any attempt to simply compare the terms and formulae used by Theodore against definitions which were solidified after his death, and which he never had a chance to comment upon, is anachronistic. Any attempt to reexamine Theodore and weigh his teaching against the teaching of the Councils must thus be done with great care. Second, the question assumes that the questioner himself knows exactly what is "enough" to constitute a satisfactory description of the unity of Christ, where the case usually is that even the questioner has a rather vague, formulaic notion of Christ's unity in his own mind. Finally, it is often forgotten that all of Theodore's phrases in describing Christ originate in Scripture. When, for example, Theodore uses one of his more common phrases to describe the unity of Christ, "indwelling of good pleasure," it is usually criticized by saying that it "sounds as if" the

---

[303] *Definitio fidei* at Chalcedon: "perfectum in humanitate."

116

Word was in Christ "in the way that one might be in another."[304] What is usually forgotten is that the origin of this phrase is not the mind of Theodore but the mind of St. Paul: "In him all the fullness of God was *pleased to dwell*,"[305] and "in him the whole fullness of deity dwells bodily."[306] McKenzie puts it pithily:

> Should one find *inhabitentem* offensive, one may pardon Theodore for taking the word from St. Paul…But Theodore cannot even quote St. Paul without risking a charge of heresy from some theologians.[307]

McKenzie's point is exactly what we said before: that Theodore's theology is from beginning to end a commentary on Scripture, and an attempt to understand Scripture as a whole. Trying to understand it otherwise, or without this consideration, is in the end to invent an opponent to defeat.

It is here that a point made earlier shows its relevance: because there are, regarding the description of Christ, different points of departure *within Scripture*, there must also be different approaches in any sincere attempt to understand Scripture. One must either start from Paul's assertion that God was pleased to dwell in Christ, and read John's assertion that the Word became flesh in its light (as do the Mesopotamians and Antiochenes), or start from John and read Paul and the Synoptics in his light (as do the Alexandrians). In other words, either the Word becoming flesh is understood as a further explication of the indwelling, or the indwelling is understood as a further explication of the Word becoming flesh. Both are Scriptural approaches, both are valid (within certain limits), and, as will be shown, both are limited. And to reduce the Christian mystery to one or the other is only to fool oneself into thinking that God has been comprehended. In the end, it will be shown that the purpose of the two approaches is to highlight two different aspects of the Christian mystery.

In any case, even the recent works written on the philosophical, theological, or anthropological assumptions underlying

---

[304] "vel in ipso esse ut alterum in altero." Canon 3 of Constantinople II.
[305] Colossians 1:19, emphasis mine.
[306] Colossians 2:9.
[307] McKenzie, 83.

and somewhat guiding Theodore's thought should be read in this light. It is correct enough to say that Theodore, and every Christian thinker since Pentecost, is thinking within a cultural context with certain assumptions and within certain linguistic and historic circumstances. Christ himself expressed his teaching in a specific language and with reference to peoples and events familiar to his audience, such as those of the Old Testament. The most pertinent question is not whether Theodore's thought is colored by his time, but rather whether Theodore or any thinker remains ultimately faithful to the truth of the faith revealed most fully and most richly in the Bible and in Christian tradition, without letting his culture and the limits that come along with it to make him stray from the truth of revelation. It is almost unconsciously that previous thinkers are judged by this standard: whether Thomas Aquinas was "too much" an Aristotelian, or Origen "too much" a Neo-Platonist, or Tatian "too much" an ascetic, or Theodore "too much" a methodologist.[308] All that these questions finally mean is whether, in their attempt to balance the truth of the whole Bible, these thinkers rejected any part of it on the basis of something outside the Faith, or whether, in the end, the Faith was their ultimate standard of measure.

Because this chapter is about Theodore, it is necessary that he be examined exclusively, since no short or cursory evaluation of Origen or Cyril or any other thinker could give them a fair trial in so comprehensive a question.[309] Thus for the sake of time the Alexandrian school must be abandoned. Even regarding Theodore, we are left a difficult situation, since we have only a few pieces of his life's work, and most of these surviving either in fragmentation or translation.

Greer gives perhaps the most succinct description of Theodore's methodology in approaching the Bible: "As a generalization, we may say that Theodore draws his theology from the text, organizes it somewhat systematically, and then reimposes the

---

[308] It is the conclusion of O'Keefe in ibid. that Theodore ultimately chooses his methodology over Scripture. I hope to counter this claim, or at least show its deficiency, using in part the conclusions of Greer, Chapter 7: "The Commentary on John – Exegesis versus Theology."

[309] I refer especially in these cases to the Scriptural passages referring strongly to Christ's humanity, such as Luke 2:52 ("And Jesus increased in wisdom and in stature and in favor with God and man"), and what it means, for example, for Cyril to interpret them according to the mode of appearance (i.e., "Christ *appeared* to grow in wisdom…"), and whether this is really to interpret them at all.

more sophisticated theological system upon the text."[310] The part of this method that seems most characteristic of Theodore is the first: drawing theology *from* the text. We discussed earlier how this contrasts with Origen's method of using a Biblical text as a kind of springboard with which to reach to an eternal truth which lies above and beyond it; Theodore uses the text more as a ladder that *in itself* touches upon a higher or nobler insight. A good example of this is Theodore's comments on Genesis 1:26-27[311]:

> This is [the reason for] the excellence of humanity's coming to be: [namely] that it came to be in the image of God. For just as in the case of these other created beings, [the author of Genesis] by his repetition made known [what is] the excellence of each one and its reason for coming to be. He twice established that He made humankind in the image of God, in order to manifest that there is indeed a matter of excellence in his fashioning – that it is in him that all beings are gathered together, so that they might draw near to God through him as an image by obeying the laws laid down by Him about showing service to him and [thus] please the Lawgiver by their diligence to him...If some king, after having created a very great city and adorned it with numerous and varied works, ordered upon the completion of everything that his image, having been made the greatest and most remarkable, be set upon the middle of the entire city as proof of his founding of the city, the image of the king who built the city would necessarily be venerated, with all in the city confessing their gratitude to their city's founder for having given them such a place to live. So the Artisan of creation has made the whole cosmos, embellishing it with diverse and varied works and at the end established

---

311 "Then God said, 'Let us make man in our image, after our likeness; and let them have dominion over the fish of the sea, and over the birds of the air, and over the cattle, and over all the earth, and over every creeping thing that creeps upon the earth.' So God created man in his own image, in the image of God he created him; male and female he created them."

humankind to serve as the image for his household, so that all creation would by their care for and veneration toward humans render the honor due to God.[312]

Several principles are at work in this commentary. First, one notices the precision with which Theodore examines the text itself: he notices, for example, the repetition of the idea that man is created in God's image ("God created man in his own image, in the image of God he created him"). The details of the passage – especially those that might seem odd, like such a repetition, he explains with reference to other parts of the passage, or similar passages in Scripture. Thus the repetition of the "image" idea is explained via man's excellence in regard to other creatures and his dominion over them, given scripturally in the following verse in Genesis,[313] as is the concept of God as Lawgiver. Next, he gives the passage theological significance, explaining *how* man functions as the image of God: by their "diligence" to man, other physical creatures can show obedience to and reverence for God in whose image man is made. Finally, Theodore gives the explanatory analogy of the king and his statue in the city by which his reader may better understand his theological insight. The remarkable point here is that there is nothing within his commentary that is conceptually exterior to the passage on which he is commenting. Every insight is drawn out *from* the passage – nothing outside it is brought in to illumine it save a very close analogy.

It is unfortunate that we have been left little or nothing of Theodore's commentaries on the Synoptic Gospels, from which a great deal of his Christology must have been drawn. Nevertheless, we can see his faithfulness to the rule of Scripture at work in his commentary on John, which should, by our own affirmations above, be the most "difficult" Gospel for Theodore to interpret, due to its varying approach to the mystery of the Incarnation. Generally speaking, Theodore is rather careful in using the *communicatio idiomatum*. Those attributes which belong to humanity he seldom affirms of the divinity without strict qualification, and vice versa. The

---

[312] Quoted in McLeod, 456-458.

[313] "And God blessed them, and God said to them, "Be fruitful and multiply, and fill the earth and subdue it; and have dominion over the fish of the sea and over the birds of the air and over every living thing that moves upon the earth.""

reasons for this will be discussed in the next section, suffice it to say here that the basic drift of Theodore's Christology is to keep the humanity and divinity of Christ precisely distinct. In commenting on John, however, Theodore is forced by Scripture to adapt the theology that we find in his other extant works. While commenting on John 11:42,[314] Theodore says: "Although these words were said from the part of man, nevertheless he shows that he has omnipotence, by that which he received from God the Word, on account of his union with Him."[315] Here Theodore attributes omnipotence to the humanity of Christ before the resurrection, which is a definite change in his Christology on account of this passage. He does this again in commenting on John 5:26-27:[316]

> "The Father," he says, "gave him the same power as His own for raising from the dead, and He gives him the same power of judgment." Well does he say this of the man, because by his union with God the Word, he receives omnipotence like the Father, for God the Word, who was in him, can do everything as the Father. Therefore, it is evident, that all this is said of the man who was assumed: because from this phrase, *for the Father judges no one,* he transfers the whole speech to the *homo assumptus.*[317]

Again, omnipotence is attributed to the humanity of Christ, showing the extent to which Theodore revered the Biblical text as the rule toward which everything else — even his own theology coming from other Biblical texts — must bend. It is true that Theodore makes a strong attempt to read John in the light of Paul's doctrine of "indwelling," but he leaves this behind, or, rather, he attributes a divine characteristic to the one who is indwelt, due to the force of John's language. Greer notes how, though Theodore attempted to retain his own strict distinction of natures in this commentary, "that

---

[314] "I knew that thou hearest me always, but I have said this on account of the people standing by, that they may believe that thou didst send me."

[315] Quoted in Greer, 146. I am indebted to Greer's ideas for this entire section on the commentary on John.

[316] "For as the Father has life in himself, so he has granted the Son also to have life in himself, and has given him authority to execute judgment, because he is the Son of man."

[317] Greer, 147.

121

he fails [to do so] is rather a tribute to his method of exegesis than a slur upon his theology."[318] A final note is that, as Galtier points out, the term *homo assumptus* was one used frequently by a great number of writers in the church including Hilary, Ambrose, Augustine and Gregory of Nyssa; the council of Toledo even anathemized anyone who did not confess that "the man Jesus Christ was assumed by the Son of God."[319]

Theodore's Christology

Having discussed sufficiently what it means to say that Theodore's theology "flows from Scripture," what remains is for us to examine his Christology itself as found in what remains of his systematic Christological works.

In the first extant fragment of *de Incarnatione*, which comes from Book V of that work, Theodore makes this absolute assertion: "[Christ] is discovered to be the same in person – by no means as the result of a confusion of natures but by reason of the union which came about of the one assumed to the One who assumes him."[320] He proceeds in his typical Scriptural way – just as the Gospels began with a simple knowledge of Christ, this man before them, and through contact with him realized that he is God, Theodore begins with Christ as absolutely One – "the same in person." The distinction of natures is only after the fact and upon further examination – one might even call it an "intellectual exercise."[321] Theodore is here as usual quite careful in distinguishing the two natures in Christ – one is assumed and one assumes. Among the reasons for this is his ongoing debate with Arians, who asserted that the Son is less than the Father, and therefore not divine. In this context, freely utilizing the *communicatio idiomatum* is confusing at best: one does not defend the divinity of the Son very convincingly by affirming that he suffered and died. Nor does it make things any clearer to say "God the Son died in his humanity." The word "humanity" denotes at best a

---

[318] Ibid., 148.

[319] P. Galtier, "Theodore de Mopsueste: sa vraie pensee sur l'incarnation," *Recherches de Science Religieuse*, 45 (1957): 165.

[320] *The Christological Controversy*, ed. R.A. Norris (Philadelphia, Fortress Press, 1980), Chapter VIII: "Theodore of Mopsuestia," (hereafter *de Incarnatione*), 113.

[321] I prefer this term to Galtier's description of the duality in Christ as "hypothetical" in Galtier, 180.

concept, and a concept does not suffer or die, nor does it heal on the Sabbath, nor can it be baptized in the Jordan nor really even encountered at all – and it is precisely these things that Theodore (and any honest reader of the Scriptures) saw Christ doing in the Gospels. Indeed, it is not a concept that does these things, but a man – the very one whom Peter describes in Acts 2:22-24:

> Men of Israel, hear these words: Jesus of Nazareth, a man attested to you by God with mighty works and wonders and signs which God did through him in your midst, as you yourselves know – this Jesus, delivered up according to the definite plan and foreknowledge of God, you crucified and killed by the hands of lawless men. But God raised him up, having loosed the pangs of death, because it was not possible for him to be held by it.

It would take a very artificial frame of mind to read Peter's testimony without realizing that he distinguishes "Christ the man" and "God." This distinction that Peter makes does not deny that Christ is at once God and man, since he soon afterward calls Christ "the Author of Life."[322] In addition to this is the Lord's own testimony in rather frequently calling himself the "Son of man." From this approach, the question is no longer "what is this concept that God has assumed?" but rather "how is this man also God?"

The discomfort that many theologians feel when they read Theodore's phrase, "the one assumed is not equal to the One who assumes him,"[323] betrays the fact that they unconsciously do consider Christ's humanity exactly as if it were a concept. If, for example, the pronoun "him" were changed to "it," so that the phrase would read: "the one assumed is not equal to the One who assumes it," the "one assumed" could be read as "the nature assumed," and Christ's humanity could be placed nebulously in the world of concepts, safely away from any supposedly "independent" existence, and it only affirmed that the concept "humanity" is not equal to the concept "divinity," which is true enough. But this does not solve the problem,

---

[322] Acts 3:15.
[323] *De Incarnatione*, 113

it only avoids it. For Theodore, a "nature" is not a concept, but a concrete, particular thing.[324] McLeod describes it thus:

> For [Theodore] Christ's divine nature was interchangeable with the Word, and his human nature was synonymous with Christ as a "man." ...Theodore considered every concrete existing nature to be real and able to function in its own right. With this kind of mental outlook, he would have found it hard to fathom what the neo-Chaldedonians meant when they asserted that the Word can be said to suffer in his humanity, with his human nature being conceived in some sense as an abstract but real nature.[325]

The humanity of Christ thus had to be taken very seriously, and could never be dismissed as an appearance or a semblance – especially because Scripture never did this. This means that Christ the man has a human intellect, a human soul, and a human will – affirmations that perhaps shocked Alexandrians during his time, but that were ultimately codified during later councils.[326]

This insight that Christ's human nature was not abstract but concrete was easily misunderstood. Theodore referring to Christ's humanity as "the man" or "him" suggests to some that he is speaking

---

[324] As will be later shown, this is not at all to imply any independent existence on the part of the man. Though describing something as "concrete" or "particular" may imply this in Scholastic terms, the distinction drawn here is between an *abstract nature* and a *particular nature*. The question of independent existence is not involved in the distinction in any way.

[325] McLeod, 453. Though he does not himself speculate what is the case, McLeod in the same place supplies some useful possibilities for the source of this insight in Theodore: "...it is not clear whether Theodore has been influenced here by an oral Jewish tradition that did not distinguish the abstract and concrete other than in the context or by an Aristotelian tradition that rejected the generic Platonic world of real forms and ideas or by what he thought to be the scriptural perspective."

[326] The human soul of Christ, for example, was defined at Chalcedon; "We teach...one and the same Son, our Lord Jesus Christ: the same perfect in divinity and perfect in humanity, the same truly God and truly man, of a rational soul and body..." This is particularly interesting read in contrast to Cyril's analogy in his third letter to Nestorius, codified at the council of Ephesus, that "[the Word] made his indwelling in such a way as we may say that the soul of man does in his own body."

of a separate, independent person who happens to be "on good terms" with God the Word. But there is nothing in Theodore to suggest that that is the case, if he is read fairly. The following passage may illustrate this:

> [The man] had an inclination beyond the ordinary toward nobler things because of his union with God the Logos, of which also he was deemed worthy by the foreknowledge of God the Logos, who united him to himself from above. So for all these reasons he was immediately possessed, together with judgment, of a great hatred for evil, and with indissoluble love he molded himself to the good, receiving also the cooperation of God the Logos in proportion to his own purpose.[327]

Two mistakes may be made in interpreting this passage from Theodore. The first is to assume that, because the Word "deemed" the man worthy to be united, that the union occurred in the course of Jesus' life – at the baptism, for example, as the adoptionists taught. To read the passage in this way is to ignore that it was by his *foreknowledge* that the Word knew the man would be worthy. Indeed, the union between God the Word and Jesus the man did not take place at any time after the conception of Christ. Later in the same paragraph, Theodore speaks of Christ "having received the union even before [the resurrection] in his *very fashioning*, by the good pleasure of the Lord."[328] The second mistake is to think that Theodore, in speaking of Christ's worthiness and his "own purpose," is dividing God and man into two independent beings. There is no such division in Theodore, but rather only a discussion of the reality of Christ's human will, which must have, if it is real in any sense, its own purpose and moral quality.[329]

---

[327] *De Incarnatione*, 118.

[328] Ibid., italics mine.

[329] This is the central thesis of R.A. Norris' doctoral dissertation *Manhood and Christ: A Study in the Christology of Theodore of Mopsuestia* (Oxford: Clarendon Press, 1963). See especially p. 233: "...the determinant element in Theodore's whole system, Christological and anthropological alike, is his interest in the problem of free rational obedience to divine law." and p. 237: "What is done in Christ must, for [Theodore], be the work of the free human will; and therefore he must emphasize the 'personal' character of Christ's manhood, the reality of his

This leads to what may be the crux of the entire question. There is in Theodore a certain ease in speaking of Christ's humanity at the same time as real and concrete on the one hand, and as united to the Word on the other — a comfort that is present in the writings of no other writer of his time. The following passage brings us closer to the matter:

> But what does it mean to say [that God dwelt in man] "as in a son?" It means that having indwelt him, he united the one assumed as a whole to himself and equipped him to share with himself in all the honor in which he, being Son by nature, participates, so as to be counted one person in virtue of the union with him and to share with him all his dominion, and in this way to accomplish everything in him, so that even the examination and judgment of the world shall be fulfilled through him.[330]

That God unites man to himself, and is the agent in every action in the above quote, shows that the Word is indeed the Subject of the man. That the man is united to God "as a *whole*," that he shares in "*all* the honor," and shares "*all*" the dominion, and that "*everything*" is accomplished in him leaves us no doubt that there is an absolute unity between the natures in Christ — but not an identity, and this seems to be the insight that Theodore gives to the entire Christological dialogue that was ignored by some of the contemporaries who read him with hostility. That is, that there can be an absolute unity between two absolutely distinct and absolutely concrete natures. In other words, there can be *distinction* of natures without *separation*; there can be completeness without independence: there can be duality without division.

If this is the case, then another question may be asked. If a divine nature can assume a human nature, and both be absolutely united yet absolutely "unconfused,"[331] and if in the same way a divine will can assume a human will, and a divine intellect assume a human intellect: why can a divine Person not assume a human person —

---

human soul, which is the subject of the obedience by which the world is redeemed."

[330] Ibid., 117.
[331] "*inconfuse*," Canon 7 of Constantinople II.

especially if understood correctly: without any understanding that "God the Word was one and the man someone quite different?"[332] Indeed, how can there be a human soul, a human intellect, and a human will, without a human person – one who is neither divided nor separate nor independent? This is what Theodore seems to have meant when he said:

> In the case of Christ the personal union is not destroyed by the distinction of natures. When we distinguish the natures, we speak of the nature of God the Word as complete and of his person as complete (for there is no hypostasis without its person). Moreover, the nature of the man is complete, and likewise his person. But when we consider the union, then we speak of one person.[333]

The final phrase of the passage suggests that Theodore had two senses for the meaning of the word "person." The first, of which there are two in Christ, seems to be a complete, concrete nature with individuality or self-reference: that which can (distinctly but not independently) say "I" – something like what the Church of the East has dubbed "*qnoma*." That Christ the man "has" something like this is indeed attested in Scripture. For example, in the Gospel of John, after the Resurrection, Christ says to Mary Magdalene: "Do not hold me, for I have not yet ascended to the Father; but go to my brethren and say to them, I am ascending to my Father and your Father, to my God and your God."[334] The second sense of person, that we come upon "when we consider the union," of which there is one in Christ, seems to be what may be called the "ultimate subject" of the union.[335] I would affirm that it was of the second sense that Constantinople II said "there is only one person,"[336] and that denying the humanity of Christ the first sense is simply to deny that it is complete. At the very least, one must admit that the phrase "when we consider the union" and the different uses of "person" in Theodore's works suggest the

---

[332] Canon 14 of Constantinople II.
[333] *De Incarnatione*, 120.
[334] John 20:17.
[335] The term "ultimate subject" is also used by Norris on p. 237.
[336] Canon 5 of Constantinople II: "*unam personam.*"

type of interpretation they were given by the Church of the East, whether or not Theodore himself intended that interpretation.

A final note about Theodore's Christology is his use of the analogy of marriage in describing the union of natures in Christ. The Second council of Constantinople condemns this analogy: "Furthermore, this heretical Theodore claimed that the union of God the Word to Christ is rather like that which, according to the teaching of the Apostle, is between a man and his wife: *The two shall become one.*"[337] It must be said, however, that this analogy must be read as proceeding from Scripture, and in Scripture, it refers not to an ordinary marriage, but to the marriage between Christ and the Church. In an ordinary marriage, especially today, it is easy to imagine how the man and the woman might separate. It is absolutely impossible to imagine this in regards to the marriage between Christ and the Church. This is even more sharply understood when we realize that the relationship between Christ and the Church is *constitutive*: the Church is *created* in her union with Christ, and does not exist otherwise. If this is applied to the Word and the man, it must be said that the man is constituted and created — in short, he exists — only insofar as he is one with the Word. And because the Word united the man to himself such that he accomplishes all through him and with him shares all dominion, worship, etc., the Word now exists only as Incarnate. Thus the man cannot say "I" apart from the Word, and the Word cannot say "I" apart from the man: there is neither a "we" nor a "one and another." The "who" of the Son of man *is* the Son of God.[338] A more complete union than this is difficult to imagine.

The union is indeed so great that it allows Theodore in the end to admit the truth in the Marian title *Theotokos*, an issue which gave Nestorius much more trouble than it ever did for Theodore. In the twelfth extant fragment of *de Incarnatione*, he states:

> When they ask whether Mary is a man's mother or God's mother, we must say, "Both," the one by the nature of the thing, the other in virtue of a relation. Mary was a man's mother by nature, since what was in her womb was a man, just as it was also a man who

---

[337] Canon 12 of Constantinople II.

[338] Mt 16:13-16: "'Who do men say that the Son of man is?'...Simon Peter replied: 'You are the Christ, the Son of the living God.'"

came forth from her womb. But she is God's mother,
since God was in the man who was fashioned.[339]

Here is Theodore's explication of the doctrine of the Indwelling as
applied to the most slippery of areas, and it seems even here, where
later Antiochenes failed, Theodore succeeded. The union of, in
Theodore's terms, "persons" in Christ is so complete and absolute
that the birth of the man from Mary is in the end attributed to God.

In making a modern judgment on Theodore's Christological
orthodoxy, several things should be kept in mind. First, there is today
no doubt whatever about Theodore's honest intention to teach
nothing but the doctrine of the Church. Even those modern
commentators on Theodore who end by affirming that he *is* the
"proto-Nestorian" never doubt his *desire* to teach the truth of the
faith. Sullivan, for example, who calls Theodore the "Father of
Nestorianism,"[340] still affirms that,

> It must be observed, however, that in asking whether
> the orthodox formula: "two natures in one person,"
> actually corresponds to sound ideology, we do not
> mean to question the sincerity of Theodore's
> intentions. There is no reason to suspect a deliberate
> attempt to conceal heresy under a cloak of orthodox
> terminology. One cannot read Theodore's works
> without being thoroughly convinced of his honest
> intention to think with the Church.[341]

A second point to recall is the importance of avoiding anachronism.
Judging Theodore is not as simple as Sullivan describes – that is,
taking Theodore's works and, by means of linguistic analysis and
inter-textual examination, trying to "fit" them into the Chalcedonian
formula. Theodore, because of his approach to Scripture and his time
in history, certainly does have a different Christological formula than
that of Ephesus and Chalcedon. The fair approach is not to judge his
formula by another formula defined after his death, but to test his
faith which he expressed in his own words against the faith of the

---

[339] *De Incarnatione*, 121.
[340] Francis A. Sullivan, S.J., *The Christology of Theodore of Mopsuestia* (Rome:
Gregorian Press, 1956), 288.
[341] Ibid., 202.

Church which she expressed in the words of the councils. These factors, along with our observations regarding Theodore's Scriptural terminology and his consideration of nature as concrete rather than abstract, must be kept in mind as we reread the condemning texts of the Second Council of Constantinople.

It is now our purpose to examine II Constantinople's interpretation of Theodore and what it saw as his "intolerable tongue,"[342] and attempt to discover whether the council read him accurately, and, if not, what exactly the council condemned. I will attempt to show that what the council condemned, though indeed a heresy, was not what Theodore taught or, at the very least, was not Theodore's teaching as interpreted by the Church of the East. The two areas of insight into reading Theodore discussed above will be used to balance the text of II Constantinople. Thus, the condemnation of analogies based in Scripture will be first examined, and second the condemnation of a *separation* of persons versus a *distinction* of concrete natures. The first text that concerns us is in the fourth canon of the council:

> If anyone declares that it was only in respect of grace, or of principle of action, or of dignity or in respect of equality of honor, or in respect of authority, or of some relation, or of some affection or power that there was a unity made between the Word of God and the man; or if anyone alleges that it is in respect of good will, as if God the Word was pleased with the man, because he was well and properly disposed to God, as Theodore claims in his madness...*anathema sit*.[343]

Several remarks must be made about this text. First, one would fain find, in Theodore's extant works, a claim that the unity in Christ is "only" *anything*. Every attempt made by Theodore to describe the unity of Christ is always in terms of "greater than." In other words, he assumes beforehand the inadequacy of his language. The text examined above from *de Incarnatione*[344] which frequently repeats the

[342] II Constantinople, *Sentence against the "Three Chapters."*
[343] II Constantinople, Canon 4.
[344] *De Incarnatione*, 117: "But what does it mean to say [that God dwelt in man] "as in a son?" It means that having indwelt him, he united the one assumed as

term "everything" testifies to this. Second, as we have already said, the term "good pleasure" originates in Scripture, not in Theodore. Third, because the above text is more concerned with describing the Word as the ultimate subject of Christ, it does not ask the question of Christ's humanity in the same way Theodore would have asked it. That is to say, though it may sound "as if" we are separating the man from the Word, is it *incorrect* to say that the man was "well and properly disposed to God?" Was Christ *improperly* disposed to God? Or is Theodore merely attempting to treat the man as real and not as a concept? The same comments may be made about the twelfth canon, which summarizes the remainder of the Christological condemnation of Theodore in II Constantinople:

> If anyone defends the heretical Theodore of Mopsuestia, who said that God the Word is one, while quite another is Christ, who was troubled by the passions of the soul and the desires of human flesh, was gradually separated from that which is inferior, and became better by his progress in good works, and could not be faulted in his way of life...*anathema sit.*[345]

Again, if we retain the Mesopotamian reading of Theodore, and say that divinity and humanity are absolutely distinct in Christ but in no way separate, it is difficult to claim that he said that the Word is one and that Christ is "quite another." This is to say nothing of the fact that all of the phrases describing Christ's humanity originate in Scripture: that he was "troubled by the passions of the soul," for example, at the cleansing of the Temple; the "desires of the human flesh" are manifest in Christ's hunger before the Temptation in the wilderness; that he was "gradually separated from that which is inferior, and became better by his progress in good works" is almost a paraphrase of Luke 2:52: "And Jesus increased in wisdom and in stature and in favor with God and man." Finally, we, as well as scholars such as we have consulted like Norris, Patterson, Greer,

---

a whole to himself and equipped him to share with himself in all the honor in which he, being Son by nature, participates, so as to be counted one person in virtue of the union with him and to share with him all his dominion, and in this way to accomplish everything in him, so that even the examination and judgment of the world shall be fulfilled through him."

[345] II Constantinople, Canon 12.

Zaharopoulos, McLeod, and others, should not be troubled by the fact that anyone who "defends the heretical Theodore" is thereby anathemized from the Church, for we are defending no such heretic, but, as it seems, a writer of orthodox teaching who lived and died in communion with the Church Universal.

It is certainly heresy to say that "God the Word was one and the man someone quite different,"[346] and this separation between the Word and the man seems to be exactly what the Council condemned. The doctrine of the Indwelling, however, and the absolute distinction between the two concrete, united natures, which are the keystones to Theodore's Christology as it is read by the Church of the East, were not condemned. The final section of this paper will deal with the question of how this Church developed the thought of Theodore of Mopsuestia.

The Church of the East after Theodore

We discussed earlier the relationship between Theodore the Interpreter and the Church of the East, and how the latter saw the former as somehow representing her own thought. The Mother Church, however, is always larger than the child theologian. Just as the Church honoring Theodore as the Interpreter perfected the weak points of his exegetical method, so did she perfect the weak points in his theology. Though I believe Theodore to be basically orthodox not only in his intention but even in his theology, there are admitted weak points in his Christology, as must necessarily be the case in any human attempt to understand a divine mystery.

The weak points in Theodore's Christology are twofold: first, Theodore is vague – though not necessarily heretical – in his treatment of the Word as the ultimate Subject of the Incarnation, and I assert that this vagueness comes from a deficiency in his terminology; second, though his description of the union of natures in Christ is in the end as sufficient as can be expected from a human intellect trying to grasp a divine reality, Theodore is generally too careful in dividing the attributes between the natures: the *communicatio idiomatum* finds little foothold in his thought. In this concluding section, I propose to show that the Mesopotamian School filled both of these gaps in Theodore's Christology. This will be done, firstly, by examining the official declarations of the Synods of the Church of

---

[346] Ibid., Canon 14.

the East, and, secondly, by examining some of her Christological writings and liturgical hymns.

A. The Synods of the Church of the East[347]

In this section I wish to show how the Church of the East, though having her own unique expression of Christology, nevertheless maintained both orthodoxy and a true concern for doctrinal unity with the Church Universal. The Church of the East clearly showed her acceptance of the Councils of Nicea and Chalcedon though none of her bishops attended; on the other hand, the Councils which had come about in questionable circumstances and had more personal attacks than theological content, namely Ephesus and II Constantinople, were taken with a grain of salt, though even in these cases, whatever dogmatic affirmations were made were not contradicted.

THE SYNOD OF ISAAC – 410 AD

It is remarkable that the first concern of the first Synod of the Church of the East, which came about after decades of severe persecution in which communication with the West was impossible, was to affirm the unity of the Church of the East with the Church of the West. Before any of its Canons, the Synod expresses the "Symbol of Faith of the Three Hundred and Eighteen Bishops," that is, the Creed of the Council of Nicea.

THE SYNOD OF MAR AQAQ – 486 AD

The Church of the East watched from Persia while the West aggressively debated the Christological question at the Councils of Ephesus and Chalcedon, and waited over thirty years to publish any official declaration. At the Synod of Mar Aqaq, we have a clear statement of Chalcedonian orthodoxy:

> But our faith in the dispensation of Christ should also be in a confession of two natures of Godhead and manhood, none of us venturing to introduce mixture, commingling, or confusion into the distinctions of those two natures. Instead, while Godhead remains

---

[347] My English source for this text is an early copy of the translation done by Corbishop M. J. Birnie, for which I am very grateful.

and is preserved in that which belongs to it, and manhood in that which belongs to it, we combine the copies of their natures in one Lordship and one worship because of the perfect and inseparable conjunction which the Godhead had with the manhood. If anyone thinks or teaches others that suffering and change adhere to the Godhead of our Lord, not preserving — in regard to the union of the *parṣopa* of our Savior — the confession of perfect God and perfect man, the same shall be anathema.

Just as in Chalcedon, the Fathers of the Synod of Aqaq affirmed a single *parṣopa* (which we will see means person) with two distinct natures in Christ.

THE SYNOD OF MAR ABBA – 544 AD

The story of Mar Abba is an inspiring one in many ways, but our concern here is with his relationship to the Western Church and the doctrinal statements of his Synod. As for the former, after Abba converted from Zoroastrianism, he visited many of the great Christian cities of the West as a representative of the Church of the East. Moffett relates that "At the Byzantine capital he is said to have been received to communion as a matter of course and in no way treated as a heretic."[348] This reflects the atmosphere of the West aside from the Church of Egypt, whose tendencies a few later would force the Emperor to begin the Second Council of Constantinople.

But nine years before II Constantinople, the Synod of Mar Abba made a strong expression of union with the West, at the same time affirming the Church of the East's unique understanding of Christology:

These things were made known with precision by the gift of the Holy Spirit upon the disciples, who learned from the Holy Spirit that Christ is not ordinary man, nor God stripped of the clothing of manhood in which he was revealed, but Christ is God and man, that is, manhood which is anointed with [the Godhead] which anoints it. As it is written,

---

[348] Moffett, p. 219.

134

"Therefore God, your God, anoints you with the oil of gladness above your fellows," the same making known his manhood. Again, "In the beginning was the Word," this showing his Godhead, which exists eternally and for ever, which created all that is seen and all that is unseen, and exists in three qnome, without beginning, without change, without passion, and without division, which are the Father, Son, and Holy Spirit. As our Lord said — for by him the eternal Trinity was made known — as he spoke concerning himself, "Destroy this temple," that is, the manhood with which he clothed himself, and again said, "My Father, who [dwells] in me, performs these works," and again concerning the Holy Spirit who is in him when he said, "The Spirit of the Lord is upon me. Because of this he has anointed me." Behold, from the title "Christ" we learned about the Father, Son, and Holy Spirit, and we have understood his manhood from the same, and in it is the seal of the entire confession of Christianity. Anyone who does not confess in this way, let him be anathematized. Anyone who introduces a "quaternity" into the holy and immutable Trinity, let him be anathematized. Anyone who does not confess that in the last time the Only-begotten Son of God, who is Christ our Lord, was revealed in the flesh, let him be anathematized. Anyone who does not acknowledge the suffering and death of the manhood of Christ, and the impassibility of his Godhead, let him be anathematized. Or anyone who seals a prayer with the name of the Father, Son, and Holy Spirit but numbers some other with them, or does not believe that in the name "Son" he refers to the Godhead and manhood of Christ together, or anyone who seals a prayer with the name of Christ and not as confessing the Trinity, let him be anathematized.

Behind this moderate Chalcedonian approach was a deep respect for Theodore of Mopsuestia, "the Interpreter," who was to be condemned almost a decade later at II Constantinople, though no persons are named in the definitions of the Synod of Mar Abba.

THE SYNOD OF MAR ISHO'YAHB – 587 AD

It is remarkable that it was not until almost forty years after II Constantinople, wherein Theodore and others were condemned by name, that Theodore is mentioned in any Synod of the Church of the East. The Synods of Mar Yawsip (554 AD) and Mar Hazqiel (576 AD) made no mention of either Theodore or of the Christological controversy. Even this Synod of Mar Isho'yahb mentions Theodore in a totally different context. Its Second Canon is entitled "A defense of the writings and teachings of the holy Theodore, and against the slander of the heretics, who have spread false information concerning him," but it has nothing at all to do with Constantinople II or Christology. Rather, it is a defense of his spiritual interpretation of the book of Job and his teaching on its authorship.

THE SYNOD OF MAR SABRISHO' – 596 AD

The first time Theodore, as a symbol of the Christological controversy and the condemnations of II Constantinople, is mentioned in the Synods of the Church of the East is in 596, 43 years after his condemnation in the West. Like in other Synods, the Christological language is moderate and Chalcedonian, but takes on a personal note:

> We also cast out and anathematize all who reject the interpretations, traditions and teachings of the approved teacher, the blessed Theodore the Interpreter, and attempt to bring in new and foreign traditions full of humbug and blasphemy...

The conclusion I would like to make in this section is that, compared to the raging controversies in the West which became personal attacks, the Church of the East was for the most part quite respectful of all dogmatic agreements while putting aside condemnations of individual writers, including Theodore the Interpreter.

B. Christological Writers and Hymns in the Church of the East

In this section I will analyze the Christological Terminology used throughout the Church, but especially that of the Church of the East, focusing more on the crucial term *qnoma*. Finally, I will present three hymns from the _Hudhra_ to show how this Christological synthesis found beautiful liturgical and spiritual expression.

We have seen how, in reaction to the Arian heresy, the Council of Nicea resorted to using philosophical, rather than Biblical, terminology in defining the Divinity of the Son of God. Though this was helpful in answering the Arians and in clarifying beyond any doubt the teaching of the Church on this question, the use of philosophical terms was to cause some confusion in the coming centuries. Both because of the passage of time and because of geographical distance, terms came to take on different meanings, especially the Greek terms *hypostasis* and *prosopon*. Before moving to the terminology of the Church of the East, this chart will help to show how complex the terminological problem became:

	hypostasis	*prosopon*
At Nicea	"nature" (**one** in the Trinity)	-
Cyril/Ephesus	"person" (**one** in Christ)	"face" or "personality" (**one** in Christ)
Theodore/Nestorious	"individual nature" (**two** in Christ)	"person" (**one** in Christ)
At Chalcedon	"person" (**one** in Christ)	"person" (**one** in Christ)

In order to understand the terminology of the Church of the East, we turn to a writer named Mar Babai the Great, who defined her terms in his book *On the Godhead and on the Manhood, and on the Parsopa of the Union*. The first term in the Aramaic usage of the Church of the East is *kyana*, which means "nature" and translates the Greek *phusis* as well as the *ousia* and *hypostasis* of Nicea. The most important terms, however, are *qnoma* and *parsopa*.

Mar Babai defines **qnoma** in the following way:

A singular essence (*ousia*) is called a "*qnoma.*" It stands by itself, singular in number, being one and distinct from many. It is not, therefore, joined [to anything else] – except, with such things as are rational and free creatures, when it receives various accidents,

137

either of excellence or evil, or of knowledge or ignorance, but with the irrational there are also here various accidents...a *qnoma* is fixed in its natural state...it is differentiated from its fellow *qnome* in the unique property which it possesses in its *parsopa* – that of Gabriel is not that of Michael, and Paul is not Peter. However, in each and every *qnoma* the whole common nature is recognized, and it is known intellectually what the one nature is which encompasses the *qnome* in general.[349]

As for **parsopa**, this definition is given in the same place:

Parsopa is also the characteristic of a certain *qnoma* which distinguishes it from others. Therefore the *qnoma* of Paul is not that of Peter, even though in nature and *qnoma* they are the same, for each of them possesses a body and soul, ad is living and rational and fleshly, yet parsopically they are distinguished from one another by the singular uniqueness which each of them possesses, whether in stature, or in form, or in temperament, or in wisdom...

The point to be made here is that having encountered the single Christ, "what is two" in him must be understood if he is to be understood, and "what is two" in him is not simply an abstract concept of a "nature" (what the Church of the East would have called *kyana*), but **this particular nature**, both in Divinity and in humanity. It was not the Holy Trinity which became flesh, but *God the Son*, who is Christ; nor was it "human nature" that was united perfectly to God the Son, but *the man Christ*.

This category of "particular nature" vs. "abstract nature" is the contribution of the term *qnoma*. This is also the reason why it is perhaps best left untranslated, since neither "person" nor "nature" nor even the Greek "hypostasis" in any of its forms does *qnoma* justice. The nearest English translation might be "individuality."

The next note to make is concerning the mode and time of the union. Though the human *qnoma* of Christ is, like all other human

---

[349] *Liber de Unione*, I.17. I again thank Corbishop Birnie for an early copy of his translation of this important work.

qnome, an individualized nature, it is in no way separate from either the *Qnoma* of the Word nor of the *Parsopa* of the Union. Though the two *qnome* are absolutely distinct, they are absolutely united, and completely inseparable; nor was there ever a moment that the human *qnoma* existed independently or apart from the Word. In fact, *the human qnoma of Christ was united perfectly to the Word at the very moment of its creation*, and conversely, *the human qnoma of Christ was created precisely at the moment of, and because of, its union with God the Word.*

Finally, the only way we know either *qnoma* is through the one *Parsopa* of Christ. In Babai's own words:

> In the same on *parsopa* of the one Lord, Jesus Christ, the properties of the two natures and two *qnome* of the Godhead and manhood of Christ are made known. As the nature of God is made manifest in the property of the three *qnome* of the Father, Son and Holy Spirit, so in the same one *parsopa* of one Lord, Jesus Christ, the two *qnome* of God and man are made known – the likeness of God and the likeness of a servant, one Son in one union in one authority, worship and Lordship.[350]

In other words, in Christ we find not only the full revelation of Divinity, but also of humanity as well. It is not only God who is revealed in Christ, but also the meaning and purpose of human life, perfected in his *qnoma*. More on this will be seen in Chapter 5, in the anthropological writings of Mar Narsai.

What this conclusion amounts to is that a full, complete humanity was assumed by God the Word, including, as is affirmed by the Councils of the Church, a created human mind, a human will, and even a human "I," though in every case the created human mind, will and "I" of Christ is always and perfectly united to the uncreated and eternal mind, will and "I" of the Word of God. This is the only way to make sense of the Scriptures, which say both that "the Father is greater than I" (John 14:28) and that "the Father and I are one" (John 10:30).

---

[350] Ibid., I.8.

Knowing Christ, in his one *Parsopa* in two *qnome*, is not a matter of mere theological speculation. It is first and foremost the salvation of the human race, and the center and fount of all our prayer as Christians. As such, I present here three Christological hymns to show how the Church of the East took her deep understanding of Christ into her heart and made it the source of her prayer and spirituality.

First, the Basilica Hymn from the First Sunday after Christmas, which is a straightforward discussion of the unity of Christ's being through the distinction of his natures:

> O Lord of all, while you are in the likeness of God, you assumed the likeness of a servant in your love, and you neither robbed your Divinity nor defrauded your humanity. Rather, in both natures you are truly one Son, undivided. Indeed, above you exist without a mother, from the Father; and below, without a father, from a mother. Thus have the prophets anticipated and predicted; thus also have the apostles preached; and thus have the Fathers taught in the Church. And so, by their pleading and in their faith, may you protect us, O God, and have mercy on us.

Secondly, a longer hymn from night prayer of Christmas Day, discussing how both natures of Christ act throughout his earthly life, and how through the distinction of operations, there is one Subject who is acting at every moment:

- The Son of God showed the revealed truth to his Church betrothed when he chose, in his love, to come to the world and proclaim and teach his Divinity and his humanity.
- For he had been in the womb of his Father, before the ages, without beginning – truly, he is God indeed.
- He came to us in the latter times, put on our body and saved us through it – truly, he is man indeed.
- The prophets proclaimed him in their revelations, the just revealed him through their mysteries – truly, he is God indeed.
- He was carried in the womb for nine months, and was also born as a man – truly, he is man indeed.[351]

---

[351] My full translation is provided in Appendix 4.

Thus the same One who was "in the womb of the Father from before the ages" is without any qualification the one who "came to us," "took our flesh" and "is indeed and truly man." In this way the Christology of Theodore, though read by the Church of the East in a way which is compatible with orthodox faith, was nevertheless surpassed in its vague or weak points. This hymn is sometimes attributed to the fifth century writer of the Church of the East, Mar Narsai, who will be examined in detail in the next chapter.

Finally, a Advent and Christmas hymn by Mar Babai himself, called *"Brykh Hannana."* This hymn is essentially a summary of the liturgical-Christological teaching of the Mesopotamian School, and is worth quoting here in full:

> Blessed is the Merciful One who, in his grace, has provided for our lives through prophecy. Isaiah saw with a spiritual eye the amazing child of virginity. For Mary gave birth to Emanuel, the Son of God, without copulation. From her the Holy Spirit fashioned the united body, as it is written, to become a dwelling and an adorable temple for the Radiance of the Father in one Sonship, and from the beginning of his incredible conception, unite it to himself in one adoration, that everything that is his will be fulfilled in it for the salvation of the people, as is fitting for him. The angels glorify him on the day of his birth, with their praises in the heights above. The earthly also offer adoration with their offerings in one honor. Christ is one – the Son of God, more honored than all, in two natures. In his Divinity he was born of the Father, without beginning and above time. In his humanity he was born of Mary, in the latter times with a united flesh. Neither is his Divinity from the nature of the mother, nor his humanity from the Nature of the Father – the natures are unconfused [lit. "protected"] in their *qnome*, in one Person of one Sonship. And wherever there is divinity, there are three *Qnome* and one Existence. Thus is the Sonship of the Son: in two natures, one Person. Thus has the holy Church learned of the faith of the Son who is the Messiah. We adore you, O Lord, in your Divinity and in your humanity which are without division.

The genius of the Mesopotamian School is expressed in its development of the term *qnoma*, which is defined as a particular or concrete nature, and, in the case of Christ, corresponds to what Theodore was forced, by lack of better terminology, to call his human "person." It is because of this weakness that Theodore had trouble describing the Word as the ultimate Subject of the Incarnation. Here the weakness is alleviated, since describing Christ as "two *qnome*, one person" at once captures all of Theodore's insights into the meaning of Christ's perfect humanity and affirms in a less confusing way the unity of his Person.[352]

Finally even the *communicatio idiomatum* and its liturgical use by the Church of the East is shown in the beginning of the closing prayer for Vespers:

> Glory to you, Jesus our just King, eternal Splendor of the Father, Begotten without beginning, above times and beings, without whom we have neither hope nor expectation, O Creator...

Here is a very clear indication of divine characteristics being attributed to Jesus without any qualification: he is addressed as the "Splendor of the Father," the one "Begotten without beginning," and even the "Creator."

---

[352] Though it is true that individual authors of the Mesopotamian School assert even two *parsope* in Christ, the official liturgical and canonical formula of the Church is two *qnome*, one *parsopa*.

Conclusion

We must end this chapter where every Christological discussion must end: in admitting the fact that whatever the sophistication of thought or terminology or formula, in the end we are grasping at a reality who is utterly beyond our comprehension, despite his descent to our race. Every formula must betray this human reality in one way or another. Where Theodore can be accused of "dividing Christ into two," many an Alexandrian can be ccused of treating Christ's humanity as a cloak or concept. Where the Mesopotamian can be criticized for placing a fourth *qnoma* within the Trinity,[353] though this *qnoma* is the human *qnoma* of the Word of God, the Westerner could be criticized for giving the Trinity a second nature. We are given consolation only in the consideration that, though every attempt to comprehend must end in failure, every sincere attempt to contemplate and adore will end in grace.

---

[353] Canon 5 of Constantinople II: "There has been no addition of person or subsistence to the holy Trinity even after one of its members, God the Word, became human flesh."

CHAPTER 5
NARSAI

Introduction

Mar Narsai, like Mar Ephrem called the "Harp of the Spirit," was born in northern Mesopotamia some time before 420, though the dates concerning Narsai's life are not absolutely certain. All sources affirm, however, that he lived a rather long life. The most common estimation is that he was born around 400 and died in 503. He wrote voluminously, though little is left of his work besides a few dozen metrical homilies and the hymns and other works which were incorporated into liturgical services. After studying in Edessa/Urhai, he moved to Nisibis in 457 and became the head of the great school founded in that city.[354] This happened because, after the Christian theological school in Edessa was shut down due to its "Nestorian" tendencies, Narsai, its head at the time, moved it from the Roman to the Persian Empire, across the on-again off-again borderline, the Euphrates River, into the city of Nisibis. After Narsai moved there, students flocked across the River to continue studies with their old mentor – indeed, the immediate popularity of the School of Nisibis is impossible to explain without attributing it in great part to the students' attraction to the genius of Narsai. I hope to show in this chapter how Narsai can be seen as one authentic continuation of what I have previously described as the Mesopotamian School. I will therefore retrieve three of the four sections used in Chapters I and II: Anthropology, Cosmology and Piety, in order to show how this is the case, assuming that his Dialectic, or his Mesopotamian reverence for Scripture, will be made clear through them.

The Assyro-Chaldean Church incorporates a great deal of Narsai's writings into her liturgical life. Among the places where Narsai's writings are used is the third day of the "Supplication of Nineveh" – a penitential three-day season in which the Prophet Jonah's visit to the city of Nineveh is remembered. The literary and spiritual peak of this season is the first "Mawtwa" of the third and

---

[354] Mar Eshai Shimun XXIII, "Introduction," *Homilies of Mar Narsai*, vol. 1 (San Fransisco: Patriarchal Press, 1970), vi.

final day, when Mar Narsai's text is used (the first two days are mostly comprised of pieces by Mar Ephrem). The text used for this liturgy is a metrical homily which I have titled "Treatise on Man," and the first section of this chapter will thus be a short commentary on it.[355]

Narsai's Anthropology

<u>The "Opening Chiasm"</u>

After a brief introductory supplication, Narsai's Sermon 16, the "Treatise on Man," presents its theme of human nature with the following verses:

11. O Painter of the world in the paint of his love [of spirit] which does not dull,
scour the filth of ignorance from <u>our image [mind]</u>.

12. O Fashioner of <u>bodies</u> and Breather of the <u>soul</u> into members,
tighten our disposition, lest we slacken before enticements.

13. O Honorer of man as surpassing all else due to his <u>love</u>,
have pity on your Honor's image lest it be shamed.

14. You have named our composition after the Name of your Uncomposed Existence.
may your honored Name not be made dull by our dullness.

15. In us you have shown your great <u>love</u> toward your works,
show not in us a sign of wrath against your handiwork.

16. In us you concluded the great name [expansion] of your workmanship,
and within our composition you have bound up <u>the earthly and the heavenly</u>.

17. In us you composed the height and the depth as one flesh:
irrational in our body, <u>rational in our soul</u> – [in] a great marvel!

---

[355] My translation of the text is appended in Appendix 1.

The underlined words, showing the significant elements in each verse, reveal a chiasm wherein Narsai summarizes his basic understanding of human nature: mind, body, and love. Hence verses 11 and 17 are about the mind or intellectual faculty, verses 12 and 16 about the union of soul and body, and verses 13 and 15 about love, with verse 14 working as a hinge, using the theme of "composition" – that is, composition of these three elements. The chiasm can be shown graphically thus:

- Mind (v. 11)
  - o soul and body (v. 12)
    - ▪ love (v. 13)
      - • composition (v. 14)
    - ▪ love (v. 15)
  - o earthly and heavenly (v. 16)
- intellect (v. 17)

The initial inquiry, then, for Narsai, is after the elements of the composition of man. They are not three independent parts, however, but rather three aspects of the single being. The three elements are given as a kind of thesis statement to the five parts of the entire Treatise, and though Narsai will deal with them more extensively later, he merely mentions them here.

"Main Themes"

Verses 25 to 30 give a particularly interesting picture of the main themes Narsai finds within human nature. While the opening chiasm gave various elements of the one man, this section gives various ways of looking at that same man:

25. I saw that the image of your composing was decorated wisely,
and I wished to uncover its gorgeous beauty before onlookers.

26. Within the image of our image I saw the whole creation tied,
and I called to man to come and see all in our nature.

27. [Our] nature pulls me to examine the natures that are tied up within it,
and how indeed this frail thing was able to hold everything!

28. In our very own nature, I saw the sciences of your Divinity,

and I reflected that there is hope for man, sinner though he is.

29. I saw the Name of your Essence dwelling in him[356] as in a temple,
and wondering seized me – how can the wretched suffice for the
   Hidden One?

30. He is wretched indeed, yet you honor him without measure,
and who would not marvel at this wretchedness you chose over all?

31. If your Love has chosen him from all and named him in its
Name,
we can therefore is be sure that you will not despise the one you have
   chosen.

For Narsai, then, these are the different ways of looking at man: as
formed wisely (25), as the completion of Creation (26), as frailty
containing greatness (27), as having knowledge of Divinity and as
such capable of forgiveness (28), as temple of God (29), as
contemptible yet honored (30), and as chosen by God (31).
      It is here that the richness of the tradition of the Church of
the East can be seen, for one can find here elements both of the
Judaism upon which Christianity in Mesopotamia was initially built
(that is, upon the Jews who stayed in Babylon after the exile), as well
as the unique-for-the-time Aristotelian outlook on the world.
Regarding the former, the frailty of man, his capacity for forgiveness
from a personal God, man understood as the temple of God, his
being contemptible yet honored and his being chosen by God are all
themes revealing a strong connection if not directly to the Old
Testament, then at least to New Testament interpretations of Old
Testament symbols such as temple, etc. Regarding the latter, the
strong concentration, here as well as in the opening chiasm, on man's
wisdom as being definitive of him, man having a natural knowledge
of divine things, and especially man as being tied to and, in some
sense, containing, the whole of creation, reveal a very poignant

---

[356] From here to verse 43, the grammatical object is (human) "nature," or
"our nature," but this becomes conceptually untenable. It is clear that, eventually,
Narsai is talking specifically about Christ from verse 34 onward (at the latest), and I
have therefore translated all pronouns with this referent "him" rather than "it."

influence of Aristotelian thought,[357] much more popular among Christians in Persia at this time than among those within the Roman empire, as seen in Chapter 3.

The "Litany of Levels"

After the "Main Theme" section, there follow ten verses beginning with the word "if." They all take a similar form: "If God has made man X, then who would not Y?" They are thus each ethical statements – if man is such-and-such, then he must act accordingly. Even in this bare form one already recognizes the Aristotelian notion of basing ethics on human nature and dignity (rather than, for example, the Old Testament notion of Law as the will of God), with the (Judeo-Christian) qualification that this nature and dignity come as gifts from God. There is also, within the Litany, a very interesting building-up or climbing of the "steps" or "levels" mentioned at the end of the Litany at verse 42. This is best shown by once again quoting in full:

31. If your Love has chosen him from all and named him in its Name,
we can therefore is be sure that you will not despise the one you have chosen.

32. [And] if your Lordship has made him lord over all that is,
who would not join himself to the yoke of his life's work?

33. If your Knowledge has called and appointed him to a high position,
who would not confess that his position and the name of his authority is true [his position is true and his authority great]?

34. If your Hiddenness reveals itself to your handiwork [servants] by his uncovering,
who would not gather his vision from all else toward his composition?

35. If you have shown in him the great mystery of Son and Spirit,

---

[357] See, for example, Aristotle's *De Anima* III.8: "…in a manner the soul is all existent things."

who would not approach the sciences hidden in his name?

36. If in him you have shown your sweetness to angels and men,
who would not take refuge in his body that pleads on his behalf [his
    living body and blood]?

37. If that Word begotten of you dwells in him in love [unites with
him],
who would not call him the emperor of height and depth?

38. If in him you have completed your provision for all,
who would not labor for his provision without weariness?

39. If through him you will judge the earth at the end of time,
who would not fear the trial that is in his hands?

40. If through him you will grant blessings [reward] to the good and
scourgings to the wicked,
who would not beg you to let him be [beg him to be] an advocate for
    his debts?

41. If he is the one with authority over this world and that to come,
who would not believe that he is the Second of Divinity [truly the
    Son of God]?

42. To these levels I saw our miserable nature raised
and my mind was stirred to journey mentally toward his misery [his
    authority].

43. The greatness of his rank forced me to dare out of order,
and to proceed on a path whose inquiry is greater than my words.

The Levels or Titles given to man (beginning in verse 32, with verse
31 as an introduction) and their corresponding edicts can be
represented thus:

Verse	"Level"	Edict
32	"lord over all that is"	Join oneself to life's work.
33	"high position"	Confess man's authority.
34	"manifestation of God"	Gather one's perceptions (in

		continence).
35	"showing of Son and Spirit"	Approach hidden knowledge.
36	"showing of God's sweetness"	Take refuge in his body.
37	"united with the Word"	Call him emperor of height and depth.
38	"completion of God's providence"	Labor in one's own provision patiently.
39	"judge of the earth"	Fear the trial in his hands.
40	"giver of reward and punishment"	Permit him to be an advocate for you.
41	"possessor of authority"	Believe he is Second of Divinity.

From the beginning of this "litany" in verse 32, there is a subtle hinting at Narsai's ultimate thesis: humanity cannot be totally understood except in reference to the perfect humanity of Christ. While the title "lord over all" could be read as referring to man's dominion over creation as established in Genesis 1:28, each succeeding title becomes harder and harder to apply to any mere man. Verse 36 begins to be more explicit, referring either to the Eucharist or to the ascended body of Christ in heaven, and verse 37 finally recalls that the "Word begotten of you dwells in him in love [unites with him]," and the following verses continue in this vein. Therefore, this is no generic humanity Narsai is speaking of; rather, it is the humanity of Christ, in which Narsai seeks to understand humanity as a whole as completed and perfected. This is, for Narsai, the Christian addition to Aristotelian philosophy: that while ethics is based on human nature, human nature is best defined by its "final cause" or ultimate goal: the humanity of Christ, toward which all men strive. That is why, beginning in verse 35, the edicts given make sense only in the context of the Christian faith, and are not simply moral statements but properly religious ones.

Man's Misery

Yes, human nature is created in God's image and fulfilled in the Messiah, but Narsai is too realistic - too human - to stop at ideas. The reality he sees before his eyes is just as solid a witness as the thoughts he finds in the Scriptures. The suffering and contingency of everyday human life is more than fascinating to Narsai; it is heartbreaking, and he offers a lengthy section of his Treatise describing it:

48. Poor and lacking is our miserable race of all good things:
sustain this miserable thing with a small crumb of your Gift.

49. He is far too weak to gather temporal sustenance,
and he is unable to work the land with his strength without your
    Strength.

50. His work is filled with great fear, as much as he works,
and there is no security for his sustenance, as much as it multiplies.

51. Sufferings and griefs accompany his toil summer and winter,
and all perils are constant for him – for him, and for what is his.

52. Much is his work, and little the reward returned to him;
great is his weariness, and miserable and lacking, the sustenance of
    his life.

53. He plants so much and harvests little of the much,
he is beaten and crushed, and by the time he enjoys himself, death
    has swallowed him.

54. In fear he plants, and in trepidation he gathers his produce,
and his heart does not rely on enjoying his labor or his gathering.

55. He casts his wheat upon the [his] field, that it may be returned to
him,
and he is afraid and distressed that perhaps he perish and his life pass
    away.

56. He works his land and he thinks that perhaps it may fail to
produce;
he walks on the path, and Death sits and waits for him.

57. Like a mother, he awaits for produce like a newborn,
and the whips of Death strike at his discernment at every hour.

58. He stands in a contest of sufferings every day and night,
and there is no end to the battlefield of his emotions.

59. A great battle is poised at all times against his disposition,
and if he falls asleep, enticements enter and plunder his freedom.

60. The wretched one is cast before two calamities, each worse than the other:
the twofold scourgings of the passions of his [the] body and the
    sustenance of life.

61. As if with leather cords, he beats himself with his inclinations,
and there is no place in him not filled completely [with the scars] of
    the passions.

62. He is suffering and weary regarding his passions [life] and
regarding his labors,
and there is no time when he does not rest with bitterness.

63. If the sun grows hot, his mind grows hot regarding his crops,
and if the rain stops, his thoughts dry up with his plants.

64. If heat gains the upper hand, thirst has killed him;
and if cold increases, he is consumed by frost.

65. If he is impoverished, he conceives depression and begets
complaining;
and if he is made opulent, he puts on pride and arrogance of spirit.

66. If he is justified, he derides and mocks sinners;
and if he sins, he is weakened and decides there is no hope.

67. If he is made wise, he forgets the clay of his wretched nature;
and if he glorifies himself, he becomes a beast without understanding.

68. In great and in small, his sufferings increase and his malice grows,
and what can he do, where can he run, who has such a brief life?

69. He is stuck wanting between neediness and excess,
and so how is it possible for him to keep his life without harm?

70. It is exceedingly difficult for men to live well,
and the course of righteousness is not made easy for the bodily.

This sadness is one regarding both the body and the soul (feeding the former and perfecting the latter) and their difficulties. But this sadness is by no means despair, because Narsai returns, after facing the hardships of humanity directly, to Christ as man's hope, the one who dwells in a temple miserable though it is:

71. Flesh – he is flesh, as much as he desires spiritual things,
and even that desire is not his, but an Other's.

72. An Other dwells in him, in a temple of corruptible clay,
and in his living, he blossoms a little before he decays.

Conclusion

Narsai represents one of the finest attempts of the Church of the East to give a solid and comprehensive understanding of man, using Aristotelian philosophy at the beginning, and completing Aristotle with Christian doctrine. Much work needs to be done to show the connection between the Syriac translations of Aristotle that were beginning during (and before) Narsai's time and their effect on the theology of the Mesopotamian School. Nevertheless, Narsai's consistency with what we have seen in previous anthropological works of the Mesopotamian School is clear: he retains the humility found in *Gilgamesh* and the Talmud, while basing his final doctrine of man solidly on Scripture and ultimately on Christ himself.

Narsai's Cosmology

The various genres found in Narsai's writings include the metrical homily, the hymn, and, among others, the *soghytha*: the "canticle," according to standard dictionary definition, or, more accurately, the dialogue. This literary device was used both as a vehicle for expressing theological insight and as a tool for teaching the faith - these dialogues were likely performed as plays in monasteries or parishes. Narsai's dialogues characteristically are extremely biblical - based upon his lifetime of meditation on Holy

Writ, as well as uniquely dramatic - using the emotions expressed by biblical characters as a starting point for extended literary development. This much will me seen in the following discussion on Narsai's "Dialogue Between the Watcher & Mary."[358] The relevance of this dialogue to Narsai's cosmology will not be immediately apparent until the teaching of the dialogue is made clear – that the ultimate virtue personified by Mary, the Second Eve, is *wonder*.

The "Dialogue Between the Watcher & Mary" is based upon, and is indeed merely a dramatic expansion of, Luke 1:26-38. By Narsai's time, the standard Biblical text in the East was the Syriac *Pshytta*, the Diatesseron having been superseded by it much earlier. As this is the text Narsai would have referred to, it is useful here to quote the passage in full, making parenthetical note of the terms expanded upon by Narsai in his dialogue:

> <26> In the sixth month, then, Gabriel the angel was sent from near God to Galilee to a city whose name was Nazareth,
> <27> toward a virgin betrothed to a man whose name was Joseph, from the house of David, and the virgin's name was Mary.
> <28> And the Angel entered toward her, and said to her: Peace be with you, O filled with grace! Our Lord is with you, O blessed among women!
> <29> But she, when she saw, was troubled [*ithrahbath*] in his word, and was thinking [*mithhashwa*] what this greeting was.
> <30> And the angel said to her: do not fear [*tidhhlyn*] Mary. Indeed, you have found favor near God.
> <31> Indeed, behold! you will conceive [*tqablyn*] in the womb, and give birth to a son, and you will call his name Jesus.
> <32> He will be great, and will be called Son of the High One, and the Lord God will give him the throne of David his father, and he will rule over the house of Jacob forever.
> <33> And there will be no end to his kingdom.

---

[358] Found in Syriac in: D. Alphonsi Mingana, *Narsai: Doctoris Syri, Homiliae et Carmina*, vol. 2 (Mosul, Iraq: Press of the Dominican Fathers, 1905), 367. My translation appended in Appendix 3.

<34> Mary said to the angel: How can this be, since man has not known [*ḥkym*] me?

<35> The angel answered and said to her: the Holy Spirit will come and the power of the High One will overshadow you, because this one who will be born from you is holy, and will be called Son of God.

<36> And behold! your kinswoman Elizabeth also has conceived a son in her old age, and this is her sixth month for her who was called barren.

<37> For nothing is impossible for God.

<38> Mary said: Behold, I am the handmaid of the Lord God; let it be to me like unto your word. And the angel departed from her.[359]

Narsai, in his dramatic reformulation of this text, divides the scene into two parts, with the hinge being the mention of the Holy Spirit and Mary's acceptance. The metrical dialogue itself has twenty-two acrostic stanzas, one for each letter of the Aramaic alphabet, with one verse each spoken by the angel and Mary per stanza. It is therefore in the center of the Alphabet, at the letter "Mym," that both events happen – the angel's mention of the Holy Spirit, and Mary's consequent acceptance of the angel's message.

There are two major themes in the dialogue. The major theme in the first half of the dialogue is Mary's being troubled – the verb "*ithraḥbath*" (root RHB) – and various elaborations on what exactly it means to say that Mary was troubled. The major theme in the second half is Mary's acceptance – the verb "*tqablyn*" (root QBL) – and various elaborations on what it means to say that Mary accepted the angel's word. As will be seen, the connecting thread between the two halves, as well as the element that marks Mary as superior to Eve, is the concept of *wonder* and all that is implied in it.

Immediately after the angel's greeting, Mary expresses her confusion: "Who are you, my lord? And what is the story you tell? What you say is strange to me, and I am unable to understand its meaning."[360] A similar idea is given in the next two stanzas, as the angel's words are "distant"[361] from Mary – indeed, a "novelty."[362]

---

[359] *Les Saints Evangiles d'Apres, La Pschitta* (Mosul, Iraq: Press of the Dominican Fathers, 1896), p. 267-8. My translation is provided in Appendix 3.

[360] Mingana, *ALAP*.

[361] Ibid., *BETH*.

Every attempt at explanation given by the angel is answered by Mary's insistence that she does not understand what he is saying. Confusion, then, is the first expression of Mary's being troubled. It is worth noting here that Mary's confusion does not end in any kind of silence, but rather in a curiosity that is seen even in Luke's short account of the Annunciation.

The angel, responding to Mary's seeming resistance, expresses "wonder" and changes the question into why she does not believe him. Mary's answer turns the dialogue to the theme of Mary as the New Eve, for she answers: "I am afraid, lord, to accept you (*eqablakh*), for indeed my mother Eve, when she accepted (*qablath*) the snake who spoke to her as a friend, was deprived of glory."[363] Thus Mary shows her good training in the Hebrew Scriptures: the very mention of a "fruit" recalls to her the story of the Fall in Genesis.

There is also here a clarification of the meaning of Mary's being troubled: it is not mere stubbornness that she has, but rather fear. Her fear, however, is not at all one of cowardice, but rather righteous fear of sinning against God as did her mother Eve. Mary's questions and concerns are therefore quite justified, as she is confident is the case, when she continues to question the angel, to his apparent amazement:

> *Watcher:* "That imposter deceived, my daughter, when
> he made her trust him. I am not like him, however,
> for I have been sent by God."
> *Mary:* "This story you tell me is contentious like that
> one – do not blame me [for arguing] – for in a virgin
> has never been found a son, nor in a fruit,
> Divinity."[364]

But the angel has an immediate response: "There are no words opposed to mine."[365] Mary is not so easily convinced, however: "Your pledge is fair, and even your word. If only nature would not shake me and make me terrified to accept you: all on account of 'a fruit being found in a virgin'"[366] In other words, there *is* a "word

---

362 Ibid., *GAMAL.*
363 Ibid., *DALATH.*
364 Ibid., *HEH.*
365 Ibid., *WAW.*
366 Ibid.

opposed" to that of the angel – one also coming from God: nature. This Mary confirms in the next stanza, in her already established courageous shyness:

> *Watcher:* "Angels tremble at his word, and, as soon as he commands, do not act insolently. But you – do you not fear to prevent something which the Father desires?"
>
> *Mary:* "I was indeed shaken, Lord, and alarmed, and being afraid, I dared not tell you that nature itself has forbidden virgins to give birth."[367]

Mary's case is thus the stronger one at this point: on her side is the indubitable authority of nature, while the angel has only his own word.

What Mary requires if she is to "accept" him (or "conceive," for the root QBL has both meanings), is a confirmation – not one to answer any kind of doubt of the power of God, but one to show her that her acceptance will not be a repetition of the mistake of Eve, one, that is, to verify that the angel does indeed come from God. Stanzas *HETH* and *Teth* repeat Mary's request for verification. The following to stanzas reveal more clearly Mary's suspicion of the angel. Finally, making explicit the vagueness that had been becoming clearer in the last four stanzas, Mary answers the angel's latest request for acceptance thus: "No, lord. I am not known of man, and I have not met with copulation, so how can it be as you say, that one without intercourse give birth to a son?"[368] This is the dramatic peak of the dialogue, placed in the center, and what follows begins the resolution:

> *Watcher:* "By the Holy Spirit, who is without suspicion, will you accept (QBL) a conception that is beyond understanding, and the power of the Most High will descend upon you, that the King may dawn from your womb."
>
> *Mary:* "Well, then, O watcher, do not turn away from me. If the Holy Spirit is coming to me, it is easy for

---

367 Ibid., *ZAYN.*
368 Ibid., *LAMADH.*

me to be his handmaid. Therefore, be it done unto me according to your word."[369]

It is, ultimately, the mention of the Holy Spirit that gives the Blessed Virgin the verification she needs in order to both "accept" and "conceive." Only he has the power to overturn or go beyond the laws of the Creation established by God.

Mary having been convinced and having conceived, the dialogue continues with her retaining her original character, except without her suspicion of the angel. That is to say, her curiosity remains. Once the initial miracle is explained in terms of the power of the Holy Spirit, Mary begins interrogating the angel about her Son: "What does he resemble? Do you know?"[370] "If he is a flame, as you say, how will my womb not be harmed?"[371] "Why is it fitting for him to dwell in a poor woman, for, behold, the world is full of the daughters of kings?"[372] "Why does he wish to come to me?"[373] "…make also clear to me the habits of my Son…What shall I do for him who will not misbehave?"[374] After this bombardment of questions, the dialogue ends with several stanzas of praise and glory to the Creator, describing the "mingling" of heaven and earth.[375]

What is worth noting here is the common strain between the first and second halves consistently and poignantly found in Mary's personality: asking questions - curiosity.

Keeping the potency of this message within the dialogue in mind, and recalling the "New Eve" imagery, we can come to a few interesting conclusions. First, we can note the strong contrast between Mary's questions and Eve's immediate acceptance of the one who came to her. The contrast here is between the rule of the mind on the part of Mary, and the rule of the desires on the part of Eve. Though Eve desired the fruit because by it she could gain wisdom, she did not consider the means by which this wisdom would be gained. Going more deeply into the matter, the contrast is even starker when we consider what the Old and the New Eve "saw,"

---

369 Ibid., *MYM.*
370 Ibid., *NUN.*
371 Ibid., *SIMKATH.*
372 Ibid., *'AYN.*
373 Ibid., *PEH.*
374 Ibid., *SADEH.*
375 Ibid., *TAW.*

respectively. Whereas the Old Eve "saw that the tree was good for food, pleasing to the eyes, and desirable for gaining wisdom," (Genesis 3:6) she did *not* see, at that moment, the larger picture of God's law in Creation. Eve's wonder, her curiosity, had ceased when presented with the temptation. At that point, her mind became smaller and her vision diminished, as all she saw was her own desire. Mary's constant questions in the dialogue may seem exaggerated or even irritating, if the *meaning* of curiosity and questioning is not kept in mind. **Curiosity in its pure form, as found in Mary, is precisely the same thing as wonder at God's Creation.** Mary, in her curiosity, remains open to accepting (QBL) the whole of Creation, and has no trouble, in stanza *MYM*, in finally conceiving (QBL) something that is "beyond understanding."[376] Eve, in her dullness, reduces her mind to simply that which she sees before her, and excludes all the rest of what is offered by God, and she and her act are the beginning of sin, as her daughter is the beginning of Redemption.

Narsai's Piety

This section will be a short commentary on the first section of Narsai's metrical homily entitled "On the Order of Creation, also Relating the Qnome of the Trinity."[377] By looking at this work, I hope to show how Narsai's Trinitarian theology represents a continuation and perfection of the Mesopotamian piety described in the previous chapters.

Introduction

The homily begins with a retelling the story of Moses' conversations with the Lord on Mount Sinai. Moses asks the Lord to be allowed see him in his Nature – asks with yearning, in fact, and making a strong rhetorical case for it: "If, then, you have chosen me for yourself as a disciple, and if you love me, show me the glory of

---

[376] Ibid., *MYM*.

[377] My translation appended in Appendix 2. In the translation of the first part of this homily, I have opted to simply transliterate the Syriac technical term *qnoma* rather than to attempt to translate it. Though in a Trinitarian context, "person" is the Western equivalent, it is misleading when used Christologically, since there are, in Mesopotamian thought, two *qnome* in Christ (cf. Chapter 4).

your Nature, and let me contemplate your hidden Radiance."[378] A common theme running throughout Narsai is his concentration on the human activity of wonder. This is, as we have seen, one of many "Aristotelian tendencies" in Narsai[379] and in most Mesopotamian thinkers.[380] In any case, the Lord is unimpressed with Moses' desire, however ardent, to see his Glory. God's intent in calling Moses is not, indeed, to reveal himself completely to him, that being impossible, but rather to use him as a messenger to announce to the people that God is the Creator of the whole world around them:

7. "You have erred greatly, O Moses:" the Lord said to him, "no mortal can see me, for my nature is above those who see."

8. "I called you unto myself in order to be taught, that you may learn that I am the Creator; not that you may learn my Hiddenness, for that is incomprehensible to creatures."[381]

Two notes may be made here. First, there does not seem to be, in Narsai, any concern with distinguishing "reason" and "revelation," since for him, as will be seen, the insight we gain into God's nature from creation is as much a "revelation" of God as Scripture. Indeed, even in this homily on the Trinity, the stress seems to be much more on the knowledge gained through creation:

21. For this is fitting in the Maker, that in his works he may proclaim his Power, and in the ordering of his creatures, they may gain knowledge.[382]

---

[378] Ibid., v. 6.

[379] See again, for example, the first words of Aristotle's *Metaphysics*: "All men by nature desire to know."

[380] For a discussion of Aristotelian influence in the Christian thought of Persia in general, see Isho'dad of Merv, *Commentary on St. Paul's Epistles*, tr. Margaret Gibson, *Horae Semiticae* 11 (Cambridge: University Press, 1916), xiii: "From the catalogue of Syriac writers by Ebedjesu...we find that the Syrians began to teach the Peripatetic philosophy at the Persian school in Edessa: here Ibas, Koumi and Probus translated the works of Theodore and the works of Aristotle..." Or, A. Voobus, *History of the School of Nisibis*, vol. 266 of *Corpus Scriptorum Christianorum Orientalium* (Louvain, 1965), "Introduction."

[381] Appendix 2, "Introduction."

[382] Ibid, "*De Deo Uno.*"

On the other hand, and secondly, the fact that there *is* a Creator is something that required a special act of God in order for "things that are made" to know. In contrast, the Scholastics would have discussed the Creator in terms of "merely reasonable" inquiry which was led by faith, while Trinitarian discussions would have begun with the revelation of the New Testament. This is not to place Narsai in *opposition* to the Scholastics, as if for him Trinitarian theology is a work of pure reason and theology of creation is one of Scriptural interpretation, but rather to stress the point that this distinction between "faith and reason" simply has no foothold at all in the thought of Narsai – the categories simply do not exist.

In any case, Narsai begins this sermon by giving himself, in our categories, a Biblical basis or starting-point. The Lord responds to Moses' request to see his Essence with a specification of what exactly Moses' role is to be – to reveal the existence of the Creator. The rest of the Sermon may be divided into three large sections: (I) Characteristics of the Unity of God, (II) Trinitarian Theology, (III) Commentary on the Six Days of Creation. This paper will deal with only the first two sections.

De Deo Uno

After the introductory discussion between Moses and the Lord, Narsai begins a discussion on what must be believed about the One Creator God. The "link" or progression from the Biblical scene to the theological discussion is subtle:

16. Forsooth, "in the beginning" the Creator began and created everything that is, and fixed the times, in his knowledge, of the beginning and the end.
17. And while not beginning in his Being (for his Nature is without beginning [in time]), he made creation in time, as he foreknew.[383]

Narsai thus uses a kind of dialectical technique in explicating his theological teaching: if God created everything, both in its beginning

---

[383] Ibid.

and end, and God is greater than what he creates, therefore God is without beginning.

The eternity of God having been established, Narsai continues along the same logical path, showing what it means for God to have eternity:

> 18. It was not a new thought that led him to make creatures, for this was set from eternity in his Knowledge and Being.[384]

The decision to create, then, though temporal in its effect, is eternal in its origin. In other words, God did not change his mind or come up with a new idea in the act of creation. He then moves from God's eternity to his perfection:

> 19. Nor was it for his own satisfaction that he constituted heaven, earth and all therein, but rather in love and mercy that he revealed his will to creatures.[385]

God did not create "for his own satisfaction," since that would suggest something lacking previously, but rather "in love and mercy." The progression of the dialectic so far is thus: God created the world → God is eternal → God is perfect → God is loving and merciful. The next step for Narsai is to move to God's power:

> 21. For this is fitting in the Maker, that in his works he may proclaim his Power, and in the ordering of his creatures, they may gain knowledge.[386]

This power is the first thing which proclaims God, through the work of creation, which proclamation is made by means of beauty and order. It is this verse that justifies the title of the sermon, which connects the order of creation and the revelation of the Trinity itself: God's work is self-revealing, therefore creation reveals God's Nature, which is a Trinitarian Nature.

---

[384] Ibid.
[385] Ibid.
[386] Ibid.

Before moving to Trinitarian theology, however, Narsai prepares the reader with a literary device whereby he begins three verses in a row with the same words:

22. His Being is without beginning; his Lordship is without end. For his creatures, however, there is a beginning, and for his creatures, temporality and composition.
23. His Being is incomprehensible by the minds of creatures; nor can it be contained by sight, for his Nature is greater than this.
24. His Being is immeasurable: for what is before the beginning? Nor is there any time when he was not, for he existed before all.[387]

This threefold structure is a common tool for Narsai, and an avid reader will have been trained to pay close attention when it is used. The three characteristics Narsai stresses just before explicitly naming the Persons of the Trinity are: being without beginning or end, incomprehensibility, and immeasurability. Each of these is then contrasted with a created nature. Thus, where God is without beginning or end, creatures are temporal; where God is incomprehensible, creatures are un-comprehending; where God is immeasurable (here meaning literally "without limit"), creatures come to exist only "after" him. This triad also serves as a preface, almost a warning, to the upcoming analogies: although we can know something about the Creator by comparison with creatures, this knowledge must by necessity be extremely limited. In any case, this threefold negative theology having been given, Narsai moves on to the major theme of the sermon.

De Deo Trino

The section of the sermon on the Trinitarian attributes of the Godhead may be divided into the following sub-sections: (A) Basic Doctrinal Trinitarian Teaching, (B) Analogy 1: Splendor, (C) Analogy 2: Soul, (D) Analogy 3: Eve, (E) Conclusion.

---

[387] Ibid.

Narsai has full access to Nicene Trinitarian dogma, and makes use of all the basic tenets of the Orthodox Trinitarian faith:

25. There was the [Divine] Nature, perfect in being, without beginning: Father, Son and Holy Spirit, three Qnome, one Power.
26. The Father, perfect, without beginning, who begat the Son without alteration; the Son is from him and like him, and there is no interval of time between him and his Father.
27. The Spirit, who is from the same Nature, is an existing and a true Qnoma; the equality of whose Nature witnesses that he existed with the Father.
28. The Begotten of the Father resembles him, for he is with his Father from eternity, and because he is with his Father, the ages do not confine the Begotten.[388]

It is worth noting that the structure of Syriac is such that the root of every word is three letters, and that the most basic form of any root is verbal. Thus what I have translated "Begotten" is literally "that which was given birth to." In any case, these verses are a simple statement of the defined dogma of the Church regarding the Trinity: that the Son and Spirit are equal with the Father in Divinity, and that they are eternal.

The first analogy Narsai uses to describe the Trinity is that of fire and its splendor:

29. The Begotten of the Father resembles him, and is with him as Light: for as is light with fire, so is the Begotten with his Father.
30. The light of fire is with it, and there is no fire without light; for through its light it is seen, and through it is light shown.
31. With the Father is also his Begotten, and the Son is with him without beginning. Neither is there Father without his Begotten, nor Son without his Begetter.[389]

---

[388] Ibid, "De Deo Trino."
[389] Ibid.

The first note to make here is that Narsai neither quotes nor makes explicit reference to any Scriptural passage. This is in part because of his audience, which was the educated student body at the school at Nisibis, who would by second nature already have passages like "I am the light of the world..." already in mind. A second remark to make is that Narsai takes the New Testament and the Incarnation for granted, and even seems to "skip over" the revelation of the Trinity by the Son at his baptism. He moves from an establishment of the resemblance between creature and Creator directly to a discussion of the inner life of the Trinity, without a reference or even a nod to salvation history. In other words, there is little or nothing to connect the Trinitarian life with human life. This is an apparent flaw in the work as a piece of systematic theology, though I hope to show that Narsai's conclusion to this section of the sermon fills in this gap.

In explaining the splendor analogy, we should first point out that the analogy does not attempt to explain the whole Trinitarian life, but rather only one aspect thereof:[390] how two or more things can exist in absolute interdependence. Thus fire cannot and does not ever exist without the light shining forth from it, just as the Father cannot and does not ever exist without the Son being begotten from him. Immediately after establishing this analogy, however, Narsai criticizes it:

32. The Son, however, is not constituted without a Qnoma, like light. Rather he is a true Qnoma and an Image that resembles his Begetter.
33. The Son does not form the Father, nor is the Son named "father;" for the difference in their Names proclaims the truth of the Qnome. [391]

The problem with the splendor analogy is that the light that is produced by fire does not have any kind of separate identity, as the Son has in relation to the Father. Here the Syriac word Qnoma is perhaps more useful than the English word Person, since Qnoma can be translated also "an individual example of a nature." Thus a particular flame can be called a qnoma of fire. Still, the Qnome of the Trinity are defined in relation to one another, and not in relation to

---

[390] Perhaps what Aquinas would call a "notion."
[391] Ibid.

the Divine Essence, since the Son is simply "he who is begotten" and the Father is simply "he who begets."

The next section regards the Spirit, and begins, like the splendor analogy, with a statement of dogmatic belief:

34. The Spirit is a Qnoma from the Father who is equal with him in everything. As the Son is equal to the Father, the Spirit is equal to the Father and Son.
35. The difference of their Names does not injure the equality. The Names are to be taken in order, but the Qnome are equal in Essence.[392]

Thus, despite the "rank" of Names, that is, in their relation to one another, the Qnome are equal as far as the Divine Nature is concerned. The next analogy is the closest Narsai comes to attempting a single "cover all" analogy for the Trinity:

36. A manifestation of the three Qnome of one Being is fastened, for us, in our soul: for the Son and the Spirit are from the Father as reason and life are from the soul.
37. Along with the soul is born reason, and power and vitality, and along with the Father are the Son and Spirit without beginning.
38. Two powers accompany the soul: reason and vitality as well; and two Powers with the Father: the Son and Spirit without beginning.[393]

This is Narsai's psychological analogy: Soul, Reason and Life = Father, Son and Spirit. It is important to avoid reading this analogy as saying more than it is intended to say. The analogy is simply showing an example in creation of three things coming by necessity from one thing. His use of the term "powers," for example, should not be read as a modalist replacement for "qnome" in reference to the Qnome of Son and Spirit, since he makes it clear in the previous analogy that nothing less than the term Qnoma will suffice.

Here the question arises, "if both Son and Spirit come from the Father, how are they distinguished from one another?" Narsai

---

[392] Ibid.
[393] Ibid.

attempts an answer by using precise terminology, probably borrowed from the Greek West:

> 39. The Son, the Begotten without beginning and the Spirit who proceeds from the Father: one Begotten One and one Proceeding One; one equality in Nature.
> 40. The Spirit is from the Father and is not named "Begotten," for though he is no stranger in Nature, such is not the order of the Names.[394]

Thus the Son alone is said to be "Begotten" while the Spirit is called the "Proceeding One." This is an admittedly vague distinction as regards the Godhead, and Narsai attempts to clarify it with his third and final analogy:

> 41. Eve was fashioned out of Adam and she is neither his daughter nor his sister, and, while from him in nature, she was called simply his wife.[395]

This third analogy, the most Scriptural of the three, is meant to show an example of how one thing can proceed from another – here specifically how one Person or Qnoma can proceed from another – and be something besides "begotten" or "sibling." If one were to take this analogy a step further than it takes itself, it would place the Holy Spirit, symbolized by Eve, as the Mother of the Son, implicitly symbolized by Adam. This is awkward at best, and seems to go beyond the intention of Narsai's analogy, which is simply to give an example of a procession that is not a begetting.

Conclusion

Narsai, as a representative Mesopotamian thinker, is very sober in his estimation of the limits of human understanding – even that enlightened by faith. Therefore, after these three simple analogies, he begins the conclusion to his discussion thus:

---

[394] Ibid.
[395] Ibid.

42. And so, he fastened an image of his Being within our nature as in a mystery, and so whoever wonders about the Son will see him explained in what is our own.

43. He has instructed us to examine his Greatness through our own nature: for if what belongs to us is not clear to us, how mysterious is his issue!

44. His very creatures are incomprehensible, and his deeds are too difficult for us. How therefore can we presume to investigate his Being which is without beginning?[396]

Justifying himself Biblically, Narsai concludes his discussion of the Trinity by making a very clear syllogism. First, he points out once again that human beings are in the Image of God. But we are incapable of understanding even human nature. Therefore, we are even more incapable of understanding the Divine Nature. Completing his argument, Narsai continues:

45. What is made cannot investigate the Essence of the Maker; and as much as he inquires "how did he begin?" he will discover that he is without beginning.

46. As much as the mind wishes to investigate his Essence, one thing alone can it handle: that it will not be comprehended by its nature.[397]

Because we as creatures or "what is made" have a beginning, we are incapable of even beginning to discover that which is without beginning – our temporality prevents us from knowing eternity perfectly. This is the case despite our desire to do so. Of course, in the Salvation granted in Christ, our desire to do so will be fulfilled by grace in heaven.

The concluding lines to this sermon make a clear connection between this conclusion and the everyday existence of human life:

47. This will suffice as regards our subject matter: that we may examine only his works, but as for the issue of

---

[396] Ibid, "*Conclusion.*"
[397] Ibid.

169

his Essence, let us treat it respectfully with our silence.[398]

The whole point, for Narsai, of Trinitarian teaching is this: that God is a Mystery utterly beyond our understanding, and this point is made not in what Narsai says but in what he does not say – in his silence. This realization brings the human being who worships God to a perfect state of piety, awe and reverence in relation to his Creator, and this state is the beginning of wisdom.

Conclusion

Man is mortal but the temple of God; the world is wonderful, and once this wonder is lost, so is our race; God is beyond our wisdom, and in realizing this we become truly wise. This is the Mesopotamian School in its true continuation, as it is found in Narsai. In him, we have a profound example of the Word of Scripture enlightening and perfecting the mind that is open to its light. Nor does the Mesopotamian School end with Narsai. This paper, however, must, with a few words of conclusion.

---

[398] *Narsai, "Conclusion."*

CONCLUSION
WHAT REMAINS TO BE DONE

From *Gilgamesh* to Narsai, and from *Enuma Elish* to Ephrem, I have, I hope, shown what it means to say that there is such a thing as the Mesopotamian School. The realism whereby the epic hero accepted his mortality; the marvel in which Ephrem beheld the created world; the practicality by which the rabbis read the Sacred Scriptures; the beautiful silence of Narsai beholding the Trinity. These are the expressions of the attitude of the Mesopotamian mind.

But, like any human reality, this thesis is incomplete, and its incompleteness is both vertical and horizontal. "Vertically," it should continue to trace the path of the Mesopotamian School through history, and discover its later expressions. This should be done both within the Church of the East, in a more thorough study of her liturgy as well as an examination of later Fathers such as Babai the Great and Timothy, as well as without, especially in studying the Medieval Moslem Philosophers of Mesopotamia through whom the realism of Aristotle was reintroduced to the West.

"Horizontally," the Mesopotamian School should be given greater definition by contrasting it *at every stage* with the other major School of thought which historically found expression in Egypt. I have done this briefly in Chapter 4 in contrasting Origen with Theodore, but it is intriguing to ask whether such a contrast exists between, for example, the ancient paganism of Egypt and that of Mesopotamia. How did the Egyptians view death, for example? Or divinity and its relation to humanity? Or the physical world? Or sciences such as astronomy and mathematics? And how existentially different was their approach to that of their neighbors in Mesopotamia?

Finally, if it is discovered that the contrast between Mesopotamia and Egypt - between Babylon and Alexandria – runs throughout history, one might ask *why*. What is it that made, for example, the Alexandrians so quick to embrace allegory both as Jews and Christians, and the Mesopotamians so quick to reject it? Was it merely a cultural precedence, as if they were simply following the local tradition that had been established before them? Or was it

something else, such as language, or even somehow the land itself —
the geography or climate? It is my ultimate hope in writing this thesis,
that these questions might be, if not answered, at least asked.

APPENDIX 1
SERMON 16:
TREATISE ON MAN[399]

[RESPONSE:
Our Lord, answer your servants in your mercies,
accept our prayer and grant our requests.]

[*Opening Supplication*]

1. O God[400] Divine, O hear our pleading heard before you,
and in your mercies, answer the permitted request of our soul.

2. O Overflowing in his mercies, show forth your love as is your custom,
lest the hater of man mock your handiwork.

3. O Richer than all, open your treasury to our neediness,
lest we be impoverished and hire ourselves out to the deceiver.

4. O Mighty of ages, sustain your order by the force of your power,
for lo, it is shaken by the severity of pains and demons.

5. O Being of whose Essence heaven and earth are filled,
may your Will fill us, and in us your holy Name be hallowed.

6. O Hidden in his Nature from physical and spiritual,
reveal your power in us, and show forth the riches of your Sweetness.

7. O Fashioner of all, who created creation from nothing,
pity your product, lest it decay because of our malice [sins].

8. O Free Sustainer, gracious Life-Giver to rational and irrational,
extend your right hand and fill our soul [us all] with your Gift.

---

[399] Found in D. Alphonsi Mingana, *Narsai, Doctoris Syri: Homiliae & Carmina* (Mosul: Dominican Press, 1905), vol. 1, pp. 257-270. I have followed Mangana's text, placing the variations of the Ḥudhra (which he has as footnotes) in brackets.

[400] "God" here translates "El," the ancient Aramaic, Hebrew and Akkadian word for God (see J. Payne Smith's *A Compendious Syriac Dictionary*).

9. O Un-Wanting One, of whose Fullness his construction is filled,
open the door of your Will, which is closed in our face, to our
   pleading.

10. O Perfect in his Essence, whose constancy has no beginning,
perfect in deed the promise of your words to our race.

11. O Painter of the world in the paint of his love [of spirit] which
does not dull,
scour the filth of ignorance from our image [mind].

12. O Fashioner of bodies and Breather of the soul into members,
tighten our disposition, lest we slacken before enticements.[401]

13. O Honorer of man as surpassing all else due to his love,
have pity on your Honor's image lest it be shamed.

[Man's Composition]

14. You have named our composition after the Name of your
Uncomposed Existence.
may your honored Name not be made dull by our dullness.

15. In us you have shown your great love toward your works,
show not in us a sign of wrath against your handiwork.

16. In us you concluded the great name [expansion] of your
workmanship,
and within our composition you have bound up the earthly and the
   heavenly.

17. In us you composed the height and the depth as one flesh:
irrational in our body, rational in our soul – [in] a great marvel!

18. May you not, O Lord, unravel this composition your love has
composed,
and may the great bind your command has bound not slacken.

---

[401] This could also translate "tighten our knot, lest it loosen…"

19. At this composition my weak rationality gazed,
and sought to journey through the rational path bound within it.

20. In this bind my meager mind was bound,
and wondered at the craft of the command that bound it.

21. Through this structure did my short thoughts wander,
to prepare words to build [relate] the story before listeners.

22. In this hope did my rationality seek after words,
that I may go out and bring good tidings of your Name to your
handiwork.

23. With this agreement I journeyed among the verses of [your]
Scriptures,
to explain to men the great story of your workmanship.

24. In this way my mind painted with the pen of [my] tongue,
that I might show [paint], for everyone, the gorgeous image of your
making.

[*Creation Contained in Man*]

25. I saw that the image of your composing was decorated wisely,
and I wished to uncover its gorgeous beauty before onlookers.

26. Within the image of our image I saw the whole creation tied,
and I called to man to come and see all in our nature.

27. [Our] nature pulls me to examine the natures that are tied up
within it,
and how indeed this frail thing was able to hold everything!

28. In our very own nature, I saw the sciences of your Divinity,
and I reflected that there is hope for man, sinner though he is.

29. I saw the Name of your Essence dwelling in him[402] as in a temple,
and wondering seized me – how can the wretched suffice for the
Hidden One?

30. He is wretched indeed, yet you honor him without measure,
and who would not marvel at this wretchedness you chose over all?

[*Levels of Honor*]

31. If your Love has chosen him from all and named him in its
Name,
we can therefore is be sure that you will not despise the one you have
chosen.

32. [And] if your Lordship has made him lord over all that is,
who would not join himself to the yoke of his life's work?

33. If your Knowledge has called and appointed him to a high
position,
who would not confess that his position and the name of his
authority is true [his position is true and his authority great]?

34. If your Hiddenness reveals itself to your handiwork [servants] by
his uncovering,
who would not gather his vision from all else toward his
composition?

35. If you have shown in him the great mystery of Son and Spirit,
who would not approach the sciences hidden in his name?

36. If in him you have shown your sweetness to angels and men,
who would not take refuge in his body that pleads on his behalf [his
living body and blood]?

37. If that Word begotten of you dwells in him in love [unites with
him],

---

402 From here to verse 43, the grammatical object is (human) "nature," or
"our nature," but this becomes conceptually untenable. It is clear that, eventually,
Narsai is talking specifically about Christ from verse 34 onward (at the latest), and I
have therefore translated all pronouns with this referent "him" rather than "it."

who would not call him the emperor of height and depth?

38. If in him you have completed your provision for all,
who would not labor for his provision without weariness?

39. If through him you will judge the earth at the end of time,
who would not fear the trial that is in his hands?

40. If through him you will grant blessings [reward] to the good and
scourgings to the wicked,
who would not beg you to let him be [beg him to be] an advocate for
his debts?

41. If he is the one with authority over this world and that to come,
who would not believe that he is the Second of Divinity [truly the
Son of God]?

42. To these levels I saw our miserable nature raised
and my mind was stirred to journey mentally toward his misery [his
authority].

43. The greatness of his rank forced me to dare out of order,
and to proceed on a path whose inquiry is greater than my words.

[Request for Aid]

44. Toward your Hiddenness that is in his uncovering I wish to be
drawn,
extend your hand to me as to Simon who approached you and
pleaded.

45. To the rational sea about our life do my thoughts descend:
let your command draw me out, lest I sink into what is improper.

46. I approach pleading for the sake of my works [defects] and those
of my friends;
empower my faculties that they may not weaken before they are
heard.

47. My will knocks [your servants knock] at the door of your mercies, who wills our life,
open to us, that we may enter and receive alms like the poor.

[*The Misery of Mankind*]

48. Poor and lacking is our miserable race of all good things:
sustain this miserable thing with a small crumb of your Gift.

49. He is far too weak to gather temporal sustenance,
and he is unable to work the land with his strength without your
    Strength.

50. His work is filled with great fear, as much as he works,
and there is no security for his sustenance, as much as it multiplies.

51. Sufferings and griefs accompany his toil summer and winter,
and all perils are constant for him – for him, and for what is his.

52. Much is his work, and little the reward returned to him;
great is his weariness, and miserable and lacking, the sustenance of
    his life.

53. He plants so much and harvests little of the much,
he is beaten and crushed, and by the time he enjoys himself, death
    has swallowed him.

54. In fear he plants, and in trepidation he gathers his produce,
and his heart does not rely on enjoying his labor or his gathering.

55. He casts his wheat upon the [his] field, that it may be returned to
him,
and he is afraid and distressed that perhaps he perish and his life pass
    away.

56. He works his land and he thinks that perhaps it may fail to
produce;
he walks on the path, and Death sits and waits for him.

57. Like a mother, he awaits for produce like a newborn,

and the whips of Death strike at his discernment at every hour.

58. He stands in a contest of sufferings every day and night,
and there is no end to the battlefield of his emotions.

59. A great battle is poised at all times against his disposition,
and if he falls asleep, enticements enter and plunder his freedom.

60. The wretched one is cast before two calamities, each worse than the other:
the twofold scourgings of the passions of his [the] body and the
sustenance of life.

61. As if with leather cords, he beats himself with his inclinations,
and there is no place in him not filled completely [with the scars] of
the passions.

62. He is suffering and weary regarding his passions [life] and
regarding his labors,
and there is no time when he does not rest with bitterness.

[*Twofold Wretchedness*]

63. If the sun grows hot, his mind grows hot regarding his crops,
and if the rain stops, his thoughts dry up with his plants.

64. If heat gains the upper hand, thirst has killed him;
and if cold increases, he is consumed by frost.

65. If he is impoverished, he conceives depression and begets
complaining;
and if he is made opulent, he puts on pride and arrogance of spirit.

66. If he is justified, he derides and mocks sinners;
and if he sins, he is weakened and decides there is no hope.

67. If he is made wise, he forgets the clay of his wretched nature;
and if he glorifies himself, he becomes a beast without understanding.

68. In great and in small, his sufferings increase and his malice grows,

and what can he do, where can he run, who has such a brief life?

69. He is stuck wanting between neediness and excess,
and so how is it possible for him to keep his life without harm?

70. It is exceedingly difficult for men to live well,
and the course of righteousness is not made easy for the bodily.

[*God's Temple*]

71. Flesh – he is flesh, as much as he desires spiritual things,
and even that desire is not his, but an Other's.

72. An Other dwells in him, in a temple of corruptible clay,
and in his living, he blossoms a little before he decays.

73. He is corruption entirely, although there is in him a portion of life,
and even this life is small compared to his afflictions.

74. So if the living that is in him is less than life,
how can he live a life without corruption?

[*Supplication for the Human Race*]

75. May your mercies come, O Lord, to the aid of our miserable race,
for its life's strength is burned away and wearied in the trial of suffering.

76. Stretch out your hand to the weak-hearted athlete,
for he realizes and admits openly that he cannot enter the match.

77. Cry out and encourage the mortal warrior,
for the fingers of his hands are too weak to hit the mark.

78. Command the intellectual natures to come and help him,
for his hand falls short of grasping even a straw of truth.

79. Call forth the heavenly legions to assist him,
before he falls and becomes a laughingstock to his enemy.

80. Write and send him an epistle of your Name above all,
that he may be strengthened to carry his sufferings through hope in
your Name.

81. Lift [your] hand in writing of his life's salvation,
and lo, sufferings and demons will be terrified to look upon him.

82. Rebuke the ranks of warriors who threaten him,
and lo, they will be dismayed by the command of the Name of your
Essence.

83. Send a watcher, as in the time of the Assyrian,
and lo, the powers of the evil one who surround him will be
scattered.

84. Send your command, as Isaiah toward Ezekiel,
and instead of figs, let it place mercies upon his [our] wounds.

85. Let us hear the voice that was heard to Ezekiel,
"Instead of life, lo, I increase the forgiveness of iniquity."

86. Yes, Lord, return us to health of virtues [of body and soul],
lest we be torn apart by the wounds of our disgraces.

[*Parables: The Good Shepherd & the Prodigal Son*]

87. Come out in search of us, like the parable your Love composed,
and we will enter and graze in the sheepfold of spiritual life.

88. Brighten your Face, and seek our straying in your mercies,
lest the splendor [beauty] of our clay, which is stamped in your
Name, decompose.

89. Rejoice in our repentance, as in the story of the younger son,
and interpret, with us, the life [voice] of hope that is signified in it.

90. With the deceitful one, we have worked for free and rejected our
pay,
and have lived wickedly on the swine-pods of desires.

91. We have sinned and enraged you; though, in fact, you have never been angered, nor are even now;
and we are unworthy to call ourselves the sons of your Name.

92. Let us become as hired hands in service of your house,
and let us receive what is just from your table as poor men.

93. And, if it is possible, fulfill in action the meaning of the parable,
and bring to light the symbol you composed [wrote] for our sake.

94. Tell us, "From death, you now live,
and from the corruption of ignorance, you have turned to me."

95. Command your pity to conceal our shame with a robe of glory,
and place a pledge of life on our hand as a ring.

96. Let your command persuade you and prepare before us the Sacrifice of your Son,
and in eating it, may we banish the bitterness of death from our members.

97. And if there is one who envies our life's salvation and our work [repentance],
let your love pacify his bitter disposition with the sweetness of life.

[*Reconciliation with the Angels*]

98. Call the angels and gladden them in our repentance,
that those once saddened by our sins may confess [rejoice] in our justification.

99. Please those who were angered because of our malice,
and turn them toward the service of our life's needs.

100. Let them shake the air with the power that is from you, as is their custom,
and make it firm to carry the waters upon its back.

101.   Let them place bridles of silence [peace] and reconciliation in its mouth,
lest it become fierce in disorderly seasons.

102.   May they themselves be as charioteers above its back,
and may they watch over the vehemence of its course over the face
    of the earth.

103.   May they watch his running like viewers in a gymnasium,
and weave, for your Name, a crown of thanksgiving in which you
    may gladden us.

[Pleading for Hope]

104.   Yes, Lord, accept the formation of our words, miserable
though they are,
and grant reward to our soul's study, dull though it is.

105.   Yes, Lord, make the word of our mouth worthy to respond
to the Word,
and let us hear from you, "repent, O sinner, there is hope!"

106.   Yes, Lord, gladden the air that was saddened by our malice,
and place a crown of drops in its mouth, that it may be pleased in us.

107.   Yes, Lord, may the sounds of our mouth be keys to your
treasury,
and may we open and receive the forgiveness of sins and the
    sustenance of life.

108.   Do not, O Lord, turn away from the pleading of our poverty,
lest our hope in you be weakened by despair.

109.   Do not, O Lord, turn your face away from us in a time of
wrath,
lest tyrannical demons mock us, as is their custom.

110.   Do not, O Lord, cast us away from your aid, as you do to the
evil,
lest the evil be exalted in our abasement, as before.

111.   Be not, O Lord, unmerciful, for you are the Merciful One,
(forgive me, Lord! You cannot be unmerciful; I spoke a saying in
weakness!)

112.   Let not, O Lord, the Name of your Greatness be reduced
because of our malice,
(though it can never be reduced, even if we are wicked a million
times!)

113.   Be not, O Lord, lacking in help and poor in treasury,
(oh, what I said of your Essence is a lie!)

114.   Be not, O Lord, as a sojourner in your creation,
nor like a guest who turns in to slumber in what is not his.

115.   Be not, O Lord, like a human, for you are God,
and not like a man who cannot save, for you are the Savior.

[God's Goodness vs. Human Wretchedness]

116.   And if our sins have prevailed more than the sins of every
age,
may you forgive because of your honored Name upon which we call.

117.   If our vices have made the face of the clear air vicious,
may you not show [us] an angry face which is unbecoming of you.

118.   If our wickedness has withheld benefits because of our
malice,
may you not, O Lord, change the Name of your Goodness, which is
unchanging.

[Weakness of Human Language]

119.   You are all Good, and you are all Just, and you hate evil;
and neither can your Goodness nor your Justice be measured.

120.   No one knows how to call you by a name that fair to your Name,
for all names are small compared to the greatness of your Glory.

121.   If we call you Good, the sound of your Justice thunders on earth;
but if Just, heaven and earth are filled with your mercies.

122.   If we call you Hidden, your works are unveiled before the eyes of all creatures;
if we call you Unveiled, there is none among products able to see you.

123.   If we call you the Hearing One, our voice is heard to you before we call,
and the Gracious and Forgiving One, your Love precedes us and our malice.

124.   We know neither how to pray nor how to glorify,
and we are afraid to speak words that may not be proper to you.

[*Weakness of Human Prayer*]

125.   How can we pray to one who needs nothing, and is completely perfect?
And how can we glorify him who exists in glory from eternity?

126.   If he is glorified, does he then increase through the glory?
And if he increases, is he made perfect by praise from us?

127.   If he is dishonored, is his dishonor greater than his glory?
If he is hallowed, does he increase his glory through our mouth?

128.   If he is angered, was the wicked man's shame hidden from him?
And if he is appeased, did we show him the way to reconciliation?

129.   If he notices something in remorse after a time,
did time constrain him from knowing something he did not know?

130.   If he did not know (that [a thing] which is blasphemy to say),
what more did he gain in knowledge of his own construction?

[*God's Perfection*]

131.   No, earthly ones, do not be content with earthly things;
there is nothing in Existence lacking from Existence.

132.   The name of every being is a declaration of his Constancy
[Essence's Name],
and insofar as he is, his knowledge is with him.

133.   He is before everything, and he is what he is,
and there is nothing missing from him, neither that was nor will be.

134.   Thus should a product think of the Maker,
and thus is it owed by a rational creature to repay the Giver of
    rationality.

[*Man's Response*]

135.   We owe a debt of love to our Constructor,
come, let us attempt to repay a little of so much.

136.   But he does not need repayment from us like a needy person,
he arranges pretexts that we may be enriched from his treasures.

137.   He possesses an unending treasure of life in his Nature,
and he longs greatly to give of it to the sons of his household.

138.   He has called our nature as sons of the inheritance of the love
of his Son,
because of this he chastises and instructs us lovingly.

139.   Let us therefore endure the methods of discipline[s] from his
Lordship [Discipline],
and never become weary of the scourgings of hunger and sickness.

140.   If the name of "sons" truly applies to our mind,
let us be sure, then, that our discipline is also to our benefit.

141.   Let us accept scourgings from our Maker without discouragement,
and let us know [encounter] the struggle of seasons without murmuring [arguing].

142.   This alone do we ask of him in the time of scourgings:
do not, O Lord, reprove us in stern anger, according to our deeds.

[King David]

143.   Like the son of Jesse, let us plead thunderously regarding our wickedness,
and in the way of his words, let us proceed to the promise of repentance.

144.   Yes, Lord, let us be worthy for that word to David,
and let us turn back to the rank of forgiveness of sin in his likeness.

145.   Yes, Lord, pass over the faults of your servants as with your servant,
and let them hear the voice of forgiveness as the just one did.

146.   David was just, but the evil one envied him and made him evil;
but he admitted he sinned and erased the name of evil from his heart.

147.   So if confession erases evil things and writes good ones,
then there is hope for the evil to become good.

148.   O Kind One who forgave adultery and murder with a word of the mouth,
forgive our disgraceful crimes as you forgive [see fit].

149.   It was you who forgave that [every] lawless crime:
forgive now also the sins we have committed without order [against love].

150.   It was you who loosened the execution given to murderers,
stop now also the tortures prepared for our injustice.

151.　You are the One who mixed mercy with wrath in every age,
and you gave no room for the haters of our people to mock us.

152.　You are the One who reckoned the greatness of your Love
upon the just,
and made them worthy to appease you though you do not require it.

153.　By your Love, you absolved the faults of our people from the
beginning,
and you gave the will of the righteous the reward of your Kindness.

154.　Because of the just, you forgave the faults of the first
generations,
indeed, you forgave before they persuaded your Kindness.

155.　You cast out Justice that the sons of men may persuade you,
that when they persuade you, they may realize that they can defeat
　　evil.

156.　Moses prayed, and you forgave the sin of the calf-worship,
and you told him, 'Lo, I have forgiven as you have persuaded.'

157.　Joshua prayed, and you stopped the course of the sun and
moon,
and placed in the book of the deeds of Joshua that 'Their course was
　　stopped.'

158.　Samuel prayed, and your command answered him in the
sound of thunder,
and you responded to him through the unseasonal rain that came.

159.　David prayed, for he saw the watcher that would destroy the
people,
and the spirit stood in awe of his pleading as he stood in awe of you.

160.　Elijah called to you, and you hardened the winds and they
carried the rain,

and you aroused the people to zeal whom the just man's words had
   bound and unbound.

161.   Elisha called to you, and by his hands you turned a dead man
alive,
and you reckoned his prophecy a victory from the mouth of death.

162.   Ezekiel called to you, and you destroyed thousands of
Assyrians,
and as this was truly happening, he won victory against the
   destruction of the watcher.

163.   Daniel also, by the power of your aid, revealed hidden things,
and the Babylonians wove a crown of praises for his will.

[*The Logic of God's Mercy*]

164.   In every age, the just ones prayed and you answered them;
in our age that is deprived of the righteous, may you persuade
   yourself.

165.   The persuasion of your Kindness is greater than all the just,
and the treasury of your mercies is incomparable to that of products.

166.   Your Love provoked the will of the just to persuade you,
so if there are no just, send your Will without the just.

167.   Yours are persuasion and the words of persuaders,
whom would you load with your own grace to the sons of your
   household?

168.   May Goodness be entirely yours, as it is,
and so grant us what you granted at the beginning of time.

169.   Who convinced you to create creation when it did not exist?
And who advised you to bind up the world in the construction of
   man?

170.   Who was such as advised you to call us your image?

And who showed you how to complete your work in our
   construction?

171.   So if in our very existence, and all existence, you needed no
help,
what help do you need regarding our wickedness – a miserable gnat?

172.   Our wickedness is a gnat compared to the greatness of your
Divinity,
and it is only a handful if compared to the sea of your mercies.

173.   Your great Pity is a great sea, and greater than a sea,
and height and depth are quite small in proportion to its greatness.

174.   'Your Pity is great:' thus do heaven and earth cry out,
for when they were not, you spoke and they came to be from
   nothing.

175.   You created everything out of nothing for our sake,
and so how could it be that you would turn away from us in a time of
   anger?

176.   And, what is even greater and immeasurable by the rational,
we have put on your Love and our portion has been raised to the
   level of your Name.

177.   (You have called our name in the assumed name of the Name
of your Being,
and now that it is so in actions, may it be for its station.)[403]

[*God Honored in Man*]

178.   Our dirt has ascended to a high station with your Essence,
may it not be lowered from its exaltation by means our wickedness.

179.   Our body is sitting at your right hand and clothed in glory,
may its glory not be shamed by the shame of our presumption.

---

[403] This verse is not in the <u>Hudhra</u>.

180.   May the rational natures not dishonor it because of its weakness,
for you have honored it with the great Name of your Divinity.

181.   May you not, O Lord, become a boast for rebellious demons,
for they wish to rule, but their hands fall short of dominion.

182.   May those who despise our people not rejoice, as is their custom,
for how is it that it rose to the great station of the immortals?

183.   It is enough that they make light of and mock the name with which you honored us,
silence them, lest they become haughty to your Majesty.

184.   Through us, they wish to mock your great Name,
and thus [through us] they think they will prevail over your Greatness [Hiddenness].

185.   The vain despisers of your Name despise our image,
and because they cannot defeat you, they defeat you through us.

186.   Do not, O Lord, be disrespected by the foot of deceivers,
and let not the deceitful building they boast of be completed.

187.   Chastise the arrogance of their minds and they will fall to the ground,
and lift up the head of our humbleness to the level of your Name.

188.   Save our nature from the hands of the corruptors,
for it is enfeebled and brought low in the difficult fight against their ranks.

[*Angelic Assistance*]

189.   Send down your hand upon our encampment lacking in power,
for lo, its number of the lovers of truth has been reduced.

190.   Brighten your face in our miserable grief-filled dwelling,

for lo, the bright light of justice has passed away from it.

191.   May your command set up a guardian over our weakness,
for lo, it has scattered the treasure it received from your Gift.

192.   Call to the spirits, and command them to support us,
for lo, demons and grievous pains enter and plunder our storehouses.

193.   Send the watchers, let them wake us from our sleeping,
for lo, we are [every man is] immersed in our disgraces as in sleep.

194.   Send the angels, let them pacify our disturbance,
for lo, all ranks are set in wars of unworthiness.

[*Christ*]

195.   And if the powers of the heights are insufficient to wake us
[aid us],
persuade the Son of our race, and let him reconcile us with your
    Greatness.

196.   He is able to help our disturbance [weakness] in the contest
of labors,
in that he is both your only Son and our Mediator.

197.   He knows how to plead on behalf of the guilty lovingly,
in that he took on the test of suffering of mortality.
198.   Indeed, he was tested in all [those things] that the nature of
mortals had [he had from the nature of mortals],
and he better knows how to help those who are tested.

199.   For the sake of peace, you chose him from all to reconcile all,
complete in act the choice of his Name for the sake of peace.

200.   Now is the time for him to show in us the greatness of his
station,
in that he show [it] at a time when our guilt has increased.

201.   If, when we were haters of your Name, you reconciled us in
him,

how much will he reconcile our unworthiness through his mediation!

202.   If you have saved us by his hand from death and the
backbiter,
how much more will he redeem us from enticements – miserable
    gnats?

203.   If Judaism and paganism were uprooted in his cross,
how easy is it for him to rebuke the sufferings that irritate us?

204.   If he will accomplish the reckoning of all at the end of time,
how much more is he able, before the ages, to dull the severity of
    scourgings?

205.   If he has authority over the treasury of your Divinity,
he has therefore power to pity the sons of his race [mankind] for free.

206. Pity our weakness, O Kind One, as is your custom,
and grant us a portion through the Son of our race, who has hold of
    your treasury.

SERMON 35:
ON THE ORDER OF CREATION,
ALSO RELATING THE QNOME OF THE TRINITY[404]
Mar Narsai

[Introduction: God and Moses]

1. The son of Amram opened a great treasury for us in his prophecy regarding when the great Power of the Creator began to act.
2. How creatures began was hidden from all, and by whose power heaven and earth and all therein were fashioned.
3. And so, Creator wished to make the activity of his Power known to rational creatures. In Moses he chose a disciple and inspired a spiritual scroll through him.
4. On Mount Sinai he showed him a marvelous vision, and made a voice heard to him while drawing him to learn.
5. The Creator desired to show himself humanly to Moses, and because of this Moses yearned to see his Nature.
6. "If, then, you have chosen me for yourself as a disciple, and if you love me, show me the glory of your Nature, and let me contemplate your hidden Radiance."
7. "You have erred greatly, O Moses:" the Lord said to him, "no mortal can see me, for my nature is above those who see."
8. "I called you unto myself in order to be taught, that you may learn that I am the Creator; not that you may learn my Hiddenness, for that is incomprehensible to creatures."
9. "I am the Lord and God, and this is my Name: I AM. With my own power I uphold heaven, earth and all therein."
10. "And because mortals are unaware that my Majesty has dominion over all, I designate you a messenger and a mediator to instruct them."
11. "Through you I wish to reveal my Essence and my works, and in you I desire to instruct the whole race of rational creatures."
12. "See, O Moses, that I reveal to you the hidden mystery of my orderings: descend and preach among mortals that I am Maker of all that is."

---

[404] Found in D. Alphonsi Mingana, *Narsai, Doctoris Syri: Homiliae & Carmina* (Mosul: Dominican Press, 1905), vol. 2, pp. 180-192.

13. For forty days the Teacher perfected the new disciple, and the mind of a mortal became able to comprehend all that is up to the limit.

14. He made the Power of the Spirit dwell in him, in which he sang wondrous songs, and heavenly and earthly creatures were dazzled at the sweetness of his melodies.

15. His word was like thunder, and both mute and rational heard it, and his phrases were like trumpets which proclaimed the Power of the Maker.

[*De Deo Uno*]

16. Forsooth, "in the beginning" the Creator began and created everything that is, and fixed the times, in his knowledge, of the beginning and the end.

17. And while not beginning in his Being (for his Nature is without beginning [in time]), he made creation in time, as he foreknew.

18. It was not a new thought that led him to make creatures, for this was set from eternity in his Knowledge and Being.

19. Nor was it for his own satisfaction that he formed heaven, earth and all therein, but rather in love and mercy that he revealed his will to his creatures.

20. He is indeed Good in his Nature, and his Nature is full of blessings. And in his grace he desired to bring everything from nothing.

21. For this is fitting in the Maker, that in his works he may proclaim his Power, and in the ordering of his creatures, they may gain knowledge.

22. His Being is without beginning; his Lordship is without end. For his creatures, however, there is a beginning, and for his creatures, temporality and composition.

23. His Being is incomprehensible by the minds of creatures; nor can it be contained by sight, for his Nature is greater than this.

24. His Being is immeasurable: for what is before the beginning? Nor is there any time when he was not, for he existed before all.

[*De Deo Trino*]

25. There was the [Divine] Nature, perfect in being, without beginning: Father, Son and Holy Spirit, three Qnome, one Power.

26. The Father, perfect, without beginning, who begat the Son without alteration; the Son is from him and like him, and there is no interval of time between him and his Father.

27. The Spirit, who is from the same Nature, is an existing and a true Qnoma; the equality of whose Nature witnesses that he existed with the Father.

28. The Begotten of the Father resembles him, for he is with his Father from eternity, and because he is with his Father, the ages do not confine the Begotten.

29. The Begotten of the Father resembles him, and is with him as Light: for as is light with fire, so is the Begotten with his Father.

30. The light of fire is with it, and there is no fire without light; for through its light it is seen, and through it is light shown.

31. With the Father is also his Begotten, and the Son is with him without beginning. Neither is there Father without his Begotten, nor Son without his Begetter.

32. The Son, however, is not constituted without a Qnoma, like light. Rather he is a true Qnoma and an Image that resembles his Begetter.

33. The Son does not form the Father, nor is the Son named "father;" for the difference in their Names proclaims the truth of the Qnome.

34. The Spirit is a Qnoma from the Father who is equal with him in everything. As the Son is equal to the Father, the Spirit is equal to the Father and Son.

35. The difference of their Names does not injure the equality. The Names are to be taken in order, but the Qnome are equal in Essence.

36. A manifestation of the three Qnome of one Being is fastened, for us, in our soul: for the Son and the Spirit are from the Father as reason and life are from the soul.

37. Along with the soul is born reason, and power and vitality, and along with the Father are the Son and Spirit without beginning.

38. Two powers accompany the soul: reason and vitality as well; and two Powers with the Father: the Son and Spirit without beginning.

39. The Son, the Begotten without beginning and the Spirit who proceeds from the Father: one Begotten One and one Proceeding One; one equality in Nature.

40. The Spirit is from the Father and is not named "Begotten," for though he is no stranger in Nature, such is not the order of the Names.

41. Eve was fashioned out of Adam and she is neither his daughter nor his sister, and, while from him in nature, she was called simply his wife.

[*Conclusion to First Part*]

42. And so, he fastened an image of his Being within our nature as in a mystery, and so whoever wonders about the Son will see him explained in what is our own.

43. He has instructed us to examine his Greatness through our own nature: for if what belongs to us is not clear to us, how mysterious is his issue!

44. His very creatures are incomprehensible, and his deeds are too difficult for us. How therefore can we presume to investigate his Being which is without beginning?

45. What is made cannot investigate the Essence of the Maker; and as much as he inquires "how did he begin?" he will discover that he is without beginning.

46. As much as the mind wishes to investigate his Essence, one thing alone can it handle: that it will not be comprehended by its nature.

47. This will suffice as regards our subject matter: that we may examine only his works, but as for the issue of his Essence, let us treat it respectfully with our silence.

[*First Creation Account*]

48. Let us heed, then, to his orderings, and praise his handiwork, for it is the duty of a creature to give thanks to the Creator for everything he created.

49. For he began "in the beginning" in creation, thus we heard from Moses, and what is before "in the beginning," how and how so, we are not to inquire.

50. Let us inquire, therefore, as intelligent men, in a search that is appropriate for creatures: what was the reason that he spoke of his orderings in a voice?

51. "In the beginning," then, he began and created heaven and earth firstly, and five other natures which he did not call by name.

52. By this word, then, fire, water, darkness and rational and mute angels were contained within the ordering of "in the beginning."

53. In this word, "in the beginning." was the ordering of angels, and that the Creator of everything made them out of nothing.

54. In that ordering of "in the beginning," he did not speak to be heard, for there was nothing made who could hear and receive teaching.

55. But when he began to make it so that natures came to be, one by one, through a whisper he desired to reveal his ordering to the angels.

56. The reason for the whisper, then, is this: that he may teach the angels that the Lord of all, who upholds their assemblies, is the one who orders.

57. O whisper mightier than all, which was spoken "in the beginning," and which drew all intellectual natures toward him in love!

58. Darkness was covering height and depth together, and the earth was covered with water before it received order.

59. The earth, in the beginning, was without visibility or order, and he calls it "formless," since it was not yet decorated with trees.

[*The First Day*]

60. The Spirit, as related, was above the water of the abysses when he called the wind of the air to blow upon the ethereal wind.

61. The Word of the Maker, then, was like the order of teaching, and he made the voice heard to angels, that there may "be light" to enlighten all.

62. O Voice from out of nothing which brought light into being! O Light which, along with the sound, formed a nature which was not!

63. Light pursued darkness which had covered creatures, and spiritual beings marveled at the power which gave it authority.

64. Regarding the Word that created light was another sound heard which praised his ordering, that he may fashion something even better.

65. O wise Craftsman who is so secure in his fashioning, who placed a limit for the light, regarding how much it may rightly rule.

66. He distinguished between light and darkness, that one may not assail the other, and he established a law for their courses in the hours of night and day.

67. He called the light "daytime," and the darkness he called "night," and in their names he named them according to the realities of their hours.

68. There was an evening and a day, then, "one day," as it is written, and he called it the first day, for there was yet none other like it.

69. He established, then, a beginning: a night for the first day, that he may guard the order of his creation, since darkness existed first.

[*The Second Day*]

70. The first day, then, is completed: night and daytime – one day. Then another voice cried out "let there be a firmament from the waters."

71. O Voice having such authority – with the word, the deed! O Power which bound and made the firm out of the liquid!

72. From the water he created the firmament to bear the waters above it, and he who was first in the beginning named it "heaven."

73. He made the firmament in the middle like a nearby ceiling, that it may be close in visibility and still divide water from water.

74. What an unshaking measure, which divided the waters equally: half for the earth for its use, and half for the ridge of the firmament!

75. What a Craftsman who fashions all, whose knowledge is incomprehensible, who knew what was useful for something before it was made:

76. He was prepared to hang up the lights, the nature of fire, in the firmament, and he gathered water above it, that [the firmament] may not be burned away by the fire.

77. The Creator also knew, before he made all that is, that another dwelling was useful for rational beings at the end of time.

78. For this purpose he created the firmament like a rooftop in the middle [of the waters], that at the end it may become a spot of land for our rest.

79. There was, then, a morning as well as an evening, and the second day was completed, and he turned and praised his fashioning, that he may fashion something even better.

[The Third Day]

80. The third evening came so that it may not differ from the first, for there was One Power which commanded that something should be, and it was.
81. "Let the waters be gathered," he said, "and let there be seas in one place, and let the surfaces of the earth be revealed, so that it may be suitable for living."
82. O unwearied Command, O unhindered Word! For once his will was commanded, the waters were gathered together into the seas.
83. The earth was brought to light and gladdened, and a command came out to it: "let the earth burst forth and sprout herbs, plants and trees."
84. The command became the deed, and the earth was adorned with fruits, and there came to be plants and trees, and the Good One praised his ordering.

[The Fourth Day]

85. There was, then, an evening and a morning, and a completed third day, and another command issued forth, commanding there to be lights.
86. There then came to be lights in the firmament above the earth, so that ages, months and years may be known by their courses.
87. The Word set out to act, and immediately there were lights, and he established a law which does not pass for the courses of night and day.
88. O Craftsman who adorns all, whose will has authority over all, for whom, from something or from nothing, it is easy to make everything.
89. Out of light he created the lights, from that first light, when he divided it into portions for the moon, the stars and the sun.
90. He did not fasten them in the firmament, lest their courses entangle, but rather he hung them like candles, and arranged the course of their hours.

91. The fourth day was thus concluded, in the limiting of the evening and morning, and another command came forth: that there may be moving things from the waters.

92. And so the waters gave birth to animals of innumerable kinds – creeping things, fishes and dragons, and deadly animals.

93. O Power to whom difficult things are easy, according to his will, who from water constructed and made innumerable species.

94. From water he created birds, the nature which swims upon the air, and while it is from the water like a creeping thing, the air carries it and it moves.

95. O Good One, how great is his love, who keeps his command for his possessions, who, at the end of their formation, supplies them with blessings:

96. "Give birth and multiply on the earth – on the sea and dry land together." And meanwhile their species' were protected in succession, one after another.

[The Sixth Day]

97. On the fifth day was completed the creation of creeping things and birds, and on the sixth day he began to create beast and cattle.

98. The earth put forth and brought out the living soul of every species: beasts, roaming and grazing, and moving things born from the earth.

99. O mute nature which budded with living things from within it! For while soil is miserable to look at, it gives birth to the beauty of all species.

100. Not that it gave birth of its own nature, but rather the power of its Maker: he who solidified earth in the beginning commanded, and it gave birth to living things.

101. On the sixth day cattle and beast were created with Adam, such that those who were useful for his work may receive their forming with him.

102. On the sixth day was completed the ordering of all that is, and the Creator showed his power in his works which he spoke and made to be.

103.   On the seventh day the Maker rested from his fashioning, and he blessed the seventh day, and called it a holy day.

104.   Not because that Power was wearied, and not because his will could be hindered: he created something from nothing – in six days, everything.

105.   It would not have been difficult for his will to make everything in a moment, but rather in one day and in many it was appropriate for him to make everything.

106.   He made his creation an ordering, just as he had known, and for the sake of teaching of rational beings he completed all in six days.

107.   For the angels saw his ordering and examined it, and whenever the word he spoke came to be, the spiritual beings cried out his praise.

108.   The Knower who knows all accomplished all in knowledge – from something or from nothing, he brought creatures into being.

109.   He created light from nothing, to show his greatness, and our soul also from nothing to show he has authority over all.

110.   He created the lights out of light – the lamps of the sun and moon – and the assemblies of angels extolled in praise to the Power who orders all.

111.   To these methods did the Creator look when he fashioned all, and he tarried for the sake of his works, in order to teach his power to the rational.

112.   With holy blessings he supplied the seventh day, that it may not be a stranger to him, for he did not wish to create anything on it.

113.   That day also became a day like the first days, and to retain his order he called it "holy," that we may not reject it.

114.   It is the knowledge of its holiness that gives rest from labor – for when we hear the word "labor," we learn who the Creator is.

115.   This day was destined to be a lesson for the seed of Abraham: for when they guard it from labor, they learn the Cause of what is.

116.   Now, to each thing that came to be from him, he made a voice heard when it came to be, and he himself praised his ordering, that he may fashion something even better.

117. Up till now there has been one voice about all things together, but at the end of his ordering, another voice was spoken:

118. "Let us make rational man, in our image and likeness, and let him have authority over all that is, for it was fashioned for his sake."

119. O Craftsman so wise, O Good One so overflowing in his love, who created and adorned everything, and then formed an heir!

120. He built him an earthy abode, and provided and filled it with good things, and he gave him mute and rational beings alike for his service.

121. In all these things he honored the mortal, in his fashioning and in his authority, in that he called him his image and subdued all existing things under him.

122. For all other things that came to be and were fashioned, he made only one voice heard, but here, in the fashioning of Adam, there was a new counsel and thought:

123. "Let us make man in our likeness, and let him have authority like us," so that through his manifest image, he may proclaim his power to creatures.

124. "In him I will reveal my Hiddenness to intellectual natures, and in him I will manifest my Lordship to mute and rational alike."

125. "I place him as a statue for products to observe, so that through love toward him, everyone may recognize me."

126. The fashioning of Adam is a marvel, and different from that of products, since he made all that is with his word, but for [Adam] he spoke through a counsel to make him.

[The Trinity in Adam's Forming]

127. Glorious is the forming of the earthly one, and there are hidden mysteries buried within it, for he did not say "let him be like me," but rather "in our image and likeness."

128. O mortal in whose forming are hidden mysteries! O earthly one who manifests three Qnome to us in his fashioning!

129.   In the fashioning of the image of Adam, he taught us as through a mystery; in [saying] "in our image and likeness," he made three Qnome known to us.

130.   The Being without beginning of the Father, Son and Holy Spirit is honored in the image of Adam as a mystery by all that is.

131.   Otherwise, to whom did he call, in equality with his Greatness, "in our image come, let us make?" He did not say so to angels!

132.   In saying "our image" he taught us about the distinction of Qnome, and in "our very likeness" about the equality of the Nature.

[*Formation and Authority of Adam & Eve*]

133.   "Come, then, let us make man, and bind all existing things within him, so that in kinship toward him, all their needs will be fulfilled in love."

134.   And so God made Adam in his image out of dirt from the earth, and breathed into it a living soul, a living and rational nature.

135.   O the love toward our race! O the honor of our fashioning! He chose in his love to breathe into us, the very life that is in us!

136.   O uncomposed Nature, O immeasurable Essence! When he fashioned our nature, he made us with hands and a mouth.

137.   He did not make us like the beasts, who were males and females, for Adam was first in his creation, and then Even from his rib.

138.   He fashioned Adam first and then the woman from Adam, to teach the power of the Maker – that he himself adorns his creation.

139.   And so the Lord God formed Adam, earth from the ground, and placed him in the paradise of Eden, that he may be an heir within it.

140.   In a beautiful and desirable dwelling he placed Adam as his image, that creatures may call upon the Maker in love through one close to them.

141. The image resembles the Creator in name, but not in nature, for he gave him as much authority over all he fashioned as the Creator has over him.

142. He becomes a father when he begets, and he begets a son who resembles him, as the Father who begot the Son in his Nature without beginning.

143. He becomes a father in time, and in time begets a son, but Existence begets without time, and there is no moment of time between him and his Son.

144. He makes something from something, and while it is not, he fashions it, like the Maker who brought all into being out of nothing.

145. He makes something from something, and resembles the Creator. He looks upon all that is on earth and his own vision is in heaven.

146. For by the symbol of his looking, he seeks his place above; in this an earthly being resembles, as a mystery, the Creator.

147. And when he commands natures, by word and life, in the name of the image by proxy, he names him the First Adam.

[Christ]

148. He becomes an Image in actuality in Christ, the Second Adam; here "come, let us make in our image" receives perfection.

149. Because the Creator took on his image and made it the dwelling of his Honor, the promises to Adam became actual in Christ.

150. *Because he called him his image and he was ruined, he returned and renewed him in Christ.

[Paradise]

151. By reason of Adam's image, the greatness of paradise was related: for Adam knew his honor because he placed him in such a glorious land.

152. The Lord God thus made paradise in Eden at the first, and he made trees grow within it, suitable for [providing] much food.

153.   One of the trees he set in the middle of paradise, and he called it the Tree of Life, that Adam may acquire life by it.

154.   Then he planted another tree, and called it "the knowledge of proprieties," since the knowledge of what was hidden was to be revealed in its fruit through Adam.

155.   It is related that there was a spring from Paradise which sprung forth, from whose greatness four springs were distributed to every corner.

156.   The first river was Pishon, which encircled the land of Huyla, where there is gold, beryl, gems and shiny pearls.

157.   The second river was Gihon, which waters the land of the Cushites, and through its overflowing it reaches the Egyptians and the Medians.

158.   The third river is the Tigris, that was made an ambassador to Assyria, and the peoples around it were pleased by its sweetness.

159.   The fourth river is the Euphrates, which passes through the middle of the earth, and it gives itself to the workers who irrigate lands by it.

160.   The prophet did not relate these things to glorify paradise, nor to praise the greatness of the rivers in it.

161.   He honored the Power of the Creator [in showing] that difficult things are easy for him – for how can paradise's spring cross the sea to us?

162.   The water passes through waters, and water does not mix with water, and this witnesses to the greatness of the Power which fashioned all.

163.   O command protecting water within water as in a jar! The water of Eden does not mingle with the troubled waters of the firmament!

164.   [Thus] mute and silent works cry out at every hour about his Power, teaching rationality that the Maker is in his works.

165.   The story of paradise reveals life-filled teaching to us, and the history of the tree brings us near rationality.

166.   Through [many] causes the Creator wished to instruct our rationality, and with the stories of the rebuke, he made known the freedom within us.

167.   Through his ordering, he taught spiritual beings that he is Existence and the Maker, while through nature he instructed us, that he may reveal his Hiddenness in us.

168.   In the beginning, he fashioned earth and heaven when they did not exist, and along with the power of the beginning, the intellectual powers came to be.

169.   He created lights while making the sound heard to the spiritual assemblies, and by the existence of light he taught that he had adorned their qnome.

170.   He made the firmament out of water, and loaded water upon it, and adorned it with brilliant marks in an adornment fit for rational beings.

171.   He gathered waters away from earth in the pool of seas and abysses, and he adorned [earth] with plants and trees for the life of man and beast.

172.   The waters made living things move, and the earth gave birth to every species, and through silent orderings, he greatly instructed rational beings.

173.   He made our nature from the earth, and breathed into us a living spirit, and in the love toward our race, he tied together the mute and the rational.

[*Pre-Knowledge of God*]

174.   All of these orderings were hidden from of old in his Intellect, and he brought them to manifestation, and showed his love to his possessions.

175.   His Will, then, was before his orderings, along with his Essence, and he knew how many natures he would make before he created.

176.   He was able to make two orders suffice for [all] rationality: the dwelling of earth for mortals, and heaven for immortals.

177.   He knew the thoughts of rational beings before they were, and hidden things which would happen after a time were [already] manifest to him.

178.   He had examined all that is before it came into being, and the works which came to be from him waited within his Mind.

[*Reason for Creation*]

179. It was not to fulfill his own need that he brought creation into being. Rather, he showed his hidden Will, and how much he loves his possessions.

180. He is the Spring filled with Life who possesses Life in his Nature, and he fashioned everything out of nothing, and gave vitality in rational beings.

181. His richness is his Will, and his great treasure is his Mind, and when the recipients did not request it, he opened up his treasuries and enriched all.

182. His Love is extended upon all his creatures, and he visits his possessions every day. He keeps his command toward natures, rational and irrational together.

183. He established a law for mortals, and they will live if they keep it, and he set a spiritual power for the service of their needs.

184. These things were established from of old in order to happen according to his will, and so through the incomprehensible Mind, he limited the time of his works.

185. Every day he proclaims his Hiddenness through the manifest things of the works of his hands, while the sun and moon in their courses relate his Greatness.

[*Reason for Thanksgiving*]

186. His orderings have a duty to give thanks to him for his gift, for he adorned them in mercies and so they should give thanks to his Essence in love.

187. Nor is it to fulfill his need that there is thanksgiving from his works; thanksgiving is to our advantage, and is not desirable to God in himself.

188. Who could have praised his Nature, when he existed eternally? And who could have offered him glory before he created creatures?

189. His glory is in his own Nature, and his exaltation is with his Essence; and he does not increase or decrease, since his Nature is above these things.

190. He makes us great when he calls us and brings us near his knowledge, for when we know him he gives us the kingdom in exchange for confession.

191. In the love of the soul, let us give thanks to the Maker for his orderings, since it was for our sake that he fashioned all – to him be thanksgiving from what it his!

DIALOGUE BETWEEN THE WATCHER & MARY[405]
Mar Narsai

INTRODUCTION

1. O Power of the Father that descended and dwelt in a virgin womb, as his Love desired, grant me a mouth to speak your great and incomprehensible story!

2. O Son of the Rich One who sent down his mercies, and who dwelt in the womb of a poor woman: grant me voice and word to speak while I marvel.

3. The mouth is too small to speak of you, and the tongue to describe you, and voice and word are weak as well, for I wish to tell your story and speak of you.

4. Help me to approach your exaltation, O Lord of all, though I am afraid: the head of the watchers announced to the virgin mother regarding your descent.

5. Come, O prudent, attend and listen to the story filled with all wonders, and sing praise to the One who was brought low to give life to Adam who was lost.

6. The mercies of the Father indicated to the Son to come down and save his construction, and he called Gabriel and commanded him to prepare a path before his coming.

7. His mercies dawned toward the daughter of David, that she may be a mother to him who created Adam and the world, whose Name is before the sun.

8. The incomprehensible Will that called and commanded the angel girt and sent him from the ranks to a pure virgin and announced to her.

9. He took the letter of the Complete One, in a mystery concealed from the ages, and he filled a young girl with peace, and all nations with good hope.

10. The spirit flew, descended and arrived to the barren one, and he fell down and adored. He gave her a greeting and announced to her regarding her conception which fills all with awe.

---

[405] Found in D. Alphonsi Mingana, *Narsai, Doctoris Syri: Homiliae & Carmina* (Mosul: Dominican Press, 1905), vol. 2, pp. 366-371.

ALAP

The Watcher said to Mary: "Peace with you, mother of my Lord; blessed are you, mother of my Lord, and blessed is the fruit in your womb."
Mary said: "Who are you, my lord? And what is the story you tell? What you say is strange to me, and I am unable to understand its meaning."

BETH

Watcher: "Blessed of women, in you does the Most High wish to dwell. Fear not. In you has Grace been pleased to pour out his mercies upon the world."
Mary: "I wish, lord, that you not insist I accept you without objection. What you say is distant from me, and I cannot understand it."

GAMAL

Watcher: "The Father has revealed it to me, and so have I revealed it to you: the mystery that is between them – between him and his Son – for which I was sent: that from you he will dawn upon the world."
Mary: "You are a flame; do not harm me. You wear burning coals; do not frighten me. O fiery one, why should I remain with you, for all you have spoken with me is a novelty?"

DALATH

Watcher: "It is a wonder that you do not believe – that you would let go the trust that has come to you, for the Begotten of the Most High rejoices to dwell in your womb."
Mary: "I am afraid, Lord, to accept you, for indeed my mother Eve, when she accepted the snake who spoke to her as a friend, was deprived of glory."

HEH

Watcher: "That imposter deceived, my daughter, when he made her trust him. I am not like him, however, for I have been sent by God."
Mary: "This story you tell me is contentious like that one – do not blame me – for in a virgin has never been found a son, nor in a fruit, Divinity."

WAW

Watcher: "O daughter, the Father pledged me to bring his peace, and [pledged] that I could trust you, for his Son will rise from your womb. There are no words opposed to mine."

Mary: "Your pledge is fair, and even your word. If only nature would not shake me and make me terrified to accept you: all on account of 'a fruit being found in a virgin.'"

ZAYN

Watcher: "Angels tremble at his word, and, as soon as he commands, do not act insolently. But you – do you not fear to prevent something which the Father desires?"

Mary: "I was indeed shaken, Lord, and alarmed, and being afraid, I dared not tell you that nature itself has forbidden virgins to give birth."

HETH

Watcher: "The Love of the Father has thus desired that, in your virginity, you shall give birth to a Son. It is meet that you accept and be open, that the will of the Father not be constrained."

Mary: "Your visage is honourable, and your story awesome, and your fire ablaze. The Love of your Lord will not be constrained, but it is difficult for me to verify this all."

TETH

Watcher: "I have brought you glad tidings – that the Begotten of the Lord will be revealed to you. O girl, confess him who has made you worthy to be his mother, as he is your Son."

Mary: "I am only a girl and not able to accept a man of fire, for your difficult story is not easy for me, nor is it easy for me to draw out and confirm what you have said."

YODH

Watcher: "Today hope has been revealed to Adam – that through you the Lord of all would be seen, that he would descend, untie, and free him. Accept these things as you confess."

Mary: "Today I have been astonished and amazed in all the things that you have said to me, but I am fearful of accepting you, for perhaps there is deceit in your word."

KAP

Watcher: "When I was sent to convince you, I heard his greeting, and came to you. My Lord is trustworthy, and desires this: that from you he dawn upon the world.

Mary: "All your words amaze me – I am allowed, Lord, do not blame me. The story you speak to me is hidden from me, and it frightens me to accept you."

LAMADH

Watcher: "He is coming to you, do not turn away. In your womb will he dwell, do not hold back. O Full of Blessings, sing canticles to him who is pleased to be found in you."

Mary: "No, lord. I am not known of man, and I have not met with copulation, so how can it be as you say, that one without intercourse give birth to a son?"

MYM

Watcher: "By the Holy Spirit, who is without suspicion, will you accept a conception that is beyond understanding, and the power of the Most High will descend upon you, that the King may dawn from your womb."

Mary: "Well, then, O watcher, do not turn away from me. If the Holy Spirit is coming to me, it is easy for me to be his handmaid. Therefore, be it done unto me according to your word."

NUN

Watcher: "Raise up your head, O maiden. Let your heart rejoice, O virgin. The second heaven is pleased in you, and earth is given peace in your Son."

Mary: "My head is raised, Lord, as you say, and I will rejoice when I see your Lord. But, if you are his servant, it is thus proper [to ask you], what does he resemble? Do you know?"

SIMKATH

Watcher: "Our ranks do not dare to look upon him who is so awesome, for he is hidden in the fire of his Father, and flame covers him."

Mary: "This shakes me very much, for if he is a Flame, as you say, how will my womb not be harmed – if a Fire dwells in me?"

‘E

Watcher: "Your very womb is filled with holiness, and your virginity is confirmed, and the sanctified place is much beloved, in the God who will be seen therein."

Mary: "O angel, reveal to me, now, why it is fitting for him to dwell in a poor woman, for, behold, the world is full of the daughters of kings, so why does he wish me to be treasured?"

PE

Watcher: "It is easy for him to dwell in a rich woman, as well as in your pure poverty, and it is by friendship that the poor he makes rich by his revelation."

Mary: "Make plain to me also, if you know, why does he wish to come to me? And if, like a fire, he is unseen, why will he dwell in me as he says?"

SADEH

Watcher: "He wishes to come and, indeed, in you to dwell. And while he is not seen, you cannot perceive. Nor do I even dare to look upon you, who are full of fire and do not burn."

Mary: "I wish, Lord, to ask you – make also clear to me the habits of my Son, who dwells within me, whom I do not know: What shall I do for him who will not misbehave?"

QOP

Watcher: "Holy, holy, holy is the Lord. Holy and glorious and exalted his Name. And all that is made is unable to say a word against your Son."

Mary: "Holy and glorious and blessed his Name, who has looked upon the abasement of his handmaid. Henceforth shall call me blessed all the generations of the world."

RESH

Watcher: "Height and depth and all therein, watchers and men, glorify him who has descended and dwelt in a virgin, that he may free all the visible world."

Mary: "Great is his Power and unending, and unable to be spoken upon lips. The sky above does not contain him, but behold: a womb below suffices for him."

SHYN

Watcher: "Heaven and earth are made one, and sing to him with one voice – even the angels and a virgin who serve the Mysteries between them!"

Mary: "Heaven above rejoices in the angels, and earth below in a virgin. And when both sides exult, they bring glory to the Son of their Lord."

TAW

Watcher: "Both sides will mingle – angels and men – and will glorify the Son who has reconciled them who were angry and agitated."

Mary: "Thanksgiving to you from all angels of fire who are unseen. From every mouth in the world, the earth sings praises to you!"

APPENDIX 4

SHRARA GALYA BADEQ
"HYMN ON THE NATURES OF CHRIST"[406]

1. The Son of God showed the revealed truth to his Church betrothed when he chose, in his love, to come to the world and proclaim and teach his Divinity and his humanity.
2. For he had been in the womb of his Father, before the ages, without beginning – truly, he is God indeed.
3. He came to us in the latter times, put on our body and saved us through it – truly, he is man indeed.
4. The prophets proclaimed him in their revelations, the just revealed him through their mysteries – truly, he is God indeed.
5. He was carried in the womb for nine months, and was also born as a man – truly, he is man indeed.
6. The angels glorified him – he is God indeed. He was placed in a manger – he is man indeed. The star proclaimed him – he is God indeed. He suckled milk – he is man indeed. The magi of Persia carried and brought him glorious gifts and offerings – truly, he is God indeed.
7. He accepted circumcision and offered sacrifices in the holy temple according to the law – truly, he is man indeed.
8. Simon called him a light to the nations and the glory of the people of Israel – truly, he is God indeed.
9. He fled to Egypt from Herod the tyrannical king full of all evils – truly, he is man indeed.
10. The shepherds ran to honor him, and they knelt on their staffs and adored him – truly, he is God indeed.
11. He grew and advanced in stature, in wisdom and in divine grace – truly, he is man indeed.
12. He was baptized in the Jordan – he is man indeed. Heaven opened up for him – he is God indeed. The Father proclaimed him – he is man indeed. The Spirit descended upon him – he is God indeed. He fasted and was tempted – he is man indeed. He put the evil one to shame – he is God indeed. He was invited and went to the banquet-house with his mother, brethren and disciples – truly, he is man indeed.

---

[406] Found in the _Hudhra_ (Trichur, South India: Mar Narsai Press, 1960), vol. 1, pp. 562-565.

13. He changed water and it became wine, and the guests drank and glorified his Name – truly, he is God indeed.

14. He entered the house of Levi, the house of Zacchaeus, and the house of Simon and ate and drank at dinners and banquets – truly, he is man indeed.

15. He healed the sick, gave health to the wounded, cleansed lepers and gave sight to the blind – truly, he is God indeed.

16. He went out to the mountain to pray, and remained there in prayer – truly, he is man indeed.

17. He gave the lame the power to walk and the paralytic the power to move limbs – truly, he is God indeed.

18. He slept on the boat – he is man indeed. He pacified the sea – he is God indeed. He went up the mountain – he is man indeed. He established a law – he is God indeed. He was weary from labor, sat on the well and asked for water from the Samaritan woman – truly, he is man indeed.

19. He revealed her secrets and her obvious deeds, her reputation and all her works – truly, he is God indeed.

20. He cried and wept over Lazarus, and asked, saying "where is his tomb?" – truly, he is man indeed.

21. He called out and resurrected him from the grave by the power of the authority of his Divinity – truly, he is God indeed.

22. He rode upon an ass – he is man indeed. The children praised him – he is God indeed. The Pharisees became jealous of him – he is man indeed. He accomplished signs – he is God indeed. The priests envied him – he is man indeed. The assemblies glorified him – he is God indeed. He went out to Bethany, outside of the city, with his disciples and spent the night there – truly, he is man indeed.

23. He cursed the fig tree, and immediately it withered, and he showed his glory and made known his power – truly, he is God indeed.

24. Mary anointed him with perfumed oil, and dried his skin with the hair of her head – truly, he is man indeed.

25. He forgave her faults and absolved her sins, he blotted out her wounds and blemishes – truly, he is God indeed.

26. He ate the Passover of the Law in the upper room with his disciples – truly, he is man indeed.

27. He predicted and revealed the evil of the deceit of the Iscariot during dinner – truly, he is God indeed.

28. He took a towel and put it around himself, and washed the feet of his Twelve – truly, he is man indeed.

29. He revealed also the one who would deny him – Simon Kepa, head of the disciples – truly, he is God indeed.

30. He sweated and prayed, and was strengthened by an angel which was made visible to him – truly, he is man indeed.

31. He approached the ear of that man who had been struck, and he healed and restored it through his great power – truly, he is God indeed.

32. He was seized with suffering and accepted spit, and a crown of thorns was placed on his head – truly, he is man indeed.

33. He cast down his captors and drove off those who sneered at him, and for their sake he fell on the ground – truly, he is God indeed.

34. He was fastened to wood – he is man indeed. He ripped through rocks – he is God indeed. Nails were fastened to him – he is man indeed. He opened tombs – he is God indeed. He was given gall to drink – he is man indeed. He tore open the temple – he is God indeed. He cried out on the cross – he is man indeed. He darkened the sun – he is God indeed. He accepted death and his body was embalmed, and placed in a tomb that was hewn in a rock – truly, he is man indeed.

35. He rose from the grave and abolished death, and shattered the bars and the ramparts of Sheol – truly, he is God indeed.

36. He ate and drank with his disciples after his resurrection, as it is written – truly, he is man indeed.

37. He entered the doors when they were closed, and requested the peace of his Twelve – truly, he is God indeed.

38. He showed them the place of the nails which were fastened in his hands and feet, and to Thomas he showed his side – truly, he is man indeed.

39. He ascended in glory to his Sender, and he is coming at the end to judge all – truly, he is God indeed.

40. The angels proclaimed that he was destined to come in unveiled body, just as he ascended – truly, he is man indeed.

41. He sent the Spirit, the Paraclete, upon his disciples, and made them wise – truly, he is God indeed.

42. Constantine traced, sought out and found the wood upon which he was crucified – truly, he is man indeed.

43. He chose a Church for himself from all the nations, and sanctified her through the glory of his Divinity – truly, he is God indeed.

44. Blessed is the one who completed his providence on behalf of the salvation of mankind! To him be glory, and upon us his mercies, at all times.

BIBLIOGRAPHY

Sources on Ancient Mesopotamia

Abusch, Tzvi. "The Development and Meaning of the Epic of Gilgamesh: An Interpretive Essay." *Journal of the American Oriental Society* 121.4 (2001): 614-622.

Bottero, Jean. *Mesopotamia: Writing, Reasoning, and the Gods.* Translated by Bahrani, Zainab and Van De Mieroop, Marc. Chicago: University of Chicago Press, 1992.

Dalley, Stephanie. *Myths from Mesopotamia.* New York: Oxford University Press, 1989.

Heidel, Alexander. Translator. *The Babylonian Genesis.* Chicago: Phoenix Books, 1951.

Huehnergard, John. *Harvard Semitic Studies* 45: *A Grammar of Akkadian.* Winona Lake, Indiana: Eisenbrauns, 2000.

Jackson, Danny P. Translator. *The Epic of Gilgamesh.* Wauconda, Illinois: Bolchazy-Carducci Publishers, 1997.

Jacobsen, Thorkild. *The Treasures of Darkness: A History of Mesopotamian Religion.* New Haven: Yale University Press, 1976.

Lambert, W. G. "Myth and Ritual as Conceived by the Babylonians." *Journal of Semitic Studies* 13:1 (1968): 104-112.

Oppenheim, A. Leo. "A Babylonian Diviner's Manual." *Journal of Near Eastern Studies* 33.2 (1974): 197-220.

_____. *Ancient Mesopotamia: Portrait of a Dead Civilization.* Chicago: University of Chicago Press, 1964.

Sandars, N. K. *Poems of Heaven and Hell from Ancient Mesopotamia.* New York: Penguin Books, 1971.

Sources on the Talmud

Auerbach, Leo. *The Babylonian Talmud in Selection*. New York: Philosophical Library, 1944.

Charlesworth, James H. "Jewish Astrology in the Talmud, Pseudepigrapha, the Dead Sea Scrolls, and Early Palestinian Synagogues." *Harvard Theological Review* 70 (1977): 183-200.

Cohen, Boaz. *Everyman's Talmud*. New York: E.P. Dutton, 1949.

Goldenberg, Robert. "Command and Consciousness in Talmudic Thought." *Harvard Theological Review* 68:3 (1975):261-271.

Holtz, Barry W. Editor. *Back to the Sources: Reading the Classic Jewish Texts*. New York: Touchstone, 1984.

Mueller, Herman. "The Ideal Man as Portrayed by the Talmud and St. Paul." *The Catholic Biblical Quarterly* 28 (1966): 278-291.

Neusner, Jacob. "How Much Iranian in Jewish Babylonia?" *Journal of the American Oriental Society* 95 (1975): 184-190.

_____. "In Praise of the Talmud." *Tradition: A Journal of Orthodox Jewish Thought* 13.3 (1973): 16-35.

_____. *Talmudic Thinking: Language, Logic, Law*. Columbia, South Carolina: University of South Carolina Press, 1992.

_____. *The Talmud: A Close Encounter*. Minneapolis: Fortress Press, 1991.

_____. "The Talmud as Anthropology," *Religious Traditions* 3.2 (1980): 13-35.

_____. Translator. *The Talmud of Babylonia: An Academic Commentary*. Atlanta: Scholars Press, 1994.

Rodkinson, Michael L. *The History of the Talmud.* New York: New Talmud Publishing, 1903.

Sarfatti, G. "Talmudic Cosmography." *Tarbiz* 35 (1965): 137-148.

Sources on Early Mesopotamian Christianity

Anikuzhikattil, Thomas. "Syriac Soteriology in the *Acts of Judas Thomas.*" *Ephrem's Theological Journal* 6 (March 2002): 33-57.

Barnard, L.W. "The Origins and Emergence of the Church in Edessa During the First Two Centuries A.D." *Vigiliae Christianae* 22 (1968): 161-175.

Brock, Sebastian. "Humanity and the Natural World in the Syriac Tradition." *Sobornost* 12:2 (1990): 131-142.

_____. "St. Ephrem on Christ as Light in Mary and in the Jordan: Hymni De Ecclesia 36." *Eastern Churches Review* 7 (1975): 137-144.

_____. "The Poet as Theologian." *Sobornost* 7:4 (1977): 243-250.

_____. *The Syriac Fathers on Prayer and the Spiritual Life.* Kalamazoo, Michigan: Cistercian Publications, 1987.

Copleston, Frederick S.J. *A History of Philosophy.* New York: Image Books, 1962.

DeBoer, T.J. *The History of Philosophy in Islam.* New York: Dover Publications, 1967.

Drijvers, Han J. W. "Facts and Problems in Early Syriac-Speaking Christianity." *The Second Century: A Journal of Early Christian Studies* 2 (Spring, 1982): 157-181.

_____. "Jews and Christians in Edessa." *Journal of Jewish Studies* 36.1 (1985): 88-102.

223

Fakhry, Majid. *A History of Islamic Philosophy*. New York: Columbia University Press, 1970.

Glenn, Paul J. *The History of Philosophy*. New York: B. Herder Book Co., 1934.

Hartin, Patrick J. "The search for the true self in the Gospel of Thomas, the Book of Thomas and the Hymn of the Pearl." *Hervormde Teologiese Studies* 55.4 (1999): 1001-1021.

Hawthorne, Gerald F. "Tatian and His Discourse to the Greeks." *The Harvard Theological Review* 57 (1964): 162-188.

Head, Peter M. "Tatian's Christology and its Influence on the Composition of the Diatesseron." *Tyndale Bulletin* 43 (1992): 121-137.

Jammo, Sarhad "The Anaphora of the Apostles Addai and Mari: A Study of Structure and Historical Background." *Orientalia Christiana Periodica* 68 (2002): 5-35.

Koltun-Fromm, Naomi. "A Jewish-Christian Conversation in Fourth-Century Persian Mesopotamia." *Journal of Jewish Studies* 47.1 (1996): 45-63.

_____. "Sexuality and Holiness: Semitic Christian and Jewish Conceptualizations of Sexual Behavior." *Vigiliae Christianae* 54 (2000): 375-395.

O'Leary, De Lacy. *The Syriac Church and Fathers*. Piscataway, New Jersey: Gorgias Press, 2002.

Olmstead, A. T. *History of the Persian Empire*. Chicago: University of Chicago Press, 1948.

Marias, Julian. *History of Philosophy*. New York: Dover Publications, 1967.

Mathews, Edward G. Translator. *St. Ephrem the Syrian: Selected Prose Works*. Volume 91 of *The Fathers of the Church*. Washington, D.C.: The Catholic University, 1994.

McVey, Kathleen. Translator. *Ephrem the Syrian: Hymns*. New York: Paulist Press, 1989.

Moffett, Samuel Hugh. *A History of Christianity in Asia*. New York: Orbis Books, 1998.

Murray, Robert S.J. Translator. "A Hymn of St. Ephrem to Christ on the Incarnation, the Holy Spirit, and the Sacraments." *Eastern Churches Review* 3 (1970-1971): 142-150.

_____. "St. Ephrem's Dialogue of Reason and Love." *Sobornost* 2:2 (1980): 26-40.

Neusner, Jacob. "Aphrahat and Judaism: The Christian-Jewish Argument in Fourth-Century Iran." *Studia Post-Biblica* 19 (1971).

_____. *Rabbinic Judaism's Generative Logic*. Binghamton, New York: Global Publications, 2002.

Peters, F. E. *Aristotle and the Arabs*. New York: University Press, 1968.

Petersen, William L. "The Christology of Aphrahat, the Persian Sage: An Excursus on the 17th *Demonstration*." *Vigiliae Christianae* 46 (1992): 241-256.

Skira, Jaroslav Z. "Circumcise Thy Heart: Aphrahat's Theology of Baptism." *Diakonia* 31 (1998): 115-128.

Yousif, Peter. Translator. "St. Ephrem on Symbols in Nature: Faith, the Trinity and the Cross (Hymns on Faith, No. 18)." *Eastern Churches Review* 10 (1978): 52-60.

Sources on Theodore of Mopsuestia
Primary Texts by Theodore

Devreesse, R. *Le Commentaire de Theodore de Mopsueste sur les Psaumes. Studi e Testi* 93 (1939).

_____. "Les Fragments grecs du commentaire sur le quatrieme evangile." Appendix in *Essai sur Theodore de Mopsueste. Studi e Testi* 141 (1948).

Mai, A. *Scriptorum Veterum Nova Collectio.* Volume 6: "Theodori Mopsuesteni Commentarius in Duodecim Prophetas Minores." Rome, 1832.

Minanga, A. *The Commentary of Theodore of Mopsuestia on the Nicene Creed. Woodbrooke Studies* 5 (1932).

_____. *The Commentary of Theodore of Mopsuestia on the Lord's Prayer and on the Sacraments of Baptism and the Eucharist. Woodbroke Studies* 6 (1933).

Nau, F. "Une controverse de Theodore de Mopsueste avec les Macedoniens." *Patrologia Orientales* 9 (1913).

Sachau, E. *Theodori Mopsuesteni Fragmenta Syriaca.* Leipzig, 1869.

Swete, H.B. *Theodori Episcopi Mopsuesteni in Epistolas B. Pauli Commentarii.* 2 Volumes. Cambridge, 1880 and 1882.

Tonneau, R. *Les Homelies Catechetiques de Theodore de Mopsueste. Studi e Testi* 145 (1949).

Voste, J.M. *Theodori Mopsuesteni Commentarius in Evangelium Johannis Apostoli. Corpus Scriptorum Christianorum Orientalium: Scriptores Syri.* 4.3 (1940).

Secondary Texts

Abramowski, Louise. "Zur Theologie Theodors von Mopsuestia." *Z fur Zirchengeschichte* 72 (1961): 263-293.

Abramowski, Rudolph. "Der theologische Nachlass des Diodor von Tarsus: (Syriac text, German translation)." *Zeitschrift fur die Neutestamentliche Wissenschaft und die Kunde der Alteren Kirche* 42 (1949): 19-69.

Anastos, Milton Vasil. "The Immutability of Christ and Justinian's Condemnation of Theodore of Mopsuestia." *Dumbarton Oaks Papers* 6 (1951): 123-160.

Davis, Leo Donald. *The First Seven Ecumenical Councils: Their History and Theology.* Collegeville, Minnesota: The Liturgical Press, 1983.

Devreesse, Robert. "Essai sur Théodore de Mopsueste." *Studi e testi* 141 (1948).

Dewart, Joanne McWilliam. *The Theology of Grace of Theodore of Mopsuestia.* Washington D.C.: Catholic University of America Press, 1971.

Greer, Rowan A. *Theodore of Mopsuestia, Exegete and Theologian.* London: Faith Press, 1961.

_____. "The Analogy of Grace in Theodore of Mopsuestia's Christology." *Journal of Theological Studies* 34 (1983): 82-98.

_____. "The Antiochene Christology of Diodore of Tarsus." *Journal of Theological Studies* 17 (1966): 327-341.

Hunter, David G. "Libanius and John Chrysostom: New Thoughts on an Old Problem." *Studia Patristica* 22 (1989): 129-135.

_____. "Borrowings from Libanius in the Comparatio Regis et monachi of St. John Chrysostom." *Journal of Theological Studies* 39 (1988): 525-531.

Kepple, Robert J. "An Analysis of Antiochene Exegesis of Galatians 4:24-26." *Westminster Theological Journal* 39 (1977): 239-249.

Kertsch, Manfred. "Eine Libanius-Reminisczenz bei Gregor von Nazianz, Or 4,99." *Vigiliae Christianae* 46 (Mar 1992): 80-82.

Lupi, Joseph. "Liturgical Symbolism in the Baptismal Homilies of St. John Chrysostom and Theodore of Mopsuestia." *Melita Theologica* 29 (1977): 29-42.

Malherbe, Abraham J. "Ancient Epistolary Theorists." *Ohio Journal of Religious Studies* 5 (1977): 3-77.

McCallum, James Malcolm. *Salvation in Christ in later Antiochene Theology, according to Theodore, Nestorius and Theodoret: a study of Antiochene Christology in Relation to Soteriology.* Berkeley, California: University Press, 1965.

McKenzie, John L. "Notes on the Commentary of Theodore of Mopsuestia o John 1:46-51." *Theological Studies* 14 (1953): 73-84.

McLeod, Frederick G. "Theodore of Mopsuestia Revisited." *Theological Studies* 61 (2000): 447-480.

Norris, Richard Alfred. *Manhood and Christ: a study in the Christology of Theodore of Mopsuestia.* Oxford: Clarendon Press, 1963.

O'Keefe, John J. "A Letter that Killeth: Toward a Reassessment of Antiochene Exegesis, or Diodore, Theodore and Theodoret on the Psalms." *Journal of Early Christian Studies* 8 (2000): 83-104.

Pack, Roger. "An Onecephalic Mask." *Harvard Theological Review* 48 (1955): 93-96.

Patterson, Leonard. *Theodore of Mopsuestia and Modern Thought.* London: Society for Promoting Christian Knowledge, 1926.

Petit, Paul. "L'empereur Julien vu par le sophiste Libanius." *Empereur Julien de l'histoire a la legende.* (1978): 67-87.

Saint-Laurent, George E. "Pre-Baptismal Rites in the Baptismal Catecheses of Theodore of Mopsuestia." *Diakonia* 16 (1981): 118-126.

Samuel, V.C. *The Council of Chalcedon Re-Examined.* London: British Orthodox Press, 2001.

Sullivan, Francis A. *The Christology of Theodore of Mopsuestia.* Rome: Gregorian University, 1956.

_____. "Further Notes on Theodore of Mopsuestia." *Theological Studies* 20 (1959): 264-279.

_____. "Some Reactions to Devreesse's New Study of Theodore of Mopsuestia." *Theological Studies* 12 (1951): 179-207.

Tapia, Ralph J. *The Theology of Christ: Commentary.* New York: The Bruce Publishing Company, 1971.

Vadakkel, Jacob. "The Origin of the Anaphora of Mar Theodore the Interpreter." *Christian Orient* 10 (1989): 55-62.

Vaggione, Richard Paul. "Some Neglected Fragments of Theodore of Mopsuestia's 'Contra Eunomium.'" *Journal of Theological Studies* 30 (1980): 403-470.

Voobus, Arthur. *History of the School of Nisibis. Corpus Scriptorum Christianorum Orientalium* 266 (1965).

_____. "Regarding the Theological Anthropology of Theodore of Mopsuestia." *Church History* 33 (1964): 115-124.

Wytzes, J. "Libanius et les lois." *Hommages a Maarten J Vermaseren* 3 (1978): 1334-1350.

Zaharopoulos, Dimitri. "Theodore of Mopsuestia: Views on Prophetic Inspiration." *Greek Orthodox Theological Review* 23 (1978): 42-52.

Lightning Source UK Ltd.
Milton Keynes UK
UKHW011213100220
358475UK00003B/1109